Canonical States, Canonical Stages

Canonical States, Canonical Stages

Oedipus, Othering, and Seventeenth-Century Drama

MITCHELL GREENBERG

University of Minnesota Press
Minneapolis
London

Copyright 1994 by the Regents of the University of Minnesota

The Introduction of this book includes excerpts from Mitchell Greenberg, *Subjectivity and Subjugation in Seventeenth-Century Drama and Prose,* copyright 1992 by Cambridge University Press. Reprinted with permission.

Published by the University of Minnesota Press
2037 University Avenue Southeast, Minneapolis, MN 55455–3092
Printed in the United States of America on acid-free paper

Library of Congress Cataloging-in-Publication Data

Greenberg, Mitchell, 1946–
    Canonical states, canonical stages : Oedipus, othering, and seventeenth-century drama / Mitchell Greenberg.
        p.   cm.
    Includes bibliographical references and index.
    ISBN 0-8166-2410-0. — ISBN 0-8166-2411-9 (pbk.)
    1. Drama — 17th century — History and criticism.   2. European drama — History and criticism.   3. Self in literature.   4. Subjectivity in literature.   5. Patriarchy in literature.   6. Power (Social sciences) in literature.   7. Psychoanalysis and literature.   I. Title.
    PN1831.G74   1994
    809.2′032 — dc20   93-27546
                                                                                                            CIP

The University of Minnesota is an
equal-opportunity educator and employer.

For Julia

" . . . May you build a ladder to the stars
And climb on every rung . . . "

Contents

A Note on Translations

Unless otherwise attributed, all translations from the Spanish and French, literary and critical, are my own. In all cases I have aimed for as colloquial a translation as possible. However, because so much of the interpretations offered in this book depend on close textual scrutiny, the reader is advised to consult the quoted literary passages in the original language as these are found in the notes.

Preface

Shakespeare's Hamlet *has its roots in the same soil as* Oedipus Rex. *But changed treatment of the same material reveals the whole difference in the mental life of these two widely separated epochs of civilization . . . In the* Oedipus *the child's wishful phantasy . . . is brought into the open . . . In* Hamlet, *it remains repressed . . .*

Freud, *The Interpretation of Dreams, Standard Edition* 4:264

"There is no document of civilization which is not at the same time a document of barbarism." With his talent for aphorism, Walter Benjamin uncovers the violence that is hidden at the heart of our most treasured cultural icons.[1] Certainly the "Theses on the Philosophy of History," written in 1940, prefigure, in more ways than one, the current debates about the ideological investments — the ferocity of exclusionary strategies — that preside over the elaboration of the Western literary canon. Removed from the empyrean of a universalizing beau ideal, those works that (since the end of the eighteenth century) have been incorporated into school curricula as representing the highest achievements of Western civilization have, under the persistent scrutiny of materialist, feminist, and psychoanalytical critics, been shown to occult, in aestheticizing masquerade, the same tactics, essentially tactics of inclusion and exclusion, by which a society empowers certain of its members and dispossesses others.

We have learned that what is at stake in the "canon" is a normalizing politics, by which I mean simply that the inchoate strands, the contradic-

tory desires, both public and private, the differences of sexuality, economic status, and race that coexist in all complex societies are papered
over in a universalizing gesture. Reducing difference to an ideological
homogeneity, the intricate drives of hegemonic culture efface heterogeneity by the very processes by which it assures the "naturalness" of its
own self-empowering.

That the seventeenth century is a pivotal chapter in the elaboration
of European subjectivity will come as no surprise to the students of that
period who read in the wake of modern cultural critics. The era that extends, I would argue, from the late 1560s to the death of Louis XIV
(1715) experiences a radical realignment of social, economic, and sexual
structures—the beginnings of the modern centralized state—that is at-
tested to in the panicked reaction of the privileged witnesses of the epoch.
In our own time those masters of contemporary critical discourse—
Foucault both in his early theory of epistemological breaks or in his later
sexual histories; Lacan, who places the origin of the "era of the ego" as
beginning, he says, "sometime around Pascal"; or those "new historians"
who attempt to re-create a rich archaeology, a study of the "strategies and
negotiations" of the politics, economies, and *mentalités* of late-sixteenth-
century and seventeenth-century Europe—all point to a nexus of interconnecting forces that shift European society away from the world of the
Renaissance and toward another: the "brave new world" of (emergent)
bourgeois sensibility.[2] Perhaps the only common denominator of these
different historical, epistemological, and psychoanalytic appreciations of
the seventeenth century's radical repositioning of subjectivity is the
recognition that despite the individual emphasis accorded economic, political, or social causes, the fact is that all these particulars worked together to produce a different nexus of social dynamics out of which a new
subject emanates, a subject characterized most forcefully as a psychological configuration of human potential. The new subject of modernity appears as an interiorized being, as a privatized sense of the self.

In what must strike us as a blatantly perverse move, this "privatized"
subjectivity arises spectacularly on the stage, that most "public" form of
representation of the emerging absolutist societies of Europe. The seventeenth century is one of the "golden" periods of theater. In each of the de-
veloping nation-states (England, France, and Spain), in those cultures
most conspicuously shedding the feudal past for an as-yet-uncernable
(capitalist) future, the theater appears as the privileged form of representation. The stage becomes the most highly invested public forum in
which the social, political, and sexual contradictions of seventeenth-
century European society are given form, "represented," in the meanderings of plot, in the constitution of character, of dramatis personae, and
in the surprise of peripeteia. The theater mediates the normalizing ideol-

ogy of absolutist culture — a patriarchal culture from which is excluded, must be excluded, all that contravenes, that threatens the imperious desire for a totalizing (that is, nonheterogeneous) subject. It can only appear as a banal truism to repeat that all culture, in order to define itself to itself, must in that gesture of definition mark a "nonself," an other who is made to stand, in relation to the community that excludes it, as its other. That the place and definition of this "other" is ambiguous, floating, constantly changeable, and that the seventeenth century disposed of many different categories of social othering (religious, sexual, racial), strikes me of less compelling interest than one particular conjunction: the anthropological gesture of othering and the representational locus of the stage in which and by which the divergent forces of social contradiction and representational imperatives come together in an especially over-determined cultural nexus. Upon the new stage(s) of the seventeenth century the age-old processes of scapegoating and sacrifice coalesce, forming a radically different "subject." The "modern" avatar of the ancient *pharmakos*, the new subject of tragedy and of comedy originates, in the theater, under the imperious, ubiquitous gaze of absolutist Europe.

I would like to suggest that what we see emerging on the seventeenth-century stage is an overinvested form of "othering" in which the inchoate anxieties of a society in radical transformation are on the one hand centripetally exploding outward as Europe leaves its contained space for the greater world of commercial, colonial adventure, and, on the other, continually brought back, in a centrifugal gesture, to a cultural myth, a legend at the heart of the West's mythology of itself, that turns it in on itself: the myth of Oedipus. Freud, of course, was the first to suggest pithily how the seventeenth century rewrites the drama of *Oedipus Tyrannos* as neurotic repression (*Hamlet*). That the myth of Oedipus is central to the theater, is inseparable from it, will only serve to show how those very chaotic forces of social change that are perceived as threatening, that must be subdued, expulsed, can be anchored in an already-there of cultural patrimony. At the same time, this patrimony, reinvested, is destined to a rather portentous progeny.

The seventeenth century collapses "othering" (and this strikes me as its particularly novel invention) into an oedipal schema, a "complex" of repression, so that sexual difference gradually emerges in and through a restructuring of subjective positions as the preponderant measure of dissymmetry, positive and negative, masculine and feminine. Represented in countless theatrical spectacles across Europe, the passionate productions of seventeenth-century drama become internalized as the mark of our own investments in sexual scenarios where "othering" always returns to the representation of sexual difference subtended by an interior dialectics of exclusionary legal, social, and economic strategies. The imperatives of unity, totality, homogeneity, so necessary for the imposition of the centralized nation-state, condemn heterogeneity to the sacrificial altar of absolutism.

Certain critical positions that at first might seem foreign to a "historicizing" (in the reductive sense of that term) analysis of the plays that I read in this book will be understood to constitute an ongoing dialogue between seventeenth-century dramaturgy and twentieth-century theories of subjectivity and subjugation. Surely the plays I discuss are of their time but they are never merely a retelling of evenemential or social history. Rather, they function as "mirrors" of their moment, holding themselves up as a model for what in the world remains pure immanence. What this means, of course, is that the theater is never just a mimesis but also, and perhaps more important, a poiesis: it is a production of certain representational parameters by which and through which we are subjectively positioned. In a sense what I am suggesting is that the very gestures of inclusion/exclusion that define the parameters of subjectivity in the larger sociopolitical forum of absolutist Europe are internalized and repeated on the seventeenth-century stage. In turn, this production, "canonized," inscribes and validates an entire network of cultural apparatuses that entrap the subjects we are within the invisible parameters of a patriarchal ideology of the "One."

In order to delineate the ways in which I understand the collusion between the seventeenth-century canon with certain subjective categories that are subsumed by it I will rely, in this study, both on psychoanalysis in its Freudian and post-Freudian avatars and on epistemological criticism and feminism to elucidate texts that for many scholars remain at a remove from these disciplines. In defense of my use of these "contemporary" critical discourses, I appeal to Stephen Greenblatt, a critic who maintains a wary distance from such disciplines but admits (grudgingly?) to the tautological twist binding the texts of late-sixteenth-century and seventeenth-century Europe to (and as the origin of) our modernity:

> If psychoanalysis was in effect made possible by (among other things) the legal and literary proceedings of the sixteenth and seventeenth centuries, then its interpretive practice is not irrelevant to those proceedings, nor is it exactly an anachronism.[3]

Surely no other discipline retains so active an involvement in the theater, is so intimately informed by theatrical metaphors and scenarios (not to mention by two of the major canonical texts of Western drama, *Oedipus Tyrannos* and *Hamlet*), as psychoanalysis. As a discipline that has at its very center the unraveling of conflicted and unsuspected scenarios, psychoanalysis affords us a privileged view of the stage, at the same time that the stage functions as the most overdetermined metaphor for psychoanalysis.

The choice of the plays analyzed in this study is perforce limited and might appear arbitrary. And in a sense it is. To anyone conversant with the enormous theatrical production of each of the national traditions (English, Spanish, French) I discuss, and with the often-prodigious output of individual playwrights (Lope de Vega, Calderón, Corneille), my choice of texts cannot but seem overly narrow. On a first level, however, these texts and my discussion of them are not meant to be "totalizing." Rather, they are invoked as symptomatic texts, highly invested symptomatic texts, whose analyses reveal, I believe, a theoretical "truth" rather than a verifiable historical reality. On another level, that of the Western literary canon, the choice of these texts was not mine. It was made for me by an entire tradition that has preselected these plays, which have, as we have been taught, "withstood the test of time," and therefore are, as their status in the canon attests, highly invested exempla of precisely those strategies of othering, sacrifice, and representation whose mechanisms my readings hope to uncover.

Each of the plays read represents an already-there of choice, a "canonical" selection, and for that very reason I was seduced into reading them within the context outlined in the Introduction. I have not attempted to discuss the history of their entry into the canon; that has been done for each of the different national traditions. The fact, however, that all of these plays represent the apogee of a certain societal selection, a selection that we know is fraught with ideological, sexual, and social prejudices, intrigued me. What is at stake in these plays? Why do we continue to read these few productions of the seventeenth century while thousands of others have fallen by the wayside? What, in other words, is the subjective investment (an investment that is changing, that is being made to change) that links these productions of almost four hundred years ago to us so that despite the cataclysmic changes in social, political, and economic structures, they still appear to be read and recognized as our own? What are our own investments in systems of othering — in scapegoating and sacrifice — that take the form of "aesthetic" pleasure, that are aestheticized and therefore in some perverse fashion legitimized and thus perpetuated through the very (exclusive) idea we have of our own "culture"? Finally, the question of subjective investment must concern us, must engage us in a conversation with our own unavowed desires, desires for subjugation, for a certain totalizing ideology that functions in and through our own investments in forms of pleasure, theatrical pleasure, that are complicitous with political power. How are we to understand what can strike us only as our own sadomasochistic delectation in the dynamics of mastery and submission so seductively produced in the plots and peripeteia of the works we have been taught to cherish as the most hauntingly beautiful productions of the seventeenth century?

The answers to these questions are complex and I can offer only a partial response within the limits of my own interests, frames of reference, and desires. What I suspect is happening in these plays, more than in others, is that we see emerging within the peculiar parameters traced by their plots, the coming together of different systems of power and representation, a new "history of sexuality," as Foucault called it, which is, and this of course is inimical to Foucault's sexual histories, at the same time a reoriginating moment of the Law, a law that is always already there, as Lacan would have it.[4] It is, I would suggest, within the multiple avatars of the myth of Oedipus as it is constantly repositioned in seventeenth-century drama that these two concepts of subjectivity are mediated. That the myth of Oedipus is inextricably bound to the theater, and that the theater as a metaphor returns so vividly in Freud's rescripting of the Oedipus legend, only seems to confirm the ways in which a certain patriarchal tradition continues to haunt our dreams with desires that are both spawned by it and necessarily sacrificed to it on the inner stage of our own dramatic fantasies.

Introduction

CHAOS

CHAOS

King, you yourself have seen our city reeling like a wreck
already; it can scarcely lift its prow
out of the depths, out of the bloody surf.
A blight is on the fruitful plants of the earth,
A blight is on the cattle in the fields,
a blight is on our women that no children
are born to them; a God that carries fire,
a deadly pestilence, is on our town,
strikes us and spares not . . .
black death grows rich in groaning and in lamentation.
                    Sophocles, *Oedipus the King*, trans. Grene, lines 23–34

Something happened in the seventeenth century. Some things in this
particularly conflicted period radically altered the ways in which human
subjectivity was created and internalized to produce what in our late
twentieth century we have come to call "modernity." We like to attribute

to this phenomenon various and often contradictory inflections, but it now seems fairly certain that there was a "crisis of the seventeenth century," a crisis that was revolutionary and that was marked, most significantly for our purposes at least by an altering of subjective sensibility.[1]

Despite the differences of religion, geography, and economic and political structures, the dominant cry that we hear echoing across Europe, from England to Holland, from Spain to France, from Italy to the northern realms of Denmark and Poland, is an anxious rumor that order is falling apart and that "mere anarchy is loosed upon the world."[2] Starting in the 1560s and continuing until at least 1648, religious wars sprung up throughout Europe, carrying with them, as the engravings of Callot vividly show, carnage, destruction, and horror. As an ancillary effect of the constant deployment of large numbers of mercenary troops across Europe, troops living in and inflicting unsanitary conditions upon an impoverished populace, pandemic diseases ravaged Europe in ways not seen since the great plague(s) of the fourteenth century. To the terrors of war and plague must be added the horror of that other battle that was simultaneously being waged against an even more formidable, and this time immortal, enemy, the Devil, who was attacked in the person of his devotees, the thousands of witches (peasant women) whom the fear and fanaticism of the century sent to their fiery deaths. During the last third of the century the scourge of the witch-hunts receded; war, however, did not. There was hardly a space of more than four years during this entire period when wars (local, national, or international) were not ravaging some corner of the European continent.[3] As in a leitmotiv of ever-crescendoing echoes from Machiavelli to Montaigne, from Richelieu to Louis XIV, from Olivares to James I, a strident clamor is raised.[4] Witness, for example, the English preacher Jeremiah Whittaker, who in 1643 tells the House of Commons that "these are days of shaking, and this shaking is universal: the Palatinate, Bohemia, Germania, Catalonia, Portugal, Ireland, England."[5] Witness the more exalted, if less flamboyantly inflamed, rhetoric of Louis XIV, who in his *Mémoires* describes for the Dauphin the state in which he found France upon ascending the throne:

> But you must try to picture for yourself the prevailing conditions: formidable insurrections throughout the realm both before and after my majority; a foreign war where because of these internal troubles France had lost considerable advantages, a prince of my own blood and of an illustrious family leading my enemies; countless plots in the Realm; the *parlements*, having acquired a taste for it, still hung on to a usurped authority; at my own court there was very little disinterested loyalty, and because of that those of my subjects who appeared the most submissive were as worrisome to me and as feared as the most rebellious . . .[6]

An anxious, pervasive suspicion that the order of things was out of kilter, that, in fact, the world was sinking into disorder, dominates European thought in the first half of the century.

The fear of chaos, especially in societies whose past had precisely been grounded in rigid hierarchical structures, is obviously exacerbated in periods of great social change. Nevertheless, this fear, although inflamed by the experience of social unrest, reaches well beyond the actuality of a particular historical event and finds its terrifying power in the most archaic strata of the human psyche. Those political theorists influenced by the work of Freud have pointed to this fear of chaos as constitutive of the dialectical relation all civilizations maintain with their own internal contradictions:

> All civilization is a struggle against chaos. Not against chaos as it
> might or might not have actually existed in prehistoric times, but
> against the phantasms of a primordial chaos, of a primeval disorder, of
> an immixture, of the undifferentiated, against an ordinary violence.
> Culture turns back onto its opposite, chaos. . . . In any case, chaos
> always points to the same danger: a world without guideposts, without
> restraints, where anything could happen and where "the worst is always
> a certainty." Chaos is the constantly retreating horizon in front of
> which all social organization and institutions are constructed. It returns
> us to our ancestral fear. We embrace any and all protection against it.[7]

Beneath the premonitions of social chaos that Whittaker and Louis XIV, as well as countless other scenarios, repeat, we can detect an ambivalent message, both a fear and a desire. Fear, of course, of total societal anarchy, a fear that was not without its tantalizing aspects; we only have to look at "baroque" paintings and sculptures, or to read the rapturous play of metaphors in the poetry and drama of the time, to see how this spiraling out of control exercises its own powerful attraction. But this baroque erotics of *éclatement* also elicits and appeals to its very opposite: a desire makes itself heard for a cessation of the whirling anarchy, for the imposition of Order upon chaos, for (and this is determined as early as Machiavelli, if not Dante) a leader, a new imperator, who, subsuming disparity in his own body, the shining "body royal," imposes unity on difference.[8] Beneath the horror and fascination with dispersion lurks an appeal to a stable unity: the monarch, in his own person and persona, is made to incarnate the contradictory hopes and desires of his people — the desire of and appeal to the Absolute.[9]

That these two apparently opposite forces, centripetal pressures of dispersion and centrifugal vectors of cohesion, coexist should not surprise us: any cultural sphere is always a space of mediation, a space in which contradictory drives, forces of progress and forces of conservation, vestiges of the past and undefinable aspirations for the future, are constantly

jockeying for control.[10] What we find perhaps more difficult to understand is the enormous attraction absolutism had for great masses of the
European populace. "Absolutism," writes Roland Mousnier, "was ar-
dently desired by the masses who saw their only chance of salvation in
the concentration of all power in the hands of a single man, the embodiment of the kingdom, the living symbol of desired order and unity."[11]
The question remains, however, of how we are to understand this appeal
to the Leader, who becomes, in the words of Nannerl Keohane, "the ordering principle of all social life, the ultimate source of authority and
energy within the state."[12]

As a state system, absolutism is perhaps the first modern avatar of
totalitarian (and I am using the word advisedly, a system that desires to
be both total and totalizing) government. Georges Balandier defines
totalitarianism in a way that I find particularly telling for beginning to
understand it as a response to the social chaos we have briefly described.
It is, he says, a form of government that desires "the submission of all and
everything to the State," where "the unifying function of power is carried
to its highest degree. The myth of unity becomes the scenario directing
the political mise-en-scène."[13] Balandier insists on "unity" as integrity of
being that would be opposed to the (fear of) fragmentation that is a first
step in fathoming the underlying desire for absolutism as a drive toward
"uniformity." This desire for closure, for a unity of being, is precisely underlined by Michel de Certeau as one of the main undercurrents of European society during this troubled period:

> Such was the situation in the seventeenth century. Divisive conflicts
> called into question heteronomous social formations. The fatal splitting
> of the former religious unity gradually shifted onto the State the re-
> sponsibility of representing for all members of society a reference point
> of stable unity. A concept of unity gradually emerged based on an in-
> clusionary strategy, subtended by a subtle interplay of hierarchies and
> mediations.[14]

But, as de Certeau has also shown us, this desire for unity that the centralizing nation-states try to impose is obtained by the exclusion of differences. All attempts at closure, at forming an integral body politic, pass
through the necessary erection as difference of whatever persons or
groups that are excluded from the integrity of the state, that the state
labels as its "other." In seventeenth-century Europe the importance of the
"other" as the necessary defining term appealed to by the nascent nation-
alisms of France, England, and Spain takes on a particularly overdetermined urgency. As in all threatened societies, this other takes many
forms. In the period that concerns us it is most clearly religious: in
France, the Huguenots; in England, first the Catholics and then the Puri-

tans; in Spain, the Jews and Moors, who are expelled. In all these countries religious minorities are hounded, persecuted, killed. With the discovery and colonization of the "new" world(s), the native peoples, be they
Native Americans or the peoples of Africa and Asia, are relegated by European imperialism to the position of dominated "other," different, inferior. Finally, more perversely and more pervasively, the feminine, the
"other" that inheres in society, in a renascent patriarchal society, must
be encircled, contained, repressed.

In order for the "integral" to exist as a social imperative, and for that
imperative to be embodied in the state, an entire symbolic, economic,
and political order must coalesce around a unitary figure, a representation that already exists within the cultural/political confines of European
civilization but which, at this key moment of transition, will be newly invested with the power and prestige, but also with the danger, of the sacred. The state, as it evolves into an ever-more-centralized bureaucratic
structure, takes on the attributes of "unity," of "integrity," that had, in
the preceding periods, been the privilege of the universal church. This
change can only be effectively relayed and experienced as a sentient reality by the embodiment, the re-creation of the representative of this state,
of its Law, in and through the person, the "persona," of the king. Ernst
Kantorowicz's important work *The King's Two Bodies* has been influential
in helping us understand the complex network of social, religious, and
institutional imperatives that coalesce in the "persona" of the king. The
king is a spectacular production, a crystallization in one person of the
transhistorical essence of the nation. The sovereign figures an immanence that is incarnated in a body, a body that is double, the body royal
and the body private. The king represents a transcendence of the merely
physical reality of individual biology: as an incarnation (that is, a
"representation") the king imposes order on social forces that, otherwise
"boundary-less," would disintegrate into chaos. "Absolutism" as a political structure of "integrity" as the order of the One, needs the material sup-
port of kingship, while at the same time it perceives that kingship "incorporated" is always a representational network of religious, economic, and
metaphysical imperatives.[15]

The appeal of absolute monarchy, the appeal to the leader, would be
impossible without an underlying metaphorical structure that equated
the king, the political/metaphysical "father" of his people, to the biological father of individual family units. All the political writers of the period
fervently worked at reinforcing this metaphorical analogy between political and familial structures and power.[16] From Bodin on, the basis of political power was shown "ab origine" to emanate from "primitive," i.e.,
Biblical, family units in which the father's preeminent position was seen
both to reflect a God-given "natural order" and to serve as a model for

all larger political groupings.[17] Theorists from Bodin to Bossuet and Filmer, to mention only the most obvious, wove a braided politico-familial metaphysics in which monarchy and paternity were inextricably intertwined in an overarching Christian framework:

> If we compare the natural duties of a father with those of a king we find them to be all one, without any difference at all but only in the latitude or extent of them. As the father over one family so the king, as Father over families, extends his care to preserve, feed, clothe, instruct, and defend the whole commonwealth.[18]

In the history of patriarchal monarchy the interchangeability of the metaphors subtending the sacred and terrestrial realms are papered over, "naturalized," precisely by the slippage the word "father" precipitates, a slippage from "God the father," to the monarch, father of his people, to, finally, the father head of each individual household. Louis XIV returns time and time again in his *Mémoires* (as James I had done in his *Basilikon Doron*) to imaging himself as the benevolent father of his people:

> I thus appeared to my subjects as a true *pater familias* who justly provides for his household and who equitably shares his provisions among his children and servants.

> This is why, far from disdaining any of the social classes or of favoring one at the expense of another, it is our duty to be a father to them all, taking care to encourage each of them according to their different possibilities to be all that they can be.[19]

In its flight away from heterogeneity toward the order of the "One" in what Foucault has called the "great confinement," the seventeenth century reinforced the image of the father/king at the same time as (again following Foucault's hypothesis) it began, through its religious and economic practices, to encircle a sexuality that in its excessive drive proved too threatening to the unitary order.

In the past twenty years modern social historians, influenced by the work of Philippe Ariès and Jean-Louis Flandrin in France, Lawrence Stone and Peter Laslett in Britain, and Edward Shorter in the United States, have confirmed this view of the seventeenth century as the period that sees a general reorganization of affective familial and sexual ties. From the more generalized idea of family as "household" (that is, an economic unit that included all the members, whether blood relatives or simply feudal dependents, living under the same roof and, therefore, under the command of a single master), the concept of "family" would gradually evolve throughout the seventeenth century to come to mean that enclosed nuclear unit so beloved of eighteenth-century bourgeois culture. With this reorganization, the way that human beings reflect their own lived

emotional and sexual experience and relate it to the sociopolitical structures in which they are born and function was radically altered.[20] In the
emergent (bourgeois) familial structuring, sexuality, newly scrutinized,
was gradually enclosed in a tightened political (i.e., juridical) circle. As
Foucault suggests, it was at this time that the family became "the interchange of sexuality and alliance: it conveys the law and the juridical
dimension in the deployment of sexuality; and it conveys the economy
of pleasure and the intensity of sensations in the regime of alliance."[21]
Precisely the inextricable involution of the state in/as the family, and the
family as the mirror of the state, allows us to understand the enormous
libidinal attraction of the king as father. At the same time, however,
when we consider Freud's hypothesis of the inherent ambivalence of all
human children to their parents, we can come both to understand the intensity of these feelings of devotion and to imagine the conflated rage and
frustration that these feelings also elicit.

In patriarchal societies, such as those in which monotheism as a religion of the father was born and as it was being reaffirmed in seventeenth-
century Europe, the blind spot of ideology is any direct attack upon the
father in any of his legal, theological, or merely familial avatars.[22] This
does not mean that the intense feelings these social organizations carry
with them simply do not exist. Rather, the more intense the attachments,
the more intense the love that is demanded, the more intense the feelings
of aggressivity and of guilt that must be repressed or sublimated into acceptable outlets. We may offer as a hypothesis, therefore, that the father,
the king, was an object of ambivalence. As an object of intense longing,
of intense desire, the king assuaged free-floating social anxiety, and contained it in his person, from which emanated a sense of stability.[23] But,
as Freud has suggested in his political musings in *Totem and Taboo*, the
other side of this intense longing for, the opposite of the love that the father inspires, is an aggressive hatred, a desire to eliminate the father and
take his place.[24]

Patricide/regicide was much too heinous an act, the king too revered
a figure to receive directly in any but extreme cases the aggressivity and
hostility of his subjects. In general, despite the myriad remonstrances
and the protests against injustice, the sacred person of the king was
spared direct attacks.[25] His surrogates, however, were not. When we
wish to see fully the wrath and anger that forms the other side of the desire for absolutism, we need only look at the venomous attacks on the
kings' ministers. It was they, the Concinis, Buckinghams, Olivares,
Richelieus, and Mazarins, who stood in for, represented, the "bad" father. On their person was the negative drive of the desire for the king
acted out. It was their taking onto themselves the hostility that could not
be directed at the king that allowed, we must believe, the king to remain

in a position of sacred inviolability. But even that inviolability was not totally immune to rage. Although the assassinations of France's Henri III and Henri IV, deeply shocking as they were, appear as acts of isolated religious fanatics, the political trial and execution of England's Charles I, the culmination of portentous political upheaval, demonstrates quite literally by Charles's beheading the vital role played for the constitution of national identity and the enormously dangerous space occupied by the king/father: both an object of veneration and (most often in his surrogates, but for one spectacular instant in his own person) the *pharmakos* of emerging, premodern Europe.[26]

SPECTACLE

Every phantasm tends to become inscribed in the real, to organize it and to produce it.

Enriquez, De la horde à l'Etat

Although in the light of our own twentieth-century experiences with totalitarian leaders many theories have been proposed to explain the tie that binds the all-powerful leader to his followers, the explanation first proposed by Freud in *Totem and Taboo* and then expanded upon in *Group Psychology and the Analysis of the Ego* strikes me as particularly acute in dealing with the erotically charged relation that joined European subjects to their (absolute) kings. Freud argues that "groups have never thirsted after truth. They demand illusions, and cannot do without them. They constantly give what is unreal precedence over what is real."[27] Freud goes on to intimate that underlying the political tie is a more primitive sadomasochistic dialectic: a group Freud implies "wishes to be governed by unrestricted force; it has an extreme passion for authority . . . and it has a thirst for obedience."[28] What is compelling in both Freud's and (as we've already seen) Balandier's different analyses of the problem of group (political) psychology is the emphasis each places on two separate but, as we shall see for the seventeenth century, absolutely interrelated aspects of the question. Each insists on the idea of the leader/king as unique — the leader represents a totality, an integrity of being, that captures the desire of his followers; and each insists on the importance of "illusion" (in the sense of "masquerade") in the fixing of the rapport between subject and ruler (compare the words "illusion" and "unreal" in Freud, "théâtralisation" in Balandier).

Ever since the Renaissance, a long tradition had associated princely largesse with its manifestation in/as spectacle: to be recognized as a king the king must always live in representation, must always offer himself to his followers (courtiers and people) as the image of what a king is. This spectacle is a dialectical projection between leader and followers in which the desire of the court is reflected back to them in and through the spectacle of the prince. This insistence on spectacle, on the king as spectacle, implies, as Enriquez has written, that "the ties binding subject to sovereign are not rational but emotional," and the political necessity of court "spectacle" was acknowledged as an essential, if masked, component of power.[29] The representation of the prince and his court is inextricably bound to a politics of spectacle (illusion), to the imaginary scenario that empowers. The very essence of a court, of a king, is "parade," an ornamentalism that enhances what is mundanely universal and, with all the attributes of artifice, with all the protocols of rank, of dress, of *dépense*, with all the prodigality of financial and sexual largesse, raises it beyond the general and into the empyrean of the unique. In this form of sovereignty, it is nothing so much as the image that defines the sovereign — to himself as well as to his subjects — as (illusorily) Other.[30] On a first level, the importance of "spectacle" for sovereignty, of a life that is theatricalized, where the sovereign is coterminously both the privileged spectator and the most compelling spectacle of his realm (compare the spectacular scenarios of court life devised by and for James I, Philip IV, Charles I, Louis XIII, and Louis XIV),[31] where the image, the imaginary of power, is relayed through a spectacular dissemination and will be reproduced in those royal *entrées* that mark all the memorable events of a reign, in the extraordinary royal entertainments — the masques, the balls, the "Plaisirs de l'Ile Enchantée" — and in the construction, beginning with the Retiro palace in Madrid but reaching its apogee in Versailles, of a spectacular architecture in which the images of sovereignty are mirrored and produced.[32]

Finally, and most important for our purposes, an indispensable link develops between the sovereign — spectacle and spectator — and the theater, a theater that (despite its on-again, off-again battle with religious and moral authorities) flourishes with stunning success in each of the three centralizing states — England, Spain, and France.[33] The theater enjoys one of its golden periods at the same time that absolutism establishes its hold on European political life. Therefore, the questions that we might ask in order to frame our inquiry into the vexed rapport between the political, economic, and sexual transformations occurring during this troubled time are, What is the relation between the emergence of the first "modern" absolutist state and theatricality? Why did the theater become the privileged form of representation of the emerging absolutist state, and why is it that this theater, whose splendor existed for a relatively brief moment, tended to be almost exclusively the theater of familial conflict — of the patriarchal family living in and under the dictates of the father/king?[34] It must strike us as symptomatically telling that European literature of the medieval and Renaissance periods is singularly lacking in familial narratives. In order to encounter familial scenarios we must return to ancient Greece, and to the theater of Aeschylus, Sophocles, and Euripides, to find a similar insistence on representing the human subject within the sexual-political confines of family. The great theatrical productions of the seventeenth century in England, France, and Spain introduced the family into modern Western literature as the privileged site of individual subjugation. In its plots and peripeteia we are called upon to witness the submission (and resistance) of every human child to those societal codes that preexist his or her entry onto the stage of social existence and which he or she must internalize in order to participate in communal existence. The family becomes the locus of tragic action at the same time that tragedy becomes the privileged form of representation in absolutist Europe.

The French psychoanalyst and critic André Green has attempted to explain the intimate imbrication of theater and family in the following terms:

> The family, then, is the tragic space par excellence, no doubt because
> in the family the knots of love—and therefore of hate—are not only the
> earliest, but also the most important ones. The tragic space is the space
> of the unveiling, the revelation, of an original kinship relation.[35]

The familial scenarios of the seventeenth-century stage become the site where the sexual and political demands of society are most acutely represented in conflict with a "personal" desire that those demands paradoxically inform. In an earlier work I suggested that the theater of seventeenth-century France functions as a heavily charged apparatus combining state and family politics in scenarios of guilt and retribution, which I call the "family romance" of French classicism.[36] I borrow the term "family romance" from Freud, who uses it to describe those fictive narratives that children invent to compensate for their own disappointments or fears about their real parents and their relation to them. These narratives are, in essence, the way a child's imagination deals with a real or fantasized conflict in his or her interdependence with the parent(s).[37] I also suggested that we might expand the term and use it as a heuristic device to describe the plots and scenarios of seventeenth-century theater as a social "family romance," i.e., those stories that seventeenth-century French society (and now I would like to extend that social sphere to England and Spain) told itself, represented to itself, as the "imaginary" projection of real, irreconcilable differences, contradictions, and social struggles that were occurring in that society and which radically altered the way individuals were interpellated, by the theater, as subjects.

It would seem that in moments of major historical change, fraught moments of history's becoming, in those periods where boundaries are fluid rather than fixed, where no clear separations of epistemic systems are possible, we see that the "place of the stage" (to borrow Mullaney's resonant title) comes to the fore.[38] Certainly in this transitional period of European history, the theater clearly situates itself as the privileged form of representation of the emerging absolutist states. It is a form of representation at once strictly supervised by political and religious authorities and yet also escaping, by the ambivalent nature of theater itself, a totally complicitous relation with institutional power.[39] The theater most intensely configures a dialectical space, where competing and contradictory ideologies act out for and through the audience a ritualized, sacrificial mise-en-scène of society's own internal struggles. These struggles, although they may take psychological form and become contextualized in/as character, represent larger conflicts, economic, social, and sexual conflicts that in reality are often impossible to discern with any clarity.

The ambivalent space that is the theater is a particularly active site in the late sixteenth and seventeenth centuries. As a social institution the theater figures the locus in which notions of individual and collective identity are impossible (or at least only with great difficulty) to distinguish clearly.[40] Paradoxically the theatrical locus is a space of identification, a term that presupposes a distinct subjectivity and, at the same time, by identification, a space of "indifference": through the process of identification, the distinction self-other is temporarily abandoned. In this boundary-less space of identification the individual psyche becomes part and parcel of the communal dramatic experience of the theater.[41]

Perhaps it is in this way that we can begin to understand the enormous hold the theater exerted on the audience, a hold both individual and transsubjective. Steven Mullaney's survey of the geographical situation of the theaters of late-sixteenth-century London insists on their position in an actual space of "neither/nor": subject to neither the corporate laws of the city of London nor the feudal legal structures that pertained beyond the actual borders of the city. He reminds us that the stage is always an "in-between" site of cultural mediation. His analysis, for all its elegant apparatus, strikes me as true, in general, of the theater's metaphysical rather than physical emplacement; contrary to the situation in London, both in Paris and in Madrid the theater was not banished beyond the city limits, it was not situated on the margins of urban life, but rather was directly and immediately sited in the heart of those two metropolitan centers. Nevertheless, the role Mullaney assigns the theater, despite its actual location, remains central to his thesis, which, following the work of Raymond Williams, insists on the transindividual aspect of this mediation, the theater as a site of conflicting social discourses:

Hegemonic culture is . . . a historical dynamic, an ongoing, diachronic negotiation between the old and the new. The dominant culture in any given period cannot hope to include or even account for all
human aspirations and energies; present culture is continually limited,
challenged or modified by culture past and culture yet to come.[42]

Franco Moretti, in a more abstract twist to this same notion, reminds
us that what the seventeenth-century theater, tragedy in particular,
mediates is not so much the "reality" of social institutions, but their
mythic (that is, ideological) relation to culture:

If the general culture of absolutism qualified the sovereign power it
conferred upon the king with countless hesitations and uncertainties
. . . tragedy surrenders such power to him wholly and without the
slightest reserve. In the world of tragedy, the monarch is truly absolute
. . . Tragedy then stages not the institutions of absolutism, but its culture, its values, its ideology.[43]

Both Moretti and Mullaney are defining the central importance of the
theater as a site of ideological mediation. The function of ideology in
both, however, remains vague, perhaps because any attempt at defining
ideology is so vexed. For the present I would like to return to the
celebrated although much-debated definition that Louis Althusser
offered when he defined ideology as "une représentation du rapport imaginaire des individus à leurs conditions réelles d'existence" ("ideology
represents the imaginary relationship of individuals to their real conditions of existence").[44] I would like to insist on his word "imaginaire" in
the sense of "unconscious." Ideology, in this sense, cannot be conceived
of as something outside the experience of social existence, nor is it the
product of that existence. Ideology inheres in the experience itself.[45]
Ideology, accordingly, would be those practices that "constitute individuals as subjects," subjected to laws, social, economic, and sexual,
that preexist the individual but which are materialized by/in those practices. The place of the stage in all its ideological ambivalence always
represents a transitional space, a space in which are mediated the sexual,
political, and economic contradictions in whose intermeshings human
subjectivity is constantly being repositioned.

The theater's dominance in periods of historical transition, in those
periods of enormous social conflict and change, seems particularly acute
perhaps because, more than any other form of representation, the theater
most actively engages individual myths—those narratives individuals
construct and are constructed by, to explain and thus situate themselves
within social and economic forces that preexist them—with collective
narratives.[46] In a sense, therefore, if we agree with Green, who defines
the theater as "situated between dreams and phantasy,"[47] we can see that

the experience of the theater is always, on one level at least, the experience of a constant re-processing and re-production (through a representation) of subjectivity — always an ongoing process of renegotiat-
ing the conflicting demands of individual desire and societal Law. It is
with this process of psychic renegotiation in mind that we will read the
production of late-sixteenth-century and seventeenth-century theatrical
subjectivity as both the "origin" and object of current psychoanalytic discourse where, as Paul Smith puts it, "the unconscious . . . must be seen
as the site where social meanings and practices are negotiated prior to
and simultaneously with any activity of the conscious agent."[48] Rather
than studying the theater as an "object" that reveals a historical "reality"
we will consider it as a process in which individual and collective conflicts
are constantly elaborating a social "truth."[49]

What I would like to suggest in the next few pages is that the relation
between what we have come to see as the originating moment of the first
"totalizing," that is, absolutist, form of government with its enormous investment in the image of the father/king and the theater as a space in
which societal contradictions are mediated produces an important aspect
of modern subjectivity. As I have submitted, absolutism reduced to an
essential metaphysical component of its drive is a desire for a unity of being. This drive manifests a unitary desire that attempts to exclude the
heterogeneous from itself at the very same time that it is frustratingly imbricated in it and needs its other(s) in the dialectics that allows it to name
itself, to set itself apart. This desire for unity, this narcissistic desire for
the Absolute, must, in order to protect itself from itself and from the
other that inheres in that self, be seen as existing in a dialectical relation
in which a highly charged dose of masochistic self-denial is coupled with
an aggressively sadistic desire for subjugation. Heterogeneity, be it religious, sexual, or political, is the fear that haunts and yet the other that
informs the centralizing projects of the emergent nation-states of Europe.

I would further like to suggest — but only to suggest — that it will be the
task of the chapters that make up the body of this book to demonstrate
that the theater represents this drive toward "unity" and the exclusion of
difference by retracing in its plots and peripeteia cultural myths that
preexist the particular inchoate demands of the seventeenth century's
radical repositioning of political, sexual, and economic subjectivity.
These myths serve as receptacles into which undefined drives can be
poured, and thus be given a form, be represented as a unity in/on the
stage.[50] When we cast our eye over those "lieux (comuns) de mémoire"
that are constantly resurrected (reinvented) at different historical moments,[51] certainly Greek mythology offers ready and seductive illustra-
tions of ambivalent sociopolitical conflicts (in the full psychosexual sense
we must give the term, that is, how individual desire and social law inter-

act to form a subject, a subject of sexual, economic, and social imperatives, a conflicted subject of radically opposed personal desires and social
responsibilities) that arising absolutism could and did allegorize as its
own. Into the (narrative) mold of ancient Greek myths, emerging absolutism, in which chaotic forces of social change tend to coalesce around
the conflicted desire of/for the father/king, cast its own inchoate contradictions. These contradictions become bound to their privileged
representation in the myths that were waiting to receive them and give
them form. Certainly no myth was more pregnant with ambivalent
meaning for a culture so invested in the relation to a newly emerging
patriarchy with its concomitant family romance than the myth of Oedipus, a myth that an entire renascent tradition of classical scholarship
had, in the fifteenth and sixteenth centuries, rehearsed and made ready
for the seventeenth-century theater.[52]

OEDIPUS

The story of Oedipus is certainly the most complete of all political myths.
Delcourt, *Oedipe ou la légende du conquérant*

*Oedipus can be a myth, a tragedy, or a dream: it always expresses the displace-
ment of the limit.*
Deleuze and Guattari, *Anti-Oedipus*

I should begin by noting that I do not mean to suggest that the influence
of *Oedipus Tyrannos* was preponderant in spawning a seventeenth-century
"age of Oedipus." Although the text of Sophocles's play was given its first
modern edition in Venice in 1502 and although we know that there were
direct adaptations of it by, among others, Giustinian in 1585, the Renaissance revival of the play was too influenced by Senecan accretions to provide the theatergoing public with an uncontaminated vision of the play.
Surely Peter Rudnytsky is correct when he writes: "Only when German
Romantic writers and philosophers, following the lead of Lessing, were
able to clear away neoclassical and Senecan excrescences, and behold
Sophocles' drama afresh as a tragedy of self-knowledge, do we enter the
'age of Oedipus' that reaches its apogee in Freud."[53] That the play was
available to a cultivated public is less interesting for my purposes than
the larger sociopolitical dimension of the myth: Oedipus as myth, before
Oedipus as a particularly invested play.[54]

At this junction we can begin, in almost tautological fashion, to understand the intimate, inextricable relation that ties the birth of individual
subjects, as subjects of a law that preexists them, to the mysteries of family in the elaboration of a social network that passes inexorably through
that most overdetermined myth of family — the myth of Oedipus, a politi-

cal/sexual myth that draws the subject into a vortex of tragedy. The conundrum of the involuted ties that bind Oedipus and his family together reaches the only resolution possible: death, represented as a cleansing ritual of self-mutilation/immolation.

Guy Rosolato has attempted to define the ways individuals who are products of their own self-narrations are also, by this very narration, implicated in larger cultural myths. In turn, he suggests these overarching cultural myths are tautologically reinscribed in the personal and thus allow the personal to be restructured by the political. His definition of the role of myth is felicitously compatible with what we have already seen to be the mediating function of the theater:

> The particular antidotal quality represented by the myth comes from a sort of unification, an attraction even, of the differences that each individual discovers in relation to the myth, and which, finally, flow together into a common stream. So that starting from a "singularity," with no future, which might even be thought of as nefarious, the subject can maintain a fascination or identification with a communal endeavor. By this process, the individual subject becomes able to accept without knowing it the social and in particular the moral laws for which his or her (psychic) structure is not suited. We can interpret this identification process as a fetishistic effect of the myth in relation to the drives of the subject.[55]

Using this definition of how myth operates as my starting point, I would argue that it is this "fetishistic" function of myth that seventeenth-century drama stages for us, representing the impossible demands of absolutist ideology for the order of the One in a subject who is always double, always subjected to difference, to sexual difference. Although I do not want to minimize the enormous complexity of seventeenth-century theater, I think that we can, for hypothetical reasons, reduce the conflicts in this tragedy to the battle for integrity in a subject whose very existence is not integral, that is not one but two. At the same time and by the same token, this duality, a duplicity, which must be removed, repressed, or extirpated, which forms the impediment propelling tragic action and informing the very being of the seventeenth-century protagonist, is at the heart of the legend of Oedipus as the myth constantly attempts to replay and refashion the journey of the subject away from forces of duality and contradiction toward an attempted (but always unsuccessful) compromise with societal laws.

The myth of Oedipus, a myth resonant with theater, inseparable from it, provides the confines inside of which the drama of the seventeenth century, in ways probably unbeknownst even to itself, elaborates certain parameters of representation, certain mimetic possibilities that I believe eventually coalesce in and around the figure of Oedipus, the sacrificial king/victim. Oedipus, "tyrannos," figures the prey both called forth by absolutism and yet going beyond the particular limits of absolutist politics to emerge as the sacred victim of an entire order of sexual and social demands. Oedipus exists as a figure of representation, a mimetic process of which he is perhaps only a lure, both a beginning and an end of a model of sovereign sacrifice, a sacrifice occulted and repeated in the new "sacred space" of the seventeenth century, the playhouse.[56]

Jean Pierre Vernant reminds us that Oedipus "without the complex" was from the beginning a double figure, a sacred figure, both a political leader (a "divine king") and a victim (the *pharmakos* of Thebes).[57] At the same time, as Marie Delcourt has illuminatingly shown, Oedipus's political role, his position of king, is inextricably tied to his erotic life, which is from the beginning predestined to the horrors of uncontrolled, incestuous sexuality.[58] From the very earliest versions of the myth, politics and sexuality are shown to form an inextricable conundrum. Oedipus enters into the world predestined by a voracious, and we must assume dangerous, sexuality that preexists him. Although it is probably a moot question which aspect of Laios's crime was for the ancient Greeks more horrific (his homosexual rape of Chryssipus or his infringement of the sacred laws of hospitality), it was this initial violent demonstration of sexuality that, transgressing both the "natural" and social laws of Greece, called down the gods' wrath upon him and upon his descendants. It is the sin of his father, an unbridled and therefore unpolitical sexual outburst, that dooms Oedipus, condemning him to that sin, to a sexuality that in its blindness undoes all the ties of familial order and therefore, for Greece, the possibility of any coherent political system. Oedipus is destined to patricide and incest. From his incestuous couplings with Jocasta will be born four children, who, in the chaotic network of relations they describe, contaminate all familial distinctions (i.e., of father, son, brother, sister, daughter, mother, grandmother) and thus eradicate the possibility of either diachronic or synchronic mappings. The myth of Oedipus exposes the fear (but also the desire?) of the corruption of that most imperious of sociopolitical divides, the separation of the generations in and through family and its return to chaos. The destruction of the family coterminously implies the disintegration of the ability of the polis to define itself through a history/genealogy. It is only by and through a non-contaminated genealogy that a history can be invoked as a "natural" order from which devolves political power and succession. Oedipus's sexuality, perversely, undoes the possibilities of family, genealogy, history, and politics.

Oedipus, therefore, as king, the hero who saves the city, cleanses it, but also is the defiler who introduces impurity into the polis.[59] From the beginning the myth of Oedipus represents the ambivalence of a political and sexual desire: the hero as liberator but also as contaminator, "Oedipus tyrannos," the ambivalence that resides in a single character who is at one and the same time father, king, and victim, an ambivalence that can be resolved only through death.

But, as we know since Hegel, Oedipus is not just the example of a man cursed by a sexuality that in its excess is profoundly disruptive of familial order, the basis of the polis. He is also the originary representative, the representation of the knowledge. He is the first "philosopher."[60] Oedipus, in his myth, is the first instance of self-reflexivity, the realization of the Delphic injunction to "know thyself." For with Oedipus's encounter with the Sphinx, that hybrid, threatening, chaotic other — the other that in its heterogeneity represents not only a dangerous, female sexuality that vampirizes men in the full flower of their youth,[61] but more generally an entire culture of oriental, feminine barbarity — is defeated and expelled from the polis. Oedipus by his mortiferous answer establishes the reign of classical, that is, masculine, cerebration.[62]

In a recent essay, Stephen Heath returns to this founding moment of Western self-reflexivity, to this moment when in the space of a syllable, Oedipus constitutes himself as the measure of all things and emphasizes what in the scene of his confrontation with the Sphinx is ideologically overdetermined:

> For Hegel, the Sphinx stands at the beginning of the history of consciousness. Or rather, that beginning comes with its defeat: Oedipus solves the riddle, flings the Sphinx over the rock, gets rid of the monstrous; philosophy, consciousness in its movement to attain true knowledge, starts from there, from that solution, the passage to the Greek world. Which means that what is put aside as Oedipus answers "man" and Hegel repeats him is the otherness — as it then becomes — to that Western term: the cultural difference of the Sphinx-Orient immobile to history, before the stirring of consciousness . . . the sexual difference of the Sphinx-Woman troubling identity in her representation, as riddling presence at the city gates, the hybrid to which man's "man" replies, ending the trouble by erasure.[63]

The politics that the Oedipus myth represents, the politics that is condensed in and on the figure of the riddle-solving perpetrator of parricide and incest, is also the originary moment of Western masculine hegemony. It is an absolutist politics that is, in the very answer "man" (which sends the Sphinx — oriental, female, monster — to her suicide), the verbal gesture of inclusion/exclusion that will mark the coming into being of Western consciousness as both consciousness of self and therefore the idea of a self that necessarily excludes its other. It is the *heimliche* from which the "*unheimliche*" (the Sphinx, and all that her monstrousness represents — the body, as difference, as chaotic, as death) is cast beyond the pale.

Oedipus's answer to the riddle is an irreversible ideological construct. The response is a masculinist imposition where what is male is predicated as self-apparent, where "I" and "man" are mutual reflections of each other. Doesn't one version of the myth simply have Oedipus, silent, point to this forehead? This gesture of reflection is supposedly taken by the Sphinx to be the "answer" [the "I" ("I" = Oedipus = "man")]. This gesture that incorporates thought as self-evidence introduces this thought in and as a masculine prerogative, as male, thus arrogating to itself the light of intelligence and casting out into the darkness all that is not "I." All that is other, all that is nonintegral — those exotic, oriental, female others, those "powerless" ghostlike presences who are, in Greek society, denied the right to politics, to power, denied the right to citizenship. They are effaced, banished, excluded from the life of the mind, from the life of the polis, from, therefore, the confines of any political, economic, or sexual empowerment by the oedipal gesture/answer. Like the Sphinx, they are condemned to self-effacement in front of this victor. Oedipus is a "conqueror" who establishes once and for all, but upon what shaky terrain, the rule, the reign of the masculine "one."[64]

Yet this "one" is also condemned to be debased, to be sacrificed. He is made to pass blindly through precisely what he does not want to see, to become the victim of his own insight. Oedipus, the *pharmakos* expelled from the city, is condemned to wander aimlessly across the marginal terrains separating the contained spaces of the polis. Cast out of Thebes, Oedipus blindly roams across the wastelands, the space of the monstrous, the deserts that exist outside the confines of culture. Only after this wandering can Oedipus come, at the end of his suffering, at the moment of his death, to that epigone of the civilized, of the masculine, to Athens, the polis of poleis. There and only there can his sacrifice be fully valorized, as an acceptance of a divine knowledge that is simultaneously the "terror," the horror of a self-knowledge that blinds. Welcomed by Theseus, Oedipus becomes Athens's "holy terror." At his death Oedipus regains a semblance of majesty. At the very moment that he is divested of his sacred suffering, the sovereignty of his fate is transferred to Theseus, the slayer of monsters and seducer of women, the hero who most forcefully represents by these dual feats the civilizing, masculine virtues of Greek society. In return for Athens's hospitality, for Athens's accepting to provide him with a sepulcher, Oedipus's hallowed secret remains with the kings of that city. It is a secret that is passed from king to king, forming a chain, an oedipal legacy of sovereignty, which triumphs in all those regions where Athens has imposed her philosophy, her art, her politics. The oedipal desire for the rule of the One passes from Thebes to Athens, and from Athens it goes on to colonize the West.[65]

It would seem, therefore, that Oedipus as king/victim, the *pharmakos* of Thebes, stands as the ur-model, the sacred loved/hated father that Freud will mythologize as the leader of the unruly band of brothers in *Totem and Taboo,* but who also returns in the organization of societal desire (an ambivalent desire) in and through the political representation of the seventeenth-century monarch. As we remember in Freud's myth, the father/king tyrannizes the mob of young men who, deprived by him of heterosexual gratification, rise up, kill him, and then, to seal their deed, devour him. This ritual killing and incorporation of the father, however, demonstrates that the father is now part of them, part of each of them, that they are all like the father.[66] What is important for our purposes is the political aspect of this myth in which social cohesion produced by guilt, that is, conscience, is born through ambivalence and identification: ambivalence, the feelings toward the leader — hate and love; identification, we are all part of the father. In a very pertinent sense it seems to me the different aspects of the Oedipus legend illustrate in condensed and then in aesthetic form, the major tenets of Freud's narrative, while also serving as a particularly seductive model for the absolutist imperative of the seventeenth century, a century that bridges the transition between (in Foucault's terms) two epistemological systems, the Renaissance order of analogy and the classical world of representation.[67]

This transition, however, is always mediated. Conflicting systems, desires, political and familial structures coexist — precisely the "chaos" we have been talking about, but here "chaos" must also be seen as an ambivalent term — not necessarily the destruction of all order, but an inchoate mixture that will be productive of new and unthought-of parameters of human potential. To figure this mediation, Oedipus is invoked precisely because he is (his legend is) an ambivalent one — a structural hinge — looking at the same time, Janus-like, backward and forward. This king who is a victim is so in/as a "spectacular" staged, social event. It is in and by his immolation that the community that desires and sacrifices him can define itself.[68] The king/victim must be loved and killed so that the polis can exist.[69] Oedipus, the political figure, the king, is inseparable from Oedipus the sexual figure, also the king. The inextricable involution of the political and the sexual winds in and through representation, a representation that is a (sublimated) sacrifice, which will provide, I believe, the transitional hinge joining and separating two world orders where the stage of the late sixteenth and seventeenth centuries assumes the role, the sacred function of the sacrificial altar. It becomes the mediating locus in which and through which a community defines itself to itself and off from its "others."[70]

The founding role of sacrifice, its constitutive function, has been analyzed in various ways by several recent commentators of the Oedipus legend. Critics as diverse as René Girard and Guy Rosolato, who despite their profound differences nevertheless derive their thinking from Freud's initial speculations, have tried to delineate the essential characteristics of the *pharmakos*.[71] In general, they propose that the chosen victim is always an ambivalent cipher: he appears on the margins of the community that expulses him, both of the community and yet foreign to it. Boundaries are blurred in the victim yet the act of his immolation reestablishes (for a time) set limits: spatial limits demarcating inside from outside, self and other, native and foreign, and also temporal limits — sacrifice is always perceived as a "new" beginning. Furthermore, the victim is ambivalent, both innocent and guilty: guilty of a difference, most often a physical or metaphorical deformity that marks him as *Unheimliche*, yet at the same time pure and uncorrupted. The victim's powerlessness accentuates the dissymmetry separating him from the force(s) to which he is sacrificed.[72]

Oedipus, of course, meets all these criteria, but more perversely, because the Oedipus legend is about perversion, I would like to insist that Oedipus as victim and scapegoat is always, in his sacrificial posture, in the role of child, the child who in this particular myth is coded as monstrous. Oedipus is punished as the son of Laios. The gods call down their wrath upon him because of his father's chaotic sexuality. In a sense, therefore, what the myth of Oedipus hides and reveals is the investment all patriarchal cultures have in punishing the child in order to spare the father. The direct attack on the father is too threatening, too politically unsettling to be given directly to representation. Instead the father is attacked in and through the son. But we must insist again that with Oedipus, and this is the reason for the enormous hold of the myth, these roles ("father/son," and so on) are blurred, so that Oedipus is always both — son, father, victim, and executioner of/to himself. Girard is correct to point out that Oedipus is always "double" and therefore always monstrous.[73] Yet the term "double" that Girard is so fond of does not begin to do justice to Oedipus's convolutions. He is monstrous because he confounds not only generational but cultural boundaries in/on his person. In this sense he is a hybrid being, and in the masculinist logic of the myth he is scandalous because he most closely resembles the Sphinx whom he destroys. But in another, more profound sense, Oedipus is monstrous precisely because he is also "everyman."[74] Oedipus is guilty because he is a "child," that is, a nonintegral being, a double, the product of two, not one, a heterogeneous being, and thus in conflict not only with the patriarchal world of the Greeks that would exclude heterogeneity from the world of the masculine, but also, and more resonantly for our purposes, from the same, reinvested drive in seventeenth-century absolutism.

No more than we can the newly emerging subject of the seventeenth century live in individuality, the impossible rupture between the interior and the exterior, between the emerging split of the private and public, without the myth of family and the family as myth. The family allows the narrative of conflict, conflict of generation, conflict of sexuality, to reinscribe the overriding imperative of the age, the flight away from heterogeneity into the order of the Father, the order of the One. Seventeenth-century drama replays over and over again this impossible scenario, which, despite the enormously different settings, either historical or mythological, in which it garbs its plots, always seems to transcend a particular historical moment and to plunge us back into a time of myth, that trembling moment that paradoxically exists before the establishment of the Law, before our subjugation to it. It is at that moment when the Law as the law of difference and denial is about to be, at that quavering moment of violence and terror when the subject is subjugated to that which he or she desires and refuses, to that moment when we become "One," in the sacrifice of our ambivalence. It is a sacrifice of our own doubleness, our own duplicity in/with patriarchal law. It is a sacrifice of the monstrous within us, of the child.

Rosolato returns to Freud's fundamental clinical discoveries to examine the irreducible importance of the role of child sacrifice in all three of the major Western monotheisms. Beginning with the Old Testament, the (interrupted) sacrifice of his son Isaac by Abraham seals the alliance between God and his chosen people. In the Christian schema, the sacrifice of the child is carried out in the putting to death of God himself, in the person of the Son, yet the sacrifice is redeemed in the myth of resurrection. Islam, too, uses child sacrifice: Ali's ritual death marks a major moment in this religion's foundation.[75] For the Greeks infanticide appeared to be the least important of familial crimes, but with the advent of the major monotheisms, all religions of the Father, infanticide becomes the central most heavily invested act, the incomprehensible, originary act of that religion, whereby each establishes its mediating role between God and the world.[76]

In patriarchal societies such as those in which monotheism as a religion of the father was born and as it was being reaffirmed in seventeenth-century Europe, the unthinkable, the blind spot of ideology is, as I have said, any direct attack upon the father. In a curiously perverse fashion the rescripting of the oedipal scenario of sacrifice, its "Christianizing" at this precise juncture of European social history, represents the desire, the perverse desire that we have already seen directed at those father surrogates — Buckingham, Olivares, Richelieu — to idolize the king but to kill him, too.[77]

The representation of this sacrifice, the stage as the altar upon which is offered up the father's child in countless seventeenth-century dramas, helps us to understand the mediating role of the figure of Oedipus — both father and son, both king and victim, a heterogeneous political/sexual subject. The transition that is mediated is, I believe, the change from the external aspect of Oedipus, his role as king/victim, a role that is represented in the Renaissance as the integral body politic, the king's body including in its metaphysical dimension the diversity of his realm, to the internalization of that figure, the coming into being of what we have come to call in one more twist of the "myth" the subject of the Freudian "Oedipus complex." What I would like to propose is that the theater, that most "public" form of representation, by mediating the conflicting demands of societal and individual narratives, traces the parameters, in and through the figure of Oedipus, by which the subject of the Renaissance, a subject defined by different familial, corporate, and religious structures, is slowly reconformed as the subject of modernity, the subject defined by and through the internalization of Oedipus's sacrifice. We move, I believe, not univocally, not unproblematically, from Oedipus the King — that is, Oedipus the "political" leader — to Oedipus the *pharmakos*.[78] The oedipal sacrifice becomes internalized, it becomes what, within the confines of emerging bourgeois culture, each individual must "immolate" of his or her own ambivalent desires to become a constitutive and reproductive member of the society into which he or she is born. The theater, in its mediating role, projects and naturalizes for an emerging premodern subjectivity the necessary sacrifice of ambivalence, the internal renouncement of sexual desires that are inimical to the pressures of a nascent bourgeois social structure, that demand (but with what tortuous oscillations) that we all be Oedipus, that we all sacrifice a part of ourselves to the reproductive order of biology and family in which and by which society, in its attempts to keep chaos at bay, assures its own perpetuation.[79]

The readings that follow are not, in any sense, meant to be totalizing. None of the plays read can be seen to "repeat" in a servile fashion the "thematics" of the Oedipus legend. Rather, what I am suggesting is that each, in its own ways, combines a dynamics of "politics" (they are all "historical" dramas, all political in that their action is completely circumscribed within the historical perspective of a "founding," that is, originary moment of a particular "state" system) with a conflicting individual desire that is shown to be inimical to the well-being of the ideology that the societal parameters of the plays represent. The conflict that provides the dramatic tension of the plays is represented within the confines of a familial scenario. The political in these dramas always turns around the personal insofar as the family is seen to represent, in miniature, the conflicting demands of individual desire and social law. In each of these plays, a sacrifice is required, a sacrifice that figures the tragic and that turns the characters of these familial plots into "dramatis personae."

Because these readings are meant to be symptomatic readings of enormous social, political, and sexual changes, they are perforce fragmentary and limited. The plays analyzed belong to different national traditions, and to different moments in each nation's development away from one "epistemic" system and toward a novel ordering of the world. At one end of the spectrum (this is not a "chronological" order, but an ideological one) we have Lope's *Fuenteovejuna*, at the other Racine's *Bérénice*. *Fuenteovejuna* is the product of a deeply divided society. Spain was perhaps the first state to begin a centralizing movement in the late fifteenth century, but, despite the enormous accomplishments of the sixteenth century and despite remaining a still-powerful military presence, was already on the decline at the beginning of the seventeenth century. *Bérénice*, written at the height of Louis XIV's absolutist enterprise, represents, to my mind, perhaps the most perniciously seductive version of personal and political sacrifice to an implacable paternal injunction. In other chapters I read works by Shakespeare, Calderón, and Corneille, each of which in diverse ways deals with the convoluted problem of politics, i.e., the forming of a "national" identity, a concept of the "self" in and through processes of "othering": the "other" — racial or sexual — is sacrificed within the dynamics of law and desire as these plays adumbrate the parameters of the absolutist subject. In all, as I hope will become apparent, this subject emerges with seductive elegance, as a memory, a shadow, retracing in its own ways the same dynamics, the dynamics of a representation in which politics and sexuality come together in the myth and drama of Oedipus. These primordial parameters, altered, different but still discernible, reemerge in the theater of seventeenth-century Europe and trace the outlines of a novel subjectivity that we have only in the recent past begun to interrogate. The readings offered in this book are but a small attempt to show how certain supposedly neutral concepts, ideas that appeal to notions of "nature" and "culture," or to masculine and feminine, which are subtended by the even more primitive antagonism that opposes chaos to order, are brought forth in/as representation, in order to impose particular ideological constraints upon the definitions of human subjectivity. It is hoped that by describing the way these constraints work their limits can be, if ever so slightly, displaced.

Chapter 1

Shakespeare's *Othello* and the "Problem" of Anxiety

Sexual jealousy . . . is fundamentally a crisis of interpretation.
Eagleton, *William Shakespeare*

In Shakespeare or Cervantes, madness still occupies an extreme place, in that it is beyond appeal. Nothing ever restores it either to truth or to reason. It leads only to laceration and thence to death.
Foucault, *Madness and Civilization*

Perhaps more than any other of Shakespeare's major tragedies, *Othello* resists interpretation. As drama it remains recalcitrant to any schema that by enfolding it within a particular analytic frame would confine it. The violence, the horror, and the pathos of *Othello* break the ties binding it to the interpretive act and return the reader/spectator to the whirling abyss, to the turmoil the play at once most fears and yet desires. It is, of course, *Othello*'s tremulous flirtation with chaos, with, that is, its fear of and attraction to the loss of limits, the suppression of those boundaries, be they ever so relative, that every society establishes between itself and what it perceives as other — both exterior alterity and inner difference — that accounts, in large part, for the continued fascination with this play. In a world such as our own, so concerned with problems of sexual/political identity, so torn by questions of social, racial, and economic aporia, *Othello* can only continue to haunt us as an uncanny projection, from the past, of our own conflicted present.

For is not the question of boundaries the central concern of *Othello*? In the most obvious political and historical sense the play dramatizes the

1

necessity of securing stable boundaries between the Christian West and the Islamic East. The drama is strategically situated at that decisive, awkward moment when one of these two rival cultures is about to emerge onto the world stage as the dominant hegemonic power. The political background of *Othello* reflects the ongoing threat that Islam poses to Christendom in the back-and-forth movement of territorial expansion and contraction that for more than two hundred years had dominated Mediterranean power politics. At the same time, and coterminous with this setting of geographic limits, the play also puts into question internal boundaries, those psychic confines constituting the parameters of subjectivity. The borders of political and sexual subjugation are fixed to a social order that authorizes its own self-empowerment by using that most slippery of abstract signifiers, "nature," to define itself, in relation to its own spoken and unspoken prejudices, as something that exists in the world rather than being produced by it. By constantly putting these limits into play through an anxious decentering of the unstable predicates that apparently govern its world, *Othello*, for its own delectation and for ours, acts out the tragedy of the chaotic dispersion of identity against the too-narrow limits that would contain it.

Gone, of course, from contemporary studies of Shakespeare's universe is the elegantly static view of the Elizabethan world.[1] Eustace M. Tillyard's dream of a pyramidal society, hierarchically structured in immutable patterns, a world of cosmically arranged stability and order, has been replaced by contemporary commentators—literary critics, historians, social demographers—with a complex depiction of a tumultuous society undergoing profound social, economic, sexual, and political changes.[2] English society in the late sixteenth and early seventeenth centuries remains in constant fear of disruption from within and invasion from without: England lives under the threat of foreign aggression and, at the same time, is riddled by internal economic and religious dissension. The apparent "homogeneity" of the late medieval period gives way, as England opens itself up to commercial adventure abroad, to the lure and the fear of the heterogeneous.

This fear of heterogeneity, another name for which would be "chaos," is at the very heart of *Othello*. Anxiety is kept at bay, right beyond the limits of the known, that is, "Venetian," world. Yet it erupts from the margins of that world into the center of the drama, abolishing all attempts to keep such seemingly innocent dichotomies like "love" and "sexuality," economics and cultural prejudice, in separate, comfortably distinct compartments. They are all shown to be confounded in the twisted elaborations of subjectivity that are central to the tragic vision of this, Shakespeare's most "contemporary" tragedy.

For psychoanalysis, "anxiety" in its most elementary definition is a "reaction to a situation of danger": the ego's integrity, its hold on the world and itself, is threatened (from without, from within?) by forces that would undo its sense of itself as a "unity," and cast it back into the horror of chaos — into the fearful fragmentation of the preoedipal, of the imaginary. To circumvent this threat the ego violently attempts to avoid the situation or to retreat from it.[3] In the face of a fantasized threat (as opposed to "fear," which would be the reaction to a real danger) to what it perceives to be its "integrity," the ego reacts with avoidance tactics, which are a "rememoration" both of a past situation of threat and of its initial ways of parrying it, ways that are the manifestation, the very symptoms of anxiety (bodily discomfit, increased heart rate, feelings of nausea or suffocation, cold sweats, and so on). In a sense we could see these symptoms, an acting out of the tragedy of the ego, as a catharsis, in its initial "medical" meaning of a purgation or an "expulsion": the symptoms manifest an attempt to externalize and neutralize an internal situation of danger. In neurotic patients this catharsis is endlessly repeatable, an acting out in the body of an interior drama of the ego. In this conflicted situation the ego becomes a "dramatis persona," caught in the scenarios of its own undoing.

Can there be, however, any analogy between the threat to the (modern) ego and a hollow, uncernable threat to an entire society's view of itself? We are all familiar with the analogy medieval and Renaissance political theorists established between the individual human subject and the "body politic." Within the political treatises of the period the corporate structure of society was figured (as demonstrated by the cover of the first edition of *Leviathan*: a kingly figure represents the perfect monarchy, and this encompassing image is imposed on hundreds of smaller human portraits) as a "body," that is, the image of an enclosed, separate individual that contained, however, inscribed within the boundaries of the body and at strategic corporal locations, locations that mirrored the caste structures of the period, innumerable component members of the social corpus. This metaphor of the body politic that was so strategically practical for both late medieval and Renaissance theologians and political theorists carries forth into premodern Europe an image that had first been employed by Plato. Throughout the sixteenth century in political treatises and in iconography, the "corporate structure" of civil and religious government was metaphorized as body, and this image of the "body politic" was ceaselessly used in political writing throughout the period to demonstrate precisely both the desire for a protective, impermeable closure, the separation of one "body" from another, and at the same time, with the predominant image of the "carnivalesque body" underpinning such analogies, the impossibility of just such a closure.[4]

Judith Butler, glossing Mary Douglas's discussion of the fear of "contamination" in *Purity and Danger*, points out that the anxiety of the "ego" and the fear of the body politic's dissolution are connected by the same underlying dread, the suspicion that no boundary is impermeable. Anxiety arises precisely on/at the limits, the limits of the body, the borders of the state. And it arises, I would suggest, at exactly that moment when in the history of Western epistemology both the body and the state are being cerned, being forced, as Foucault would have it, into a new model/mold of closure, into the illusion of impermeable "difference," into discrete, be it national or personal, identities.[5]

The pervasive sense of "social anxiety" of sixteenth-century Europe has also been underlined by modern historians of English society and the family. Lawrence Stone, for instance, writes:

> The unity of Christendom had been irreparably shattered by the Reformation, and the pieces were never put together again. The result was that from henceforth there were various options in terms of religious ideology, faith and practice and no one could be completely certain which was right and which was wrong. The first result of this uncertainty was extreme fanaticism. Internal doubts could only be appeased by the most ferocious treatment of those who disagreed. The authoritarian family and the authoritarian nation-state were the solutions to an intolerable sense of anxiety and a deep yearning for order.[6]

As for literary historians, Stephen Greenblatt, one of the most incisive critics writing on Elizabethan literature, describes the social structures of Shakespeare's England and concludes that "anxiety" appears to pervade sixteenth-century English society. He finds it in the religious sermons of the period (see his analyses of Latimer) and notices it generated and controlled in/on the stage of Elizabethan and Jacobean tragedy.[7] "Why," Greenblatt asks, "should Renaissance England have been institutionally committed to the arousal of anxiety?"[8] The question of why Shakespeare's England was committed to anxiety's arousal strikes me as perhaps less interesting than the ways in which social anxiety permeates the cultural productions of the period as both a symptom of anxiety's power and presence and, of course, as an attempt at its containment: a "cure," if we wish to think of a symptom as both a sign of an internal malaise and the attempt of the "body" politic to effect its own healing. A "symptom" is always a double signifier — both of illness and of (attempted) cure.

That "anxiety" appears the correct word to describe the social situation of the body politic of Shakespeare's England, a society still reeling from the civil wars of the preceding century and from the religious strife of its own, seems, when we read both contemporary and modern chroniclers of the period, an accurate diagnosis of the political situation. Yet how this anxiety is controlled, harnessed, turned into a productive rather than an inhibiting social symptom, is less easily understood.

Much recent theoretical work on the way(s) society deals with anxiety has focused on the process of scapegoating.[9] Returning to his theme of marginality in *The Place of the Stage*, Steven Mullaney summarizes in one pithy sentence what we can take as a paradigmatic anthropological truism: "Any culture defines itself in terms of its Others, whether imaginary or real; what a given culture excludes as alien can, however, come back to haunt it."[10] Certainly Elizabethan England was no stranger to the harrowing violence that accompanied religious and sexual upheaval. Successive sovereigns demonstrated the ferocity of institutional intolerance toward those considered religious heretics, either Protestants or Catholics, and the spate of witch trials and executions reminds us of the sexual scapegoating visited upon the recalcitrant feminine other. It will not come as a particular novelty to suggest that the theater not only does not avoid the elaborate ceremonial surrounding the identification and expulsion of the *pharmakos*, but as the most active and dialectical of social spaces often (in fact, we could argue, almost exclusively in tragedy) acts as an especially overdetermined social space within whose borders, in almost infinite variations, the convoluted theme of scapegoating, sacrifice, and redemption is repeatedly acted out. An entire society stages, for its own horror and pleasure, its attempts to deal with the other that inheres in its very self and from which it desperately tries to be freed. It is in the representation of this refusal of the heterogeneity that is within itself that society, through theatrical ritual, a ritual of bloody exclusion, attempts to define the parameters of its own conflicted identity.

> *Perdition catch my soul*
> *But I do love thee! And when I love thee*
> *not, Chaos is come again.*
>   *Othello* (III, iii, 98–100)

Let us think of *Othello* as a meditation on the theme of "limits," in all the various metaphoric resonances the word has not only for a world whose limits have been exploded—the world of late Renaissance England, poised at a moment of enormous economic and colonial expansion, poised at the moment when it is about to become the center of a "new world order," the order of, in Braudel's terms, the "Atlantic hegemony"— but also for the way these exploded limits are internalized in the production of the new human subject, in whom and through whom these limits are redefined as, perhaps, the subject's own internal ambivalence, ambivalence of sexual and economic identities, unstable, floating, defying the closure of borders.[11]

If one were to try to represent this anxiously drifting situation, what better place to choose than that fabled city of wealth and power, of sexuality and exoticism — Venice.[12] For is not "Venice," as an idea, precisely a space that defies definition? It is a perfectly mythic space, a space (certainly for late-sixteenth-century English society) both coveted and feared, a space of conflicting socioeconomic and historical desires. Venice, of course, represented at once "commerce"; it had been the most powerful trading nation in the West and thus served as a model for what England was aspiring to become. But more than a mere ideal of what England aspired to, Venice was a fabled site, a place that was always other in the most obvious sense of its being a place of "neither/nor," neither land nor sea, neither east nor west, but rather a place where opposites intermingled, a mixed, heterogeneous space, a city of "and/and," water and land, east and west, rhetorical refinement and political brutality. A cultural crossroads, Venice could serve as a screen for England's projections of difference: a space of devious politicos, of subtle courtesans, a space where, because of their "rhetorical" inventiveness, sexuality and politics promiscuously intermingled so that it was impossible to distinguish between them. Venice serves as a space of "indifference" and danger (dangerous because indifferent). But because the underlying fantasy of Venice, a cultural projection, is one of "indifference," within the cultural sphere that is *represented* as Venice, difference must be imposed, must be constructed. For Venice to exist, it too — at least as it is created in the mind of English playwrights and audiences — must impose a difference, must define itself as a "this" and not a "that," in order to be the foil of Renaissance England. It is perhaps not entirely fortuitous, therefore, that for his two plays that most acutely articulate the problems of cultural difference, *Othello* and *The Merchant of Venice*, Shakespeare chose "la Serenissima" as the site of his dramatic fantasy.

With *Othello*, however, the acuity and importance of the "site" is exacerbated as the action moves from Venice to Cyprus. By transferring the scene of his tragedy Shakespeare moves in a sense within the same, already-shaky cultural sphere, from center to circumference, and to a circumference that even more than the "metropole" is extremely permeable. We are displaced by the drama to the frontiers of the Venetian empire, frontiers that reproduce by textual underlining the anxiety of floating borders with the same fabled elements of mythic Venice (sea/land, east/west).[13] Cyprus is an outpost of Venetian (Occidental) society in the midst of an Oriental (Turkish) sea. This outpost is extremely vulnerable to the oscillating movements of any boundary separating and yet intermingling two antagonistic world systems, systems of political, sexual, and economic rivalry. This is an unstable, ever-shifting area of immixture and indifference, and thus becomes marked both as a metonymy for the "greater" world stage and as a metaphor for the situation of that world — a world divided in and among itself in which this division must be papered over, must be assimilated as if it were the very center of the dominant cultural order.

But this is, of course, only the background, the mythic cultural scene upon which the tragedy of *Othello* is played out. It is not an indifferent backdrop, however, but rather, it seems to me, an essential, if muted, cultural presence that informs the very heart of the play's tragedy.[14] Two critical dicta continuously return in readings of *Othello*. The first is that this is the most "contemporary" of Shakespeare's great tragedies, the second, that it is the least "political," the most "domestic."[15] The fact that *Othello* is the "mise-en-scène" of sexual paranoia, domestic violence, and racial prejudice, reduced to the tightly constricted circle of marriage, does not, especially following the recent and rich work of both feminist critics and cultural historians, exclude it from the political.[16] Rather, precisely because the tragedy focuses on the impossibility of separating questions of cultural stereotypes that are at once racial and sexual within an economic context ("marriage"), it allows us to see that this domestic tragedy is most acutely "political," if by political we mean the ways in which a society negotiates, within its definitions of subjectivity, the way power is manipulated so that certain groups are always empowered (economically, sexually, socially) and others, the "others," disenfranchised.[17]

The play's opening scene, the dialogue between Roderigo and Iago, rhetorically lays out the dominant "economic" metaphors that underline the two obsessive strands of "Venetian" society, linking together in an inextricable knot the "two currencies," commercial and sexual, that legislate the social life of the Republic. The constant references to "purse," "price," "debitor," and "creditor," metaphors of commercial life, are intermingled with that other pervasive "currency," sexuality, as Roderigo's desire for Desdemona becomes entangled in Iago's own disillusioned narrative of his career as Othello's "ancient." At the start, we are presented with an already-there of both an established order — an economy of sexuality and politics — and that order's disruption (dysfunction). A transgression in the apparently monolithic structure of this economy has occurred and through this breach in the dominant order the entire ideological apparatus of Venetian society is undermined, thus setting in motion the tragic machinery of the play.

"Marriage," that social institution in which the two currencies, sexual and economic, overlap so that it is impossible to separate "love" and financial interest, has been destroyed. Desdemona has eloped with Othello. Othello has seduced Desdemona. In whichever way we choose to assign the agency of this "strange" coupling, whether it be the work of a too willful, too desirous female, or the activity of "an extravagant and wheeling stranger," the essential social unit upon which all of society rests has been demolished. The text's initial reaction to this fait accompli is to articulate through the violent metaphors of Iago an entire order of racial and sexual stereotypes. Iago's extreme images, which reduce sexuality to bestiality and revolt ("Even now, now, very now, an old black ram / is tupping your white ewe"; "you'll have your daughter covered with a Barbary horse"; "Your daughter and the Moor are now making the beast with two backs"; "Your daughter . . . hath made a gross revolt"), besides giving us an initial insight into this character's "perverse" relation to rhetoric and sexuality, underlines the power, and therefore the threat, of this union. Besides being degraded as a form of bestiality, that is, unnatural sexuality, it is equated, rhetorically with economic duplicity, theft ("Awake! What ho, Brabantio! Thieves, thieves, thieves! / Look to your house, your daughter, and your bags! / Thieves, thieves!") — sexuality and money coupled once again, but now as perversion.

From the beginning the "altar and the throne," the two bedrocks of Venetian society, have been subverted, and society's reaction to this threat, the threat to the Father and thus to the Law, is a civil commotion, an anxious nighttime "alarum." The only answer to so "gross a revolt" is the call-up of a militia: "At every house I'll call; / I may commend at most. — Get weapons, ho! And raise some special officers of night." Heard out of context, these lines would make us think that rather than the trifling, "private" matter, the elopement of two lovers, this must surely be a response to an enormous threat to the res publica. At the very least the Turks are in the lagoon and civilization itself is threatened.

The play's rhetorical strategies from the start exclude any simple separation of the public from the private, of sexuality and politics. Both are interwoven. In this interweave, Desdemona and Othello, presented, like all the major characters of the play, on one level as opposites, are shown to be not other but "same," two sides of the same coin, or rather two parts of the one "other" that threatens society and that society, that the play, must sacrifice in order to save itself.[18] What is curious in *Othello* is the ambivalent way marriage, separating and joining, circumscribes sexuality to politics and politics to sacrifice. Marriage is made to represent both "being in society" and exclusion from community. It is both a controlled difference and a sign of a radical otherness.

In "Venetian" society (as in most precapitalist European societies, including that of Shakespeare's England)[19] marriage is an exogamous institution, though socially and economically limited to a more or less homogeneous group. What this means is that sexuality is defined as what is not permitted by "Law" among certain (infinitely varied) consanguineous members of an extended family, but is sanctioned among other nonconsanguineous members of the group. At the same time these "others"

are acceptable partners, acceptable "other" because although legally not
related by blood, they are related by economic and political interests. In
these marriages sexuality is folded over (and usually under) economics.
The "other" in the marriage contract, the marriage contract per se, charts
out not so much a space of difference but one of similarity — not only of
similar economic interest but more metaphysically of the similarity of
"history," of "race," and therefore of "nation." Marriage ratifies both the
past (a familial lineage), which is made immanent in all the new
couplings, and a hereafter — the extension of the family/race/nation into
the unlimited expanse of time.

What is interesting about this Venetian marriage is that by establishing limits (the "laws" of consanguinity, the "incest" taboo) it legislates the
concepts separating "self" and "other"; the other that is thus circumscribed is really a "nonother," that is, ideologically it is a "same." What
is particularly radical (and therefore "mortiferous") about Desdemona's
elopement with Othello is that it takes the system at its word. By her
selecting and thus revealing the "other" as a truly radical (that is,
threatening) other whose sexuality as difference, as non-Venetian, as
black, is continually underlined in and by the excessive rhetoric that
describes and defines him, the Moor's difference is constantly reinscribed
in the text as a different economy — as an economy of sexuality, rather
than as a sexualized economy (of Venetian exchange).

Desdemona's choice, therefore, is a choice of marriage that stands the
timid othering inherent in Venetian (European) ideas of marriage on its
head, and thus uncovers several ideologically unthinkable (for Venetian
society) conflicts. First of all, her choice uncovers the otherness of the
other in herself. It reveals the forces of a sexuality that works through her.
Second, it uncovers desire as something that cannot be limited to an
economy of bilateral exchange, the economy of the marketplace, of commercial Venice. It also reveals that the desire for the Other is something
inherently uncontrollable, and therefore inimical to the Law of the Fa-
ther/State. Finally, and perhaps most radically, it uncovers desire as
death (the killing of the father), and thus the placing of the self in the
space of retribution, of sacrifice.

It is, however, the "excessive" nature of her choice (of her desire) that
at first shocks Desdemona's incredulous father:

> For I'll refer me to all things of sense,
> If she in chains of magic were not bound
> Whether a maid so tender, fair, and happy,
> So opposite to marriage that she shunned
> The wealthy curlèd darlings of our nation,
> Would ever have, t'incur a general mock,
> Run from her guardage to the sooty bosom

> Of such a thing as thou — to fear, not delight.
> (I, ii, 65–72)

The excessiveness of his daughter's choice of a marriage partner is equated by Brabantio to witchcraft, to magic, to "charms." It is obviously not a "natural" desire, but rather an unnatural love.[20] The fact that he can understand his daughter's actions only as the effect of magic ("thou hast enchanted her"), as well as the textual insistence on "drugs, minerals, foul charms," etc., signals us that for the world of Venetian economy (sexual and political) something incomprehensible has entered the system and destabilized it. Othello is therefore circumscribed (by the text) from the beginning as first a thief, then a sorcerer. Even before these accusations, in the play's initial dialogue, and then in all subsequent acts, he is created by the text as excessive, sexual, other, and this despite his own pleas to the contrary.

The two forms of excess that the text constantly points to are the sexual excess of seduction (the seduction of Desdemona by Othello, of Othello by Desdemona) and the excess of rhetoric. And yet, as we listen to the story of Desdemona's seduction, recounted in different ways by Othello, Iago, and Desdemona, we quickly realize that any separation of sexuality and rhetoric is tendentious at best: Desdemona is "debauched" by Othello's tale. In this play discourse is eroticized and sexuality is a question of "narration." What this means is that language and sexuality are presented in the world of *Othello* as a coterminous production of difference. Othello is seductive as a "narrative," a discourse that goes, as the French say, "de bouche à l'oreille" (from the mouth to the ear) but in that very process points out that this kind of seduction, a seduction of orifices, underlines the cannibalistic, destructive aspect of eroticism:

> She'd come again, and with a greedy ear
> Devour up my discourse . . .
> My story being done,
> She gave me for my pain a world of sighs.
> She swore, in faith, 'twas strange,' twas passing strange,
> She wished she had not heard it, yet she wished
> That heaven had made her such a man.
> (I, iii, 152–66)

It is his rhetoric that was sexy, that won her love ("I saw Othello's visage in his mind / And to his honors and his valiant parts / Did I my soul and fortunes consecrate"). Two things, rhetoric and desire, are intermingled in Othello to a degree that must strike us also as strange, if not "unnatural," when we consider that so powerful a rhetorical and sexual subject claims in the play to be neither sexually active nor rhetorically subtle. Othello first tells the doge and the assembled senators that he is unskilled in verbal expression ("Rude am I in speech, / And little blessed with the soft phrase of peace"), and then goes on to confess that he is not (is no longer) particularly interested in sex:

> Let her have your voice,
> Vouch with me, heaven, I therefor beg it not
> To please the palate of my appetite,
> Nor to comply with heat—the young affects
> In me defunct . . .
> (I, iii, 263–67)

There is an obvious contradiction, which is the ambivalence of theatrical representation itself, between what a character is made to say, what language is attributed to the character as a "psychological" subject, and what unbeknown to him or her (as character) the text is saying, speaking through the character. In other words, the character is always both a subject and an object of representation. In a sense, of course, all the characters are but textual constructs through which the "voice" of the (ideological) other speaks. It seems to me that in this chiasmatic confusion between character as "verisimilous" representation (which makes us forget that it is representation) and character as textual knot (spoken by a language that is transindividual, that cannot be assigned a "subjective" position) resides the hidden crux of the play's perverse intrigue—the confusion that the play itself is not able to resolve, trapped as it is, as we all are, in the illusions of "representation," in the illusions of individual, "free" subjectivity.

The contradiction between what Othello says about himself and the way he says it has been underlined by almost all commentators of the play. Despite his claim to be "rude in speech," his role contains the most florid rhetoric, the most metaphorically lush passages in the play. What I find interesting, and this takes us to the very heart, the duplicitous heart, of this theater, the place that defies logic, the place of sacrifice and death, is the textual contradiction between what a "character" says (as if a person) and how a character is constructed, how a character is both a subject and object of representation.

Stephen Greenblatt is rhetorically astute when, in his discussion of the play, he says of Othello that "he comes dangerously close to recognizing his status as a text," but Greenblatt then goes on to build his analysis of the play upon the same premises that allowed him to "reconstruct" the self-fashionings of a More, a Wyatt, a Spenser.[21] He analyzes Othello's "self-construction" as precisely due to his manipulation of rhetoric. The anomalies of this analysis are too blatant not to escape the notice of so talented a critic. It is an analysis that is, in essence, a "psychological" description of a character: Othello, given in representation, is interpreted as a "full subject" (a "sujet plein" in the Lacanian sense), when obviously Othello is not that. He is not, also just as obviously, a "subject," but merely a textual construct that, in the illusion that is the theater, passes itself off as a subject. Greenblatt's analysis, however interesting and rich, is subtended by, among other things, the ideological presence of the Cartesian ego.[22] Although such a perspective can and does afford us an interesting "comparative" reading of the play, I think we might just as easily, and perhaps more justifiably and with more radical results, turn around the initial premise — "Othello constructs himself as text" — into its contrary: "the text constructs Othello as subject (self)."

As the text constructs Othello, it simultaneously produces him as other. In a psychologizing interpretation of the play, critics point to Othello's "flowery, overblown" rhetoric. They point to the "text" Othello speaks as if it originated in the person "Othello" and thus reveals to us something of his states of mind. But because we know that there is no "person" there, and therefore no (individual) psychology, we can turn this around and say that what we have is a particular linguistic situation that through its opposition to the other rhetorical "knots" in the play (the other "characters") constructs "Othello." In other words, "Othello" is a product of displacements and condensations, put into a chain of constant oppositions to other rhetorical structures. In this case what we must be attentive to is the question, As *what* does this rhetoric construct Othello? The character cannot be separated from what constitutes him, cannot be taken out of his text. And what does this text construct but an object of "poesis," a production of difference? This difference is a difference of excess, a verbal "dépense" (the extraordinarily rich and dense textuality of Othello's speeches), which indicates a different verbal (and, if we wish, psychic) economy, an economy of metaphor, which is always an economy of excess, of overlap, of ambiguity. In this verbal economy Othello is produced as a sign of both excess and lack. He is a "more" as a sign of exuberance, ornamentation, loss of control, but at the same time a "less." He is "less" controlled, less rational, less given to "sublimation," and, therefore, less political and, of course, hopelessly "less Venetian."[23]

The text's construction/production of the character "Othello" always already produces him as other in relation to the more circumscribed, economically "cerned" rhetoric of the Venetians. In a perverse way, then, we might say that the text inscribes Othello's difference in its origins (that is, in the very rhetorical material that produces him) and then doubles back upon itself to represent his "origin" as difference. The narration of his beginnings, the fabled, mythic, and florid tale of his youth, is his seductive "tail," the immateriality of rhetoric by which he procures the "materiality" of the body, his seduction, the folding of rhetoric onto/as sexuality:

From year to year — the battles, sieges, fortunes,
That I have passed.
I ran it through, even from my boyish days
To th'very moment that he bade me tell it,
Wherein I spoke of most disastrous chances,
Of moving accidents by flood and field,
Of hairbreadth scrapes i' th'imminent deadly breach,
Of being taken by the insolent foe
And sold to slavery, of my redemption thence,
And portance in my travels' history,
Wherein of antres vast and deserts idle,
Rough quarries, rocks and hills whose heads touch heaven,
It was my hint to speak — such was my process — And of
the Cannibals that each other eat,
The Anthropophagi, and men whose heads
Do grow beneath their shoulders . . .
    (I, iii, 132–47)

Besides the obvious allusions to travel diaries and to those explorers'
and missionaries' narrations that were pouring into Europe throughout
the sixteenth century, what we hear more strangely resonating in
Othello's narrative is the evocative and seductive echoes of the Orient.
These are tales the West has heard told, has told itself about the oriental
other in a strangely perverse cultural "dialogo d'amore." In Othello's
wondrous tales we hear the distant, enticing strains of the *Arabian Nights*:
Othello is a Scheherazade in drag and he, like Scheherazade, seduces
through "the ear" — "She'd come again, and with a greedy ear / Devour
up my discourse." (I will return to the importance of "aural" seduction
in a moment.) Through his narration he is constructed as an oriental ad-
venturer who comes from a never-never land of exotic "discourse" into
the midst of prosaic Venice. But he comes as a "text," an exorbitant,
seductive tale that leads the economy of Venice astray. In so doing he (as
text) reintroduces danger, sexuality, and death where they had been excluded by/from Venetian economy. His narration seduces but it also
kills: Brabantio will not survive the loss, the elopement, of his daughter.
Othello's stories are a form of patricide, and we know how in Renaissance
Europe patricide is dangerously indistinguishable from regicide.[24]

At the same time, then, that the tale seduces it continuously transgresses the Law of the Father/land. Thus, from his very origins, from his
originary tale, Othello is produced as a transgressive element. He is a
sexualized rhetoric, a dangerous, deadly rhetoric. Once we understand
how Othello is constructed by the discourse he speaks (and the discourse
that speaks him), we can also understand how this construction authorizes the text's discursive strategies, which will evolve to reveal what at

first was but immanent, into what by the end of the play becomes apparent. The play will, like a Möbius strip, develop the character "Othello"
from a narrative of difference, of "other," into an other—alien and
alienated (mad)—character. The death that was occulted in the narrative, the "otherness" of the character, and thus his difference, his "madness"(paranoia), will gradually and inexorably become manifest as the
play unfolds. By turning Othello into what the text had always marked
him as—"black," satanic, other—*Othello* acts out a tragic scenario of sacrifice and death. What I am suggesting here is that the play, on what we
can describe as an "archaeological level," that is, a level beyond or before
"representation," a level that we might call the "textual unconscious,"
constructs its protagonists in a particular way that predestines their "sacrifice" to the ideological imperatives of the text.

In a larger sense we may look at the "tragedy" of Othello as just one
more example of the classic Aristotelian "hero" who is brought down by
a flaw in his own character. This certainly is true, but what strikes me
as more interesting is the way this flaw is constructed, and to what purpose. Why is Othello produced as an object of sacrifice, and how is this
ritual "mise-à-mort" accomplished? Finally, why sacrifice? The answer to
this last question is perhaps the most obvious. In this play that is constantly, anxiously questioning its own political, historical, and sexual
limits in a time of convoluted transitions, where so much of the dramatic
tension is produced by the conflicted imperatives of a drive toward the
"integrity" of absolutism, and the still-resistant centripetal decentering of
the Renaissance, the figuring of this "indifference," where so much of the
dramatic uncanniness of the play is produced through odd doublings
(characters that are so opposite as to appear as simple, symmetrical
reversals of each other), sacrifice most spectacularly imposes limits,
defines an inside from an outside. By so doing, the limits that sacrifice
imposes also situate the act, "temporally," as a moment of a "new beginning," an attempt to locate itself as a new point of departure, an origin.[25]
How the play accomplished this sacrifice depends on the way the economies of rhetoric and sexuality are blurred in a process of doubling. In this
blurring an entire world is undone while another, perhaps only dimly
perceived, begins to emerge.[26]

Upon a first reading of the tragedy what is particularly intriguing is
the way the world of the play is divided into rigidly separated camps of
masculinity and femininity. These two camps are symmetrical but, as we
can expect in any patriarchal culture, unequal.[27] The three (main) male
characters, Othello, Iago, and Cassio, are coupled with and opposed to
Desdemona, Emilia, and Bianca. In a sense we might say that this heterosexual pairing is a heavily invested example of the importance "doubling" takes in play. The characters are, if we wish, structurally placed

in sexual division, each in front of the other (Othello-Desdemona, Iago-Emilia, Cassio-Bianca): in this tragedy "for every he there is a she." What the "doubling" figures, though, is ambiguous to the very degree that it is "sexual." The "double" is usually interpreted as representing an uncanny reflection of the subject, which in certain cases can be perceived (narcissistically) as a reassuring presence. More often, and by the very same token, however, the double is a mortiferous harbinger of the ego's dissolution, of its destruction. On the most basic level, doubles are feared (consider the fear in primitive societies of twins) because they represent the collapse of the unicity, the destruction of the ego's "integrity." In this perception they come to represent "death."[28] In a sense, then, the "sexual pairing" in *Othello* can be seen as a doubling in which the frightening representation of the subject's disintegration is already encoded, as part and parcel of the sexuality, as inseparable from the drive of heterosexual desire. The very fact of (heterosexual) division would seem to imply the already-there of death, a death that is occulted in but also moves within the meanderings of desire.[29]

Within each sex there is nevertheless a hierarchy of station, age, beauty, and virtue that is not necessarily equally paired with the corresponding member of the opposite sex. The asymmetry of Othello and Desdemona [black vs. white, "old" vs. young, *unheimliche* (exotic) vs. *heimliche* (Venice)] is the most striking, as it underlines the social "unnaturalness" of the choice, the perversion of all order. This textually accentuated difference not only underlines and thus reinforces sexuality as division, it tends paradoxically to normalize it. By the underscoring of their "difference," by the holding up of the couple Othello/Desdemona as the most different, these two characters are encoded as the most sexual couple, but also, we must assume, the most deadly. We should be attentive to this anxious stressing of sexual division, this relentless separation of the sexes that the play both posits as an already-there and constantly reproduces in its rhetoric because this division is neither as stable nor as "natural" as the text would have us believe. On the contrary, as Jacqueline Rose reminds us,

> the lines of that division [i.e., sexual difference] are fragile in exact
> proportion to the rigid insistence with which . . . culture lays them
> down; they constantly converge and threaten to coalesce.[30]

Sexuality is a constantly renewed societal production: it is not given in nature, but staged in culture. The boundaries of sexuality do not necessarily converge with the limits of biology; rather, they are determined by the entire sociopolitical map that is continually being recharted as societies evolve in time.[31]

Shakespeare is indisputably the English canon's most important "transitional" writer, and *Othello* is perhaps Shakespeare's most transitional play. By "transitional" I mean that, situated as it is upon the meandering fault line that both separates and joins the Renaissance from what will become "neoclassical" Europe, the play inscribes within itself the ideological and discursive elements of two (to borrow Foucault's terms) conflicting "epistemes": the "old" order of Renaissance discourse, an order of "analogy," and the "new" discursive order of classical ("Cartesian") representation. *Othello*, like *Don Quixote*, is one of those key texts that was both written at and exemplifies the moment during which, as Foucault has written,

> that uniform layer, in which the *seen* and the *read*, the visible and the
> expressible, were endlessly interwoven, vanished too. Things and
> words were to be separated from one another. The eye was thenceforth
> destined to see and only to see, the ear to hear and only to hear. Dis-
> course was still to have the task of speaking that which is, but it was no
> longer anything more than what it said.[32]

It seems to me that the distinction Foucault establishes between the "visible" and the "speakable" (and thus the hearable) is helpful for understanding the dynamic dislocation of discourse and sexuality that forms *Othello*'s tragic crisis. We have already commented briefly on the flowery oratory of Othello: it is essentially a discourse of metaphor, a rich discourse by which and through which the world's "reality" is always rhetorically created as a metamorphosis. Metaphors are always both more and less than the object, the idea, they would express. This "otherness" of metaphor makes it perhaps analogous to desire itself, always other, always "more" (but also always "less"). Metaphor attempts to "visualize" the world, make the comparisons "seeable" as images. In a sense a "metaphoric" discourse paints the world, but in so doing it reveals its own investments in an order of "visibility" that remains opaque. Things are in constant mutation, turning, kaleidoscope-like, into something else, something marvelous but something that is essentially unknowable — a discourse of analogy needs the proof of the ocular in order to fix its own mutability, in order to impose being (although imposition is an illusion) on what is inherently a becoming.

I would argue first that Othello's rhetorical re-creation of the world reflects what Foucault calls the analogic order of Renaissance referentiality, and I would go on to argue that it is a discourse that does not understand, and is defeated by, the nascent discourse of absolutism.[33] This latter is the discourse of invisibility, or abstraction. It is a discourse of emergent institutional "power" functioning in absence, a rhetoric that is manipulated most successively, and most perversely, by Iago. Nevertheless, the play would be too simpleminded if it merely opposed in a stichomythic fashion "two characters" and "two discourses." What gives Iago his truly satanic dexterity is that he alone of all the characters manipulates both the discourses together, confounding them in a mortiferous embrace in which sexuality and rhetoric are intertwined in an inseparable, deadly conundrum.

Iago is the spokesman of sexual anxiety, the character who, at first, is most intimately associated with the fear of sexuality as something that is both transgressive and female. Iago's witty rhetorical joustings betray the fear that in this world, in the "transitional" space of the tragedy, sexuality is what most easily escapes those structures meant to contain it. Iago's terror of (female) sexuality (women are voracious and insatiable) and his worry about his own incapacity repeatedly resurface in suspicions that everyone (Othello, Cassio) has slept with his wife (and thus, of course, that his wife, as "female," is sexually voracious): "I hate the Moor; / And it is thought abroad that twixt my sheets / He's done my office" (I, iii, 387–89); "I do suspect the lusty Moor / Hath leaped into my seat" (II, i, 296–97); "For I fear Cassio with my nightcap too" (II, i, 308). His rhetorical bantering is made up of equal parts in which women, sexuality, misogyny, and anxiety are indiscriminately mixed. Therefore, we must turn to the convoluted space wherein sexuality surfaces as rhetoric and rhetoric is sexualized in order to understand, if we can, how in this tragedy "love" turns to "paranoia" and then to murder.

"I am not what I am," "He's that he is." The entire tragedy of *Othello* can be situated in the space separating and joining these two enunciations. They are both, curiously enough, spoken by Iago, although Desdemona also states that she is not what she appears: "I am not merry, but I do beguile / The thing I am by seeming otherwise." It is the space of passage, separating a world of illusion, of "seeming," of masquerade and unknowability, from a world in which what we say is, is, where there is a direct, "invisible" link between a word and the thing to which it refers. In the first case there are no absolute ties between "seeming" and "being," there is only the appearance ("visual sign"); in the second, there is an already-there of an absolute connection, a unity of being. We have moved in the space separating these two statements from the world of the Renaissance to the totalizing world of absolutism.

In a strange sense the play reproduces this opposition and yet commingling of "epistemes" in the same way it has underlined the interconnection of sexuality and death in the textual insistence on doubling. In the conflicted and complicitous couple Othello-Iago there is both the separation of identities and their confusion — Iago opposed to Othello, Othello mirrored in/by Iago. I believe that my own metaphor of the mirror is fundamental for understanding how these characters, these discourses, function in tandem with each other, and how, in great part, the tragedy's incomprehensibility is precisely the uncanny presence in all the characters of a rhetorical/sexual commingling that sets them apart and yet confounds them too.

Act III, scene iii, for example, the central scene in the play, the scene that divides the play into a before (Edenic, "presexual" romance) and an after (sexuality, madness, and murder), is an elaborately structured scenario of seduction, in which Iago functions as Othello's "acoustic" mirror, reflecting and distorting his own words (and therefore his own subject position, his position as sexual and political subject) back to him.[34] The entire seduction begins with verbal echoing:

> IAGO: My noble lord—
> OTHELLO: What dost thou say, Iago?
> IAGO: Did Michael Cassio, when you wooed my lady,
>   Know of your love?
> OTHELLO: He did, from first to last. Why dost thou ask?
> IAGO: But for a satisfaction of my thought;
>   No further harm.
> OTHELLO: Why of thy thought, Iago?
> IAGO: I did not think he had been acquainted with her.
> OTHELLO: O, yes, and went between us very oft.
> IAGO: Indeed?
> OTHELLO: Indeed? Ay, indeed. Discern'st thou aught in that?
>   Is he not honest?
> IAGO: Honest, my lord?
> OTHELLO: Honest. Ay, honest.
> IAGO: My lord, for aught I know.
> OTHELLO: What dost thou think?
> IAGO: Think, my lord?
> OTHELLO: "Think, my lord?" By heaven, thou echo'st me,
>   As if there were some monster in thy thought
>   Too hideous to be shown.
> (III, iii, 100–120)

What is peculiar to this passage is that the echoing reflects not only Othello in Iago, but Iago in Othello. Placed in opposition the two men are confounded in and through the mediating couple (the "mirror") Cassio/Desdemona. It is the fear/desire of *their* sexuality that parasitizes the interchange of Othello/Iago. (Cassio and Desdemona, within the frame of Iago/Othello's desire, function as objects of private passion, but— young, beautiful, and courtly—they are also cultural objects of desire, icons of an entire society's social and sexual stereotypes.) Iago and Othello are joined in the oscillation of the echo in whose reverberations they are merged. Effectively what the echoing does is to break down the difference separating the two men. Their "bodies," the barrier to their merger, are penetrated by desire's introduction by and through the ear. (Once again, in *Othello* seduction is always an "aural" affair.) As it did in Desdemona ("with a greedy ear / [she'd] devour up my discourse"), desire enters Othello through the ear, through the insinuating echo that rebounds off Iago and comes back transformed into Othello.[35] What we have here is a curiously doubled phenomenon. First, the similarity of "seduction" seems to point to a "sexuality" that floats free of an anchoring in gender difference. People, male and female, are subject to seduction as if "sexuality," in the universe of the play, were "free-floating," not yet rigidly structured within the limits of heterosexuality, which on another level the play posits as "natural." Second, on yet another level the "seduction" of Othello by Iago is curiously analogous to the creation of a transferential scenario, whereby Iago, by pretending to be a sounding board, merely repeating the words Othello utters (words uttered in/as anxious interrogations), creates a warped "subjectivity" in the very act of answering/questioning.[36] The power of Iago's subjective positioning of Othello is produced by one more instance of doubling. His entire manipulation of discourse can be reduced to the force of the double entendre. Everything Iago says, but especially his mere echoing, is open to two interpretations, a perfectly innocuous, that is, "transparent" one, and an opaque, suggestive (because open to metaphorical interpretation) one, *grosso modo* a discourse that "swings" both ways, back to the Renaissance and forward to classical "representation." It is precisely because Iago knows Othello, an "erring barbarian," to be incapable of the latter kind of interpretation — lost as he is in a fading discursive order — that he is certain of ensnaring him. Othello is destined always to "see" more than exists in the reality of an enunciation, and less, too ("the Moor is of a free and open nature, / That thinks men honest that but seem to be so"). The echoing produces clusters of overdetermined meaning that entrap Othello. At the same time, and equally perversely, this echoing, by its interweaving, its coming and going in and between the two men, traverses those subject/object distinctions that separate them, produces them as separate "subjects" and confuses them, blends them together in an "echo" of indifference. This "indifference" I believe can be read as their mutual, inchoate desire (of/ for Desdemona/Cassio?) that surfaces first as anxiety (sexual anxiety) to be transformed into total paranoia.[37]

It is, of course, not novel to talk about the "suppressed" homosexuality of Iago/Othello. The famous "dream scene" where Iago acts out for Othello Cassio's acting out on him (Iago) of his lust for Desdemona has elicited endless comment. At the same time that we can interpret Othello's and Iago's hostility as a (repressed) passion for Cassio, we can also see how that passion mediates their own mutual yearning:[38]

And then, sir, would he grip and wring my hand,
Cry, "O sweet creature!" then kiss me hard,
As if he plucked up kisses by the roots
That grew upon my lips; then laid his leg
Over my thigh, and sighed, and kissed, and then
Cried, "Cursèd fate that gave thee to the Moor!"
(III, iii, 436–41)

What strikes me as ultimately more important is not so much the sup-pressed (homo)sexual desire of one or the other, or all, of the "characters" as much as the significance and presence of a "sexuality" that circulates in the text as a force that precisely undoes any attempt to erect those boundaries of (sexual) difference and thus supports a particular structure of social and political positioning. There is in *Othello* an instability of sex-ual boundaries that refuses, in a radically disconcerting way, the limits of "bourgeois" subjectivity toward which the text, on the level of diegesis, imperialistically moves.[39] When Othello and Iago both fall to their knees and exchange, under the auspices of divine providence, vows of eternal fidelity and mutual succor, ("Witness, you ever burning lights above" . . . "Now by yond marble heaven, / [kneeling] In the due reverence of a sacred vow / I here engage my words") can we not see this finally as the culmination of their mutual "seduction," the parody of a homosexual marriage?[40] The effect of the parody suggests the instability, on yet an-other level, of both "marriage" — that is, the institutionalization of a het-erosexuality whose domain, as we know, extends and is inseparable from politics, economics, and "power" — and sexuality itself. It is, I believe, the anxiety caused by the unstable boundaries of sexuality, boundaries that affect the central institutions of the "state" (society) that resurface in the confused seduction, desires, and jealousies of Iago/Othello and ulti-mately in their paranoia. I say "their" paranoia because it is important to underline, as I have already suggested, that besides their mistrust of women and a corresponding flight into the "security," the narcissistic security, of male-mirroring, both characters, in different ways, exhibit a paranoid relation to the world. Iago's paranoia, rather remarkably the way Freud suggested, turns into antisocial aggressivity not as a result of an obvious homosexual crisis, but rather more mundanely because of (perceived) social slight: Othello preferred Cassio (promoted him) to Iago — sexuality and economy, once more intermingled, once more in-separable.[41]

Othello's paranoia is also at first more apparently "social" than sexual. He is an outsider, an alien other who has been accepted into a hege-monic, that is, totalizing, society, because that society has a particular and temporary need of certain services he can render. Although Othello, perhaps like all colonized peoples, believes, must believe, that he has become a part of that society, he also carries his "blackness" as the constant sign that he can always be distinguished, always readily cast back out into the margins from whence he came when he no longer fulfills his role. That this role is from the beginning of the play already undermined by his sexual/rhetorical transgression is something he only dimly and gradually perceives, perceiving his own being as a transgression, in the very return of the transgressive (sexuality) onto/in himself as an excess, his madness, his othering.

The floating social angst that becomes "embodied" as paranoia, as a form of paranoid jealousy, is necessarily directed, at first, outward onto the most vulnerable member (for a patriarchal system) of that society, both its sexual and cultural "other." Desdemona is positioned by the text as the requisite victim whose destruction appears imperative to appease the anxious drifting of a system in transition.[42]

Typically, despite the infinite variety of forms "sacrifice" can take in any given society, the victim of the sacrifice generally fulfills certain invariable criteria that establish his/her role as other by dialectically situating him/her both within and without the confines of the "polis." What this means for our purposes is that the victim/scapegoat is always perceived as "double"—both insider and outsider, in whom and through whom passes the line of separation, the interior difference that becomes exteriorized in the ritual killing. In general the chosen victim betrays some sign of "difference" (physical handicap, foreignness, and so forth) that apparently opposes him/her to the political ideal (that may or may not be embodied in the image God or King) that informs social Law. In this sense we can understand both Girard's as well as Rosolato's insistence that the victim be perceived as "innocent," meek, the "other" when compared to the Law, all powerful, in the name of which the victim is struck down.[43] We can also intuit how, in this context, the victim of *Othello*, necessarily double, necessarily ambivalent, is not just the fair, pathetic Desdemona, but rather the "double" other destined by the text for destruction: Desdemona/Othello.

Just as Othello's rhetoric attaches him to the discourse of the "Renaissance," his sexual anxiety, or at least the provocation of that anxiety, is facilitated by his having a culturally archaic, although pervasive, vision of female sexuality. He shares the vision of Iago, in which "women" are feared because they are "known" to be sexually voracious and duplicitous. This leads him to "see" his young wife erroneously through codes that pertain to an entire tradition of male anxiety about female sexuality, a tradition that was still very much alive in Shakespeare's day.[44] At the same moment, however, a counterdiscourse, with its roots in early-sixteenth-century treatises defending the "fair sex" and extolling female virtues, was being popularized in aristocratic circles through the writings of Italian, French, and English humanists.[45]

Desdemona is described as a "subtle Venetian," and although this is meant pejoratively, with all the negative connotations of cultural stereotypes that adhered to both words ("subtle" = devious, and "Venetian" = reputedly both sexually and politically perverse), we surely can also hear, if only grudgingly, the echoing praise that almost a century of courtly literature had attempted to bestow on the aristocratic Renaissance woman. Desdemona is, on one level at least, the product of all those courtly manner books, the most famous example of which is perhaps the *Cortegiano:* she is educated, gracious, conversant with the gallant subtleties of refined, flirtatious lotharios.[46] Desdemona figures the fair icon of "high" culture. She is also, for the virulently misogynistic world of Iago (and Othello), a shocking, modern woman, who throws all conventions of feminine propriety to the wind by eloping with Othello. This aspect will prove her undoing. It is precisely her love of Othello, which the men interpret as her "lust" for him — what better proof than her betrayal of paternal prerogative — that returns as a perverse proof of her lechery and guilt. Her father's last words resound like a curse upon the horizon of their marriage — "Look to her, Moor, if thou hast eyes to see. / She has deceived her father, and may thee" — and resound in the theater as a warning to the males, a warning that this wayward, wanton daughter can and will undo them all.[47]

But who has the "eyes" to see? Or rather how can we "see," that is, know, the other in the one? With what eyes, with what codes can the truth, the truth of "sexuality," the truth of one's own deepest investments, be seized, fixed, turned into an eternal verity? Upon what base can an identity be secured? Surely, this is the maddening dilemma with which Iago confronts Othello in his dizzying manipulation of discourse and sexuality.

The "eye" is the most concupiscent, and perhaps because of that the most duplicitous, of organs. It is at once the "opening" by and through which we take in the objects of our covetousness, and the window from which our own desire is revealed to the world.[48] From the writings of the early church fathers on, the eye has been the object of the most intense mistrust of the appointed guardians of social and moral propriety. There is an inherent ambivalence in which the physical organ's "duplicity" extends into the realm of metaphysics: what is the relation between what we perceive (visually) and what is? Trapped, as I believe him to be within the receding limits of an epistemology of the "visible," the Renaissance order of "analogy," Othello in his anxious panic retreats into an appeal to the "seeable" as the ultimate mediator between reality and truth. And yet it will be this lure of what is, the inherently unstable lure of vision, that will prove his undoing.

> Villain, be sure thou prove my love a whore!
> Be sure of it. Give me the ocular proof . . .
> Make me to see' it, or at the least so prove it
> That the probation bear no hinge nor loop
> To hang a doubt on . . .
> (III, iii, 375–82)

Othello's confusion, his inability to separate seeming and being, is articulated as a reinscription of sexual difference. Who is he to believe, Desdemona (that is, his own love for her) or Iago (that is, his love for him)—"I think my wife be honest and think she is not; / I think that thou art just and think thou art not." How is he to choose between the woman and the man, that is, what position is he himself to assume in this triangulation of desire that seems to echo in oddly proleptic tones that other stage of conflicted lust—the oedipal scenario of Freudian yearning? When Othello anxiously appeals to "ocular proof," within the frame of desire that the drama has been elaborating, we hear a muffled plea whose echoes resonate on the tragedy's several levels, on the level of diegesis and on that "other scene," that unconscious textual dynamic where the conflict between being and seeming turns around the sorting out of sexual positioning.

Othello wants to see what remains beyond or behind sight, and Iago knows this.

> IAGO: I see, sir, you are eaten up with passion.
> I do repent me that I put it to you.
> You would be satisfied?
> OTHELLO: Would? Nay, and I will.
> IAGO: And may; but how? How satisfied, my lord?
> Would you, the supervisor, grossly gape on?
> Behold her topped?
> OTHELLO: Death and damnation! O!
> IAGO: It were a tedious difficulty, I think,
> To bring them to that prospect. Damn them then,
> If ever mortal eyes do see them bolster
> More than their own. What then? How then?
> What shall I say? Where's the satisfaction?
> It is impossible you should see him,
> Were they as prime as goats, as hot as monkeys,
> As salt as wolves in pride . . .
> (III, iii, 407–20)

Instead of "ocular proof" Iago promises to "satisfy" Othello with another vision of (his) desire: he recounts his dream, the famous dream already quoted in which there is a strange layering of desire on desire, a strange confusion of the sexes and sexuality (Cassio and Desdemona, Cassio and Iago, Iago and Othello, Othello and Desdemona, Othello and Cassio). Rather than the "satisfaction" Othello asks for, rather than the blinding vision of sexuality as proof, proof of crime but also of difference, Iago gives Othello sexuality as origin—the conflicted, tangled dream, which reestablishes desire as a strange commingling rather than a separating out, and actually no "sex" at all.

What Othello asks for, what he wants to see, is what we have come to call the "primal scene" of adult (hetero)sexuality.[49] What is particularly striking in the fantasmatic production that the "primal scene" represents is the ambivalent desire of the young (boy) child, in which the positions of sexuality are both sorted out and confused in a scenario of sexual violence. What this "originary scenario" attempts to script is both the origin of the subject (that is, the subject as product of an already-there of sexuality, of sexual division) and the confusion, the indivision (in the violent commingling) of sexes. For this reason it is an impossible vision and can only be represented as another fantasy, the jealous illusion of Iago's (fantasized) dream.[50]

Othello is denied the proof, the blinding vision, that would, he believes, make order out of the chaos into which he has fallen. His anxiety wants the world reordered along divisions he can see, a vision that would ease his anxiety. But no vision is forthcoming that would return the world to the order he understands. Iago reflects to him only renewed anxiety and offers him just one image. The only "thing" that Iago allows Othello to "see" is his handkerchief:

> IAGO: Have you not sometimes seen a handkerchief
> Spotted with strawberries in your wife's hand?
> OTHELLO: I gave her such a one. 'Twas my first gift.
> IAGO: I know not that; but such a handkerchief—
> I am sure it was your wife's—did I today
> See Cassio wipe his beard with.
> OTHELLO: If it be that—
> IAGO: If it be that, or any that was hers,
> It speaks against her with the other proofs.
> OTHELLO: that the slave had forty thousand lives!
> One is too poor, too weak for my revenge.
> Now do I see 'tis true.
> (III, iii, 449–59)

The handkerchief, which substitutes for the primal scene that is denied his sight, is the most overdetermined mediator in play. It not only signifies sexuality, representing for Othello's heated imagination the sheets upon which Cassio and Desdemona have trysted, but it also goes beyond them to represent what the primal scene also "shows," the sexual origin of the subject (Cassio and Desdemona as "father and mother"), his beginning, in and as the handkerchief inscribes "what the father gave the mother." Even this, however, is not spared the ambivalence of doubling, for Othello twice tells of the handkerchief's origin, and in each telling the source becomes enmeshed in sexual ambivalence. In the first telling it was an "Egyptian" who gave the handkerchief to his mother as a talismanic "love charm" ("That handkerchief / Did an Egyptian to my mother give"). As long as she kept it the charm would bind his father to his mother, and thus assure the permanence of the heterosexual "ur-couple." In the second telling his father offered the handkerchief to his mother ("It was a handkerchief, an antique token / My father gave my mother"). Whose legacy is the handkerchief, the father's or the mother's? Into what lineage of parental devolution does Othello fit? In the first version, his is the mother's legacy, in the second the father's. In this impossibility to determine the true origin of the handkerchief, and therefore of his own situation in the schema of desire it represents, Othello, like the handkerchief, drifts from hand to hand, from meaning to meaning. The handkerchief that provides him with the "ocular corroboration" he desired ("I saw the handkerchief," Othello tells Desdemona, as proof of her infidelity, just before he kills her) proves to be simply an "empty signifier." It can be compared to that "object" Rosolato describes as an "objet de perspective," and which Tom Conley has glossed in the following way:

> The term applies to the way subjects . . . visualize or indicate through the bias of speech nodal points in their descriptive relation to the world they see and live. . . . It figures a concentrated point of attention that captures what a subject chooses to see, simply because in it resides what cannot, because of its paradoxical evidence and accessibility, be seen.[51]

The "handkerchief," for all its innocuousness, becomes the focal point of this tragedy in which the episteme of the analogous and the emergent episteme of transparency are opposed. It is a perspectival point in which the "world" captures Othello. It fixes him to this one image, an image that conflates desire and power, sexuality and law, and by so doing, the "world" itself is obscured. All that Othello cannot see (the "truth" of sexuality), all that cannot be seen (fidelity), vanishes in the image of the handkerchief. The world is reduced to the blush of a strawberry, and in that crimson-spotted blank Desdemona and Othello are undone.

The innocent ambivalence of the handkerchief is the most intense example of Othello's inability to exist in a world that is no longer legible. Desdemona, who has, for the reasons we have already discussed, become the most heavily concentrated textual example of masculine anxiety, a woman presented as both virgin and whore, is situated by the handker-chief's recalcitrant illegibility at the paroxysm of Othello's loss of the world, loss of himself, as the tragedy's designated victim. The entire drama in all of its sociosexual predicates prepares and calls for her immo-lation so that the anxiety that has been generated about her may be ap-peased. In his paranoia, Desdemona's death is necessary for Othello to reestablish order out of chaos.[52]

In a broader, social sense, however, it is clear that Othello's anxiety is not just a personal issue. It is the anxiety of an entire patriarchal cul-ture, the culture of late Renaissance Europe, which was going through a tumultuous reorganization of its religious, political, and sexual presup-positions. With the ever-greater tendency toward centralization comes a reinforcement, on the level of political and social rhetoric, of the patriar-chal family and, by extension, of the patriarchal monarchy. Absolute monarchy, as it was developed in Europe in the late sixteenth and early seventeenth centuries would be impossible without a constant appeal to patriarchal metaphors. In the history of absolute monarchy, the inter-changeability of the metaphors subtending the sacred and terrestrial realms is papered over, "naturalized" precisely by the slippage the word "father" precipitates from "God the father," to the monarch, father of his people, to finally the father, head of each individual household (this "slip-page" functions in both ascending and descending order).[53] On one level, Othello's anxiety is the anxiety of an entire paternal order for which, in Cyprus, Othello stands "in loco parentis." Othello in his marriage to Desdemona assumes the place of the Father, a place that she has already usurped. To this metaphoric role must be added his political and military role as chief commander of the Venetian military on Cyprus. For all in-tents and purposes within the confines of Cypriote society, Othello conflates in his person both the "real" and metaphysical attributes of the Law.

It is as defender of the Law that he claims he is "sacrificing" his errant wife. It is to save "man"kind from further chaos (from sexuality) that Desdemona is brought forth as the sacrificial victim of Othello's para-noia. And as this social paranoia is inseparable from sexual anxieties, it is here, in the chiasmus between the public and the private, in their in-separability, that we understand the specific perversity of this sac-rifice/murder ("makes me call what I intend to do / A murder, which I thought a sacrifice"). For in a very significant sense Othello is bound to Desdemona, they are in their own configuration a conflation of "mon-strosity" — they are both "parricide," he by his seductive narration, she by her narrative seduction, they are a doubled anomaly, a threat to the he-gemony of Venetian, patriarchal economy. The sacrifice of Desdemona by Othello must therefore be understood as an attempt on Othello's part (as male) to rid himself of himself, of a part of himself, an "other" that inheres in him and that gets figured as a dangerous "difference," a sexual, gendered difference in and through Desdemona.

The scene of Desdemona's murder takes on the ambivalence of the "sacred" rites of sacrifice precisely by reinscribing the difference and the commingling of the two protagonists. They are both separated and joined by sexuality underlined as difference, difference between innocence and guilt, female and male, white and black. At the same time there is a further, cataclysmic chiasmus that is at work in the catharsis this scene, on one level, plays out. Just as Othello has wanted to see the "primal scene," the scene that would both confuse and delineate his anxiety, so too, I propose, has the audience's desire been whetted to understand, that is, "see" represented, the "ur-zene" of Othello and Desdemona, situated, as they are by the text, as the most heavily invested example of heterosexuality. Throughout the play, almost as if this tragedy were a "farce de boulevard," we have been kept wondering— "Has this marriage been consummated?" That is, has that line that the text's scandalized rhetoric constantly underlines, the transgressive line that their elopement represents, been crossed? Have the Moor and Desdemona actually infringed the social taboo? And in each instance our question remains suspended. Our voyeuristic desire, informed not only by the virulent "scopic" drive intrinsic in theatrical representation, but by a "scopic" drive enchafed by social and racial stereotypes to "see" their desire, is constantly rekindled and deferred. At each textually underlined moment, at each moment of sexuality, something in the plot interferes, creating a doubt and a "confusion." The audience, that silent but not passive participant in this tragedy, remains frustrated by the central epistemological/sexual conundrum that abides unresolved. Its desire to "know," "to see (more)," is exacerbated by this frustration.

Finally, the only scene the play allows us to witness, the only object offered to our own "voyeurism," is an intimate scene of intense pathos and violence. The "sex" we are finally given to see is not "sex" but ferocity, the murder/sacrifice of Desdemona. Desdemona (as woman) is killed because Othello cannot "read" her, can no longer interpret the "sight" of her. Is she the innocence she claims to be, the sight of her asleep, or is she the cunning, voluptuous temptress that he sees in his mind's eye? It is precisely her "mutability" that he cannot tolerate, that causes his "eye" to lose all control, to be set free, and "roll" from any fixing, any permanent truth in the world ("you're fatal then / When your eyes roll so"). For this reason, then, in order to quell the anxiety her double-being causes in him, he must arrest her change, must kill her by turning her to stone—"smooth as monumental alabaster."[54]

Surely Othello's demented slaying of Desdemona, and her plaintive attempts to remain true to him, to protect him even in death, is one of the most horrifying and pathetic scenes in world tragedy. Yet I would propose that for the purposes of this "transitional" tragedy, the horror of Desdemona's death functions as a textual "come-on," a scenic "objet de perspective." In a sense Desdemona's death corresponds in the scenic "tableau," that is, the play, to the handkerchief that blinds Othello. Desdemona on her deathbed is analogous to the strawberry(s) of the handkerchief, our eyes riveted on this scene of "pathos" and loss. The audience's sight focuses on the sacrifice of the woman as a "primal scene," an originary re-presentation of the founding moment of patriarchy — the woman as other. This capturing of our gaze by the overinvested image of Desdemona nevertheless also turns our eyes from the larger issues of ideological othering this play mediates.[55]

When, in one harrowing revelation after another, the scales are stripped from Othello's eyes, when, presented with the duplicity of his confidant, he finally "sees" the truth of the world he has up until now misread, Othello kills himself. His suicide comes as the culminating "point" of his last "oriental speech":

> I pray you, in your letters,
> When you shall these unlucky deeds relate,
> Speak of me as I am; nothing extenuate,
> Nor set down aught in malice. Then must you speak
> Of one that loved not wisely but too well;
> Of one not readily jealous but, being wrought,
> Perplexed in the extreme; of one whose hand,
> Like the base Indian, threw a pearl away
> Richer than all his tribe;
> Of one whose subdued eyes,
> Albeit unusèd to the melting mood,
> Drops tears as fast as the Arabian trees
> Their medicinable gum. Set you down this;
> And say besides that in Aleppo once,
> Where a malignant and a turbaned Turk
> Beat a Venetian and traduced the state,
> I took by th' throat the circumcisèd dog
> And smote him, thus.
> (V, ii, 350–66)

Othello's last speech returns us, echolike, to the Orient, the threatening Oriental-other. His last great foray into rhetoric reconfirms him as the excessive other into which the plot has turned him and, in and through that confirmation, kills him. He dies, identified with the Turk he slew. But who is this Turk? Who is this Othello that at the end can say, "That's he that was Othello. Here I am"? Finally, what does this

Othello who goes out in a blaze of rhetoric have to do with Iago, the subtle, treacherous Venetian — the Venetian who leaves the play, leaves our view, alive but forever "silent"? ("Demand me nothing. What you know, you know. / From this time forth I never will speak word.")

We have already discussed Othello's underlying drive to have the ocular proof of Desdemona and Cassio's infidelity as pertaining to the Freudian oedipal scenario. On another level, that of tragic victimization and tragic catharsis, Othello bears still more striking resemblances to the "archaeological Oedipus" (in J. Pierre Vernant's term, "Oedipus without the complex"), the sacrificial victim of tragedy.[56] Both Oedipus and Othello share certain common traits that align them with the entire tradition of sacrificial victims we have briefly outlined. Both are of mysterious but noble birth. Both come into the "polis" (Thebes, Venice) as saviors of the state. Both are marked by a sign of difference (Oedipus's handicap, Othello's blackness). In the most uncanny fashion both are stamped with ambivalence, and each seems to concentrate in his person "exterior and interior marginality."[57] Each, in his own way, is "ignorant," and for each ignorance is represented as a failure of vision; it is "blinding." Finally, both assume the place of the Father, actually or metaphorically. Each, therefore, in relation to patriarchal ideology, is situated, for a limited time at least, within the very constrained limits of the Father's Law. Each is politically (but also, and inseparably, sexually) the Law's representative, the "simulacrum" of the Law. For both protagonists, the role they are called upon to play situates them in the space, the constantly displaceable sacrificial space, of the Patriarch. As the "leader" (king/general), Oedipus/Othello becomes the object, the focal point of both the amorous and mortiferous desires of the people (nation, state) he heads, both the people's idol and its hated victim.

In times of great social unrest, times of religious, economic, and sexual drifting, the theater is called upon to bear witness to, to represent, the "sacrifices" that arbitrate social changes. It reflects the conflicting social values it represents, and by so doing produces changes in those values.[58] As Ubersfeld reminds us, the theater "is always in some way the response to its audience's desire," and precisely on this level, in the dialectics of desire, can the theater's mediating role between history and ideology best be understood.[59] One of the most conventional ways of reproducing that ambivalent dialectic of history/ideology and representation is seeing the theater as re-creating on its stage the sacrifice of that member (those members) that a society at a particular moment in its evolution defines as its "other." Historically speaking, for instance, we know that in Elizabethan England there were black people in sufficient quantity to be perceived as a threat and to become the object of an edict of expulsion.[60] Much has been written on the exact nature of Othello's "blackness." The gamut runs from those who ignore or deny the importance of the question of race to those for whom Othello's blackness is the essential element of his character.[61] It is commonly accepted by most contemporary students of the play that Othello was created and perceived as a black African. Yet for Elizabethan England the choice of a racial other is clearly more convoluted than the simple fact of racial difference. That difference is both a "stage prop" and also a device that reaches deep into the social "psyche," to the origins of the constitution of subjectivity, a construction dependent on a subject-object dialectics in which the very notion of "subject" as a difference is integrally dependent as much on what is excluded as on what is included within the parameters (however varied they might be) of both the conscious and unconscious that frame that subjectivity. All societies attempt to alleviate their anxieties about the other that inheres in them by expelling, killing, or in other ways marking the "obvious" differences as anathema—"Any culture defines itself in terms of its Others," writes Mullaney in talking about the way the Renaissance stage dealt with its own phantoms.[62] This is undoubtedly true, but it would be a bit too facile to see in *Othello* simply the reflection of a "real" historical occurrence, the exclusion of the Moor as the rejection of the racial other.

Othello is the sacrificial victim of *Othello*; the theater as mediation, the tragedy as transition. On one level, as I have suggested with my comparison of the different "oedipal" layers the play unfolds, we can see this ambivalent transition in the production of emergent "modern" subjectivity, in the way the play attempts to mediate the transition from an "external" Oedipus (the "archetypical" *pharmakos*) to the "internalized" Oedipus of emergent bourgeois sexuality. The oblique commentary on the status of marriage, and of women, as a cause of social anxiety for Shakespeare's society reflects the difficult passage, in and through the other, of a reconstitution, or better, a gradual reorganization of the drives, social and sexual, that will eventually issue in the late seventeenth century as the emergent structure of the nuclear family.[63] *Othello* prefigures this shift in its anxieties, its paranoia, and its violence. Othello traduces in his madness the moment of "chaos," sexual and social, in which one oedipal structure is evolving into another, and in that evolution traces the parameters of the "divided" modern subject. The play transcribes in its ambiguities echoes of both the mythic Oedipus, the *pharmakos* victim of ancient tragedy, the other who is sacrificed, and the sexual other, who is also lost in a scenario that, unable to be mastered, transforms him into a victim of his own sexual anxiety. At the same time, on yet another level of the text, Othello's sacrifice signals the originary act of a new moment in history: the state is instituted, but as an invisible distant power, silent arbitrator, and perhaps "first cause" of these social changes.[64]

Finally Othello is sacrificed to the text that created him as other all along. He is sacrificed as the excessive — sexually and rhetorically — other that the drama has constructed in relation to a "same" that is only negatively figured: "Venice," in all its abstract political, economic, and social strictures, "Venice," the empowered state, that is represented by the subtly corrupting rhetoric of Iago. Othello was created by the text in the fantasized position of a Renaissance ideal that is no longer tenable in a world that is radically changing, and he was created in that awkward position as the flawed "hero/son" of the state — its guardian and its enemy. Othello, Venice's adopted son, was also its parricide. He, in and with Desdemona, killed Brabantio the father, but also Brabantio the "senator," the dual embodiment of the patriarchal politic structure of society. By so doing, Othello, like Oedipus, takes the (his) father's place in a "polis" that needs him to protect it against the barbarians at the gates, and yet eyes him suspiciously as one of those very same barbarians. For this reason the state, modernity's newly incarnated Patriarch, will sacrifice its children to assure the triumph of its law.[65] Venice, Venetian society, can no more tolerate this extravagant, sexual, uneconomical other than can Brabantio. In order to save itself, Venice (England) must rid itself of what it most fears in itself. But before it can afford to do away with its excessive barbarian, it uses him to destroy that other threat to Patriarchy, the willful independent female, whose act of sexual and political "free thinking" shook the foundations of society. Othello rids the state of this "female trouble," but this act situates him as the criminal-victim the state can now expunge. The newly emerging state — a strong, self-confident Venice — can comfortably sacrifice its own (adopted) son to a renascent "patria." Patriarchal ideology, an ideology that finally the tragedy espouses, kills its son in order not to sacrifice the Father (the "State").[66] The prince in the society that is emerging from the cauldron of *Othello* is, as Goldberg has written, "unobservable."[67] He has become invisible within the reflection of his own power. Venice, the state, remains beyond the horizons of the affairs and violence of Cyprus, and yet its presence is felt everywhere on Cyprus. Everything that transpires there, both in the private and the public domain, is, or will be, known. The state has disappeared into the transparent order of "raison d'Etat," into the evolving order of absolutism: it sees all but remains unseen. Othello has been brought out upon the stage to figure the confusion, the fatal sexual/political confusion of a dying world. He is the Other who inheres in the very constitution of a new world order that both needs him to define itself, and yet in that definition has to eliminate him in order to be. It strikes me as perversely resonant that the tragedy ends with the sacrifice of this leader/prince, his self-immolation in defense of the values of a state that looks approvingly but silently on as he eradicates himself from the world's stage.[68] In the horror and fascination of Othello's death, after the orotund rhetoric of his final speech fades, all that is left as the curtain falls is the originary silence of a new beginning—the silence in which the absolutist state and its new subject are born, the triumphant silence of Iago.

Chapter 2

Fuenteovejuna: The Ideology of Loss and the Myth of History

"El mundo se acaba, Flores."
("The world is coming to an end, Flores.")
Fuenteovejuna, line 1048

The phantasm of the One, the State as a unified body in which the nation in its diversity finds its corporal envelope, cannot be constructed without imagining an enemy.

Enriquez, *De la horde à l'Etat*

Spain, as they say, is different. For almost two centuries this difference shocked and dazzled her rival nations of Europe as Spaniards burst from their homeland to colonize a large portion of the recently discovered "new world." The wealth and energy of these discoveries fueled Spanish political and economic hegemony on the European continent: in the sixteenth century, the Spanish Hapsburgs presided over Europe's most powerful military apparatus during a period of momentous epistemic change. Nevertheless, by the first decades of the seventeenth century, despite all the attempts to check it, the signs of the decline of Spanish military, political, and economic power were clearly evident, and with this decline Spain had already begun to withdraw from her leading role on the stage of international politics, ceding her preeminent position to those traditional rivals France and Britain.[1]

Curiously, this retreat from the stage of world history is marked by history's invading the stage of Spanish drama. In play after play authors of the late sixteenth and early seventeenth centuries return to the chronicles, histories, and "romances" of late medieval Spain for the subject matter of their *comedias*. If we were to engage in great generalizations, and for the moment I would like to risk this, we might say that despite the enormously varied production not only of Lope de Vega but of all the major writers for the stage in the period 1575 to 1675, what strikes us as particularly compelling is the rescripting as drama of events, incidents, and conflicts of the (national) past. History, in other words, becomes the authorized subject matter of the theater at the very moment that theater becomes the privileged form of representation and of nationalist self-representation, not only in Spain but across Europe. It has been claimed, quite convincingly, that the Spanish stage constituted itself as the single most important "public" arena of the period. In this arena, that is, in the extraordinarily overcharged dialectic space that connects the world of the stage and the world of the parterre, the theater, we are told, projects an idealized vision of a distant glory to occult the untenable realities of the present:

> An age of gold and misery that, despite the efforts of the Count-Duke, refuses to confront reality, except perhaps in its attempt to make its tensions disappear by never looking any problem squarely in the eye, and by hiding the sordid social realities and sharp economic and political decline under the guise of a collective spectacle that is motivated by enormous compensatory ideals, totally alienated from reality, and that rigidified and tightly codified all social interactions.[2]

This predominance of historical material over mythological sources is not, of course, unique to Spain; it is a generalized phenomenon of the European stage, including Shakespeare, Corneille, and, to a lesser extent, Racine. It is striking precisely because what we witness in a perverse chiasmus is a "mythologizing" of history. Staged history, that is, historical drama, becomes a new myth, whether we accept Lévi-Strauss's definition of myth as a culture's attempt to represent the harmonization of its own irreconcilable contradictions, or if we follow Jean-Luc Nancy's recent rethinking of myth:

> The Greek "muthos" becomes myth when it is charged with an entire series of values that amplify, swell, and ennoble this word, giving it the dimension of a narration of origins and an explanation of destiny. In myth the world becomes conscious of itself, and it acquires this self-consciousness by an act of declaration or by a complete and decisive revelation.[3]

History, theatricalized as drama, takes on mythic proportions because it appears in its representation as a communal celebration of an "origin," in and through which a people can think of themselves as a "community," a nation.[4] This phenomenon, "history as myth," is intriguing in its own right, if only because it would seem to represent the symptomatic pressures of a realignment of ideological forces that was being traduced onto the Spanish stage not as something exterior to, or simply calqued onto, the theater, but rather as the raison d'être of that theater itself.

In Michel Foucault's panoramic scheme of epistemological evolution from the Renaissance to the classical period (see *Les mots et les choses*, *Histoire de la folie á l'époque classique*), he offers the hypothesis that it was during the late sixteenth and early seventeenth centuries that the general restructuring of the political, social, and sexual parameters inside which a society can think itself became manifest in (among other ways) different rhetorical strategies. These different strategies reflect, on the political and religious levels, the shifting of the major European nation-states away from a no longer viable "contractual" (i.e., feudal) monarchy and toward the emerging absolutist system of precapitalist Europe. One example of this rhetorical restructuring emerges in the new forms that historical writing takes, first in Italy in the writings of Machiavelli and Guicciardini where we see a novel discursive relationship emerge between the "historian" and his subject(s). History becomes a mediating locus between those who make history, and those who, subjugated to those makers, narrate it. According to Michel de Certeau, whose *The Writing of History* has been influential in my thinking about the relation between historiography, dramaturgy, and ideology, in this new form of historical discourse the emergent concept of "raison d'Etat" is first articulated around the pivotal figure of the prince, image and symbol of national unity. The reinvigorated monarchies that at the end of the sixteenth century emerge from more than a century of religious and political dissension are only shakily establishing their authority. The tenuousness of this emergent new order, its hesitations and uncertainties, is reflected in the writings of theoreticians, where we see both the fear of the continuing disintegration of the social fabric and a desire for order, for a suturing of difference, for, in a sense, an impossible return to a world that exists only now as a fantasy of a corporatist society, as an Edenic body politic. This image/fantasy of unity is at once a political, sexual, and social icon, an object of desire. The desire incarnated in the princely body would subsume the divergent aspects of communal life and unite them in a seamless whole.[5]

Recent scholarship on the Spanish government in the first decades of the seventeenth century has, for instance, made us aware of the attempts (only partially successful) of the Count-Duke of Olivares to elaborate a strengthened form of monarchy around a newly empowered "absolute" monarch. J. H. Elliott reminds us of Olivares's many endeavors to achieve what was perhaps impossible: the unification of the various realms of the Spanish Crown into an integral nation. Writing to his master, Olivares outlines this absolutist scheme:

The most important piece of business in your Monarchy is for Your
Majesty to make yourself King of Spain. By this I mean, Sir, that
Your Majesty should not be content with being King of Portugal, Aragon, and Valencia, and Count of Barcelona, but should work and
secretly scheme to reduce these kingdoms of which Spain is composed
to the style and laws of Castile, with no differentiation in the form of
frontiers, customs posts; the power to convoke the Cortes of Castile,
Aragon and Portugal wherever it seems desirable, and the unrestricted
appointment of ministers of different nations both here and
there . . . And if Your Majesty achieves this, you will be the most
powerful prince in the world.[6]

This drive toward unity, toward unification, toward the absolute order
of the One, necessarily and tautologically appeals as a symbolic integrity
to the figure of the prince, the new King/Father of the (proleptically)
united nation.

The relation between princely power and discursive practices was first
elaborated among the Italian historians of the sixteenth century. De Certeau describes that what is being reconfigured in the emergence of modern historiography is a new constellation of discursive power in which the
historian, in his writing practice, places himself in an imaginary locus
that can never be his — the locus of princely power, the locus of the real.
His history, then, is "condemned," according to de Certeau, to being an
alienating fantasy: the writer writes from the place of the prince, from
a locus of power he can never occupy. He is always only a surrogate of
a power he represents but cannot have.[7] At the same time, of course, and
dialectically, this new historiography becomes urgently necessary for the
emergent nation-states in their absolutist forms, for history grounds,
naturalizes, and legitimizes a radical realignment of the monarchal
system.[8]

Although the complex relations between the prince and the role of the
"subject" at the service of the prince receive their first theoretical elaboration from Italian historiographers, it is on the stage of seventeenth-
century European theater that this relation is given its most complex and
seductive development. In the *comedia* the imbrication of history and
drama forms a locus of overlapping and at times contradictory forces that
circumscribe the emergence of a new "subject(ivity)," by which I mean
the coming into awareness on the part of individuals of the way they exist
as political beings, subjected to and subjugated by societal laws, laws of
sociality, laws of economic and sexual constraints that are inimical to individual desire(s). A passage (perhaps a new passage) must be navigated
between those desires and their inscription in the polis. This subject, I
would argue, is implicated in the forms that pleasure and power take in

the new dramaturgy as this dramaturgy reflects and traces the parameters of the emerging absolutism of seventeenth-century Spain.

As the prince becomes the focal point of politics, of history, of the social well-being of his realm, so too does he become the symbol of an integral subjectivity, the vanishing point of legal, social, and sexual authority. At the same time, and paradoxically, as the object of desire of his subjects, the prince also serves as the vanishing point of individuality. Any conception of individual difference, that is, the possibility of the subjects to represent themselves as existing outside the forms of sociality that define them — those hierarchical values that situate the subject both synchronically and diachronically as pertaining to a transhistorical "national" essence — are foreclosed as this sociality becomes inextricably bound to the subjugation of the citizenry to the prince's history. Subjects and monarch are bound together, "incorporated" in a seamless transparency of the ideology of the One, where all subjects look to their prince to give them both a meaning and a place — to subjugate them — and where, of course, in mirror reversal, their appeal to the prince corroborates his position as sovereign.[9]

When seen in these terms, the relation between history and the theater, as it was brought to the stage by Lope in his revolutionary dramaturgy, becomes for Spanish society of the early seventeenth century particularly charged with significance. The theater becomes the locus where the conflicting demands of individual pleasure and societal renunciation meet. By tracing in its internal strictures the social changes that inform its parameters, the stage becomes the mirror of a highly charged, conflicted "subjectivity" directly connected to the ideological imperatives that Lope's dramaturgy with its enormous popular appeal elaborates for and through the pleasure of the spectator.[10]

It would be an error, however, to create too tendentious an analogy between what are, after all, different rhetorical modes — historiography and dramaturgy. The theater is not, cannot simply be reduced to, a mise-en-scène of historical events. Rather, the theater's particularly significant role as a dialectical nexus situates the stage as a highly charged site of ideological investments in which various and often contradictory imperatives that cannot find adequate expression in less tendentious forms of representation are allowed to be essayed in this most public forum.[11] The theater thus takes up and, in the illusion of representation, abolishes the contradictions of historiography — the fact that in attempting to resurrect the past the historian is always reinscribing the present. The writing of history is always the ideological explanation of the present by the past; it can be seen as the imperialistic colonization of the past by the present.[12] The theater, however, and that particular form of historical narrative that Lope perfected for the theater, presents itself disguising its present as past. In a strange crisscrossing, history and dramatic representation contaminate each other, history being the origin of drama and drama the end of history. The points of their intersection, the meeting of the two unassimilable terms of this opposition, is in the immediacy, the always *now* of the moment of spectacle. There is no contradiction between past and present in the spectacle. Rather like the Freudian notion of the unconscious that refuses chronology, the theater as spectacle ignores the past: every theatrical event is an experience of the present.[13]

What interests me, therefore, in Lope's choice of the 1476 revolt of Fuenteovejuna against its feudal lord is not specifically why this choice may or may not be resonant with analogous meaning for the first decade of the seventeenth century or even the more prosaic explanations of how and why this event is used either to shore up or to infirm a "conservative" monarchal regime, only poorly put in place.[14] I am more interested in exploring what I will term the "ideology of subjectivity" that the play represents, all the while aware that ideology is a particularly elusive and illuding term. I would like for the purposes of the present discussion to recall Althusser's famous (and hotly debated) definition of ideology, which I quoted in the Introduction to this book as "the imaginary relationship of individuals to their real conditions of existence" while insisting on the word "imaginary" as the bivalent hinge uniting the individual spectator to the represented universe and, at the same time, to those other spectators, that is, his or her reality, around him or her.[15] The exploration of the ideology of the play, therefore, would be an exploration of its "textual unconscious": forces in the text that are not reducible to an extratextual reality, and yet maintain with that exteriority very real and tendentious ties. Only in this way, in this crisscrossing of the textual universe and its historical context, might we be able to resolve one of the major dilemmas facing any commentator of a text that arrives (through what circuitous paths) in our present as a transhistorical fragment, a symptom of a vanished world. I would propose that these "imaginary" structures, underlying the represented universe, appealed to the Spanish audience of 1612, and continue to appeal to modern audiences across centuries of revolutionary change, centuries that situate us economically, socially, and spiritually in a radically different place from the Spaniards of the early seventeenth century.

Any attempted historical reconstruction of the society of the time, no matter how thorough, seems to me doomed to failure precisely because it ignores the radical difference between the two audiences of the particular play, the seventeenth-century audience and today's. Yet I do not propose to discuss some merely "transhistorical human essence" that would abolish historical difference and allow us to commune with the play in a transparent immediacy of representation.[16] Rather, I propose in this chapter an archaeological reading of the imaginary of the play, that is, of the historical read as the mythological. Thus, this is an attempt to decipher what is at stake for us, a "postmodern" audience, in the representation of a peasant revolt of 1476, written in or close to 1609.

Historically, *Fuenteovejuna*, the play and the "event," is situated as a moment of passage. This passage is the radical change between two world orders, the old order of feudality, of a fragmented and divided kingdom, and the new order of emerging absolutist monarchy, the "union" of the various crowns of the realm, imaged in the sexual/political union of the Catholic Monarchs. We might generalize by saying that the reign of feudality, a "contractual" form of monarchy, corresponded to the long, back and forth but always ongoing, *reconquista*. During nearly eight hundred years, a "national" identity was forged in large part as a negative difference, a "difference without": the "other" over and against whom the "Spaniard" constituted his identity was "clearly and openly visible,"[17] a "racial" and religious split separated "Spaniard," Jew, and Moor. In the newly reconquered kingdom, the kingdom of the Catholic Kings, the "other" has become internalized. If we are to believe Américo Castro and his disciples, the *conversos*, those *nuevos cristianos* who live among the general population, whose "unclean blood" threatens a universal contamination, become the target, the symptom of a national malaise. This new world, a "united" Spain, remains divided, "split within." Perhaps this "internal division" gave the lie to the myth of national unity, which we see represented in so much of the literature of the Golden Age, but in disguised, repressed forms. Castro remarks, and Albert Sicroff's work corroborates his thesis, that the situation of the *conversos* was never dealt with directly on stage, but that, like all the repressed, it returned in disguised form.[18]

In a sense, therefore, we must look for this symptomatic repressed, for the process of "othering" that is at work in the dramatic universe of *Fuenteovejuna* as that universe represents the movement from the old feudal order based on "difference without" to the new absolutist monarchy, with its difference within. In this passage an old order dies and a new one is born. The moment of passage between these two orders is a moment of dramatic trembling, marked by the breakdown of those sexual, political, and social laws that have heretofore obtained and the emergence of new, as yet untried social configurations. Thus the threat, the primordial fear that society will be plunged into an elemental chaos from which it will never extricate itself, that the play both proposes and, apotropaically, forestalls. *Fuenteovejuna* narrates this passage while simultaneously inscribing within itself, as its "drama," all the symptoms of the passage, symptoms of sexuality, transgression, and sacrifice.

In a well-known essay, Leo Spitzer, with his considerable scholarly weight, enters into an ongoing debate about the "real" significance of *Fuenteovejuna*. The play's essence, he states, approving the thesis of Joaquín Casalduero, "does not have a political (or revolutionary) aim as Menéndez Pelayo claims, but rather deals with a metaphysical or moral dilemma."[19] I would like to suggest that this opposition is untenable: only the most ingenuous use of the word political would oppose it to "metaphysical" (and, of course, only in the Platonic sense upon which the premises of Spitzer's arguments in this article are grounded). Political, in its first and most important articulation, concerns the way human beings cohabit in a complex structure of individual and collective demands; the articulation of that structure is always based on the sublimation of the individual in the collective, a sublimation that is, in essence, metaphysical. The sublimation surfaces in those "ideals" — nation (patria), honor, duty — for which and through which the individual becomes (most notably through one's own disappearance, death) a member of a transindividual communality. A polis is both a physical and metaphysical organization, where the metaphysical must be incorporated into the physical, and where the physical must reinscribe itself in the metaphysical presuppositions that found the collectivity. In other words, every society imposes on its members "Laws," which must be internalized if the individual is to become a subject, an economic subject, a sexual subject, a "political" subject.

This imperative of renunciation to the Law forms the underlying dilemma that the play articulates in and through the representation of its protagonist, the Comendador, the central pivot uniting not only the disparate dramatic peripeteia of the play but its metaphysical, and thus political, imbroglio as well. All the modern commentators of the play underline the fact that Lope's rescription of the historical narrative he found in Rades's *Crónica de las tres Ordenes y Caballerías de Santiago, Calatrava y Alcántara* is quite faithful to that account. Nonetheless, Lope inserts one small but critical invention of his own, as Francisco López Estrada explains:

> The notes that we find in the edition show how closely he follows the
> text of the chronicles, and only allows himself one necessary innovation
> in order to give unity to the two plots (of the play): he makes Fernán
> Gómez both the advisor counseling the young Maestre in rebellion
> and, at the same time, the Comendador of the city.[20]

The first two scenes of the play establish Fernán Gómez's position as one of perversion, a perversion in which it is impossible to separate political treason and sexual aggression. The scenes are placed in sexual and political opposition. The first is the masculine world of the Order of

Calatrava, the world of the "historical, active, public" sphere of noble military men. It is clearly placed under the sign of blood, of death ("Unsheath your white sword / dye it red in battle 'til it matches the cross on your chest . . . "). The second scene presents us with the more privatized, feminine space of "community," the world of the village of Fuenteovejuna, to which we are introduced by the dialogue where Pascuala and Laurencia decry the dishonoring sexual excesses of the Comendador. The center of each scene, however — explicit in the first, implicit in the second — is the Comendador. And in each scene, in obviously opposite ways, the Comendador represents "disorder." In the first scene he represents "political" disorder as he counsels the young Maestre of Calatrava to side with Alfonso of Portugal against the Catholic Kings in their bid for the Castilian throne, thus situating himself and his order on the wrong side of historical evolution. In the second scene he is the haunting specter of sexual disorder, of sexuality in its most blatant and excessive form. It is a sexuality that "uses" the village women to sate his lust and thus undoes social hierarchies at the most basic level, undermining the elementary social order of family and its metaphysical correlative, honor:

> LAURENCIA: What good would it do me to love Fernán?
> Do you think I would marry him?
> PASCUALA: Of course not.
> LAURENCIA: Well then, I condemn infamy.
> Too many girls hereabouts have trusted the
> Comendador only to be ruined by him.
> (189–95)[21]

The two faces of community, the external ("politics") and the internal (the sexual) are combined in the person of Fernán Gómez. He is the only character who joins the exterior to the interior, the outside world of Castilian history to the inside world of the village, bringing the one into the other. Yet, in a dramatic twist he represents this "join" as perversion. On both levels and in the inextricable immixture of them in his person, Fernán Gómez represents a perverted political/sexual being, a tyrant, the "evil one," the devil:

> LAURENCIA: Go, pursue your deer, and God be with you.
> You persecute me so that were it not
> for the cross you wear I should think
> you were the devil.
> (810–13)[22]

Before continuing with our reading of the play, two interesting threads need to be mentioned. It is a commonplace of *comedia* criticism to remark that in Lope's theater, unlike its French or English counterparts, we do not find individuated "dramatic" characters, but rather "dramatic situations."[23] The corollary to this in Lope's theater presents us with an unindividuated "social" corpus, in which the characters are rather conventional "types." There is as yet no verisimilous psychological "hero." This would seem to be only partially accurate in *Fuenteovejuna*. It is true that in this play all the characters except one seem to be rather stock figures: the kings are icons, stiff hieratic images of a "King," and the peasants of the village also fall into bucolic literary stereotypes—the young lovers, the *gracioso*, the wise elders. The only character who takes on (to some degree) an individualized profile is Fernán Gómez, the Comendador, and he is individuated as "evil." In a certain sense, we might say that in this pre-Cartesian universe, only Fernán Gómez exists, and only he can say "I am 'bad' [perverse, a traitor], therefore I am."

This textual centering of "being" on Fernán Gómez should retain our attention, because it has repercussions for the entire ideological substructure of the represented universe. In a first and simple sense, this incarnation of evil in the protagonist helps to establish the first "metaphysically" charged dichotomy of the play, the division of the represented universe into two opposing camps: villainy and innocence. This division predicates the other dyadic oppositions that reflect the moral and political universe of the play, the divisions between male and female, between town and country, between good king and bad king, between nature and culture.

In an intriguing sense, the play always returns to its most highly volatile, uncontrollable central locus, the character of Fernán Gómez, for its dramatic energy, for the energy it needs to work itself out. It is Fernán Gómez who joins and confounds, in his person, these same divisions that his character helps to articulate. His character unites the "two" in one; thus he is represented always as a heterogeneous, dual being. In this world that wants, and desires, the order of the One, of the absolute, Fernán Gómez is perhaps the marker of the Other, a *malo cristiano*, a "split being," and thus in some fashion the precursor of a modernity that the play can only dimly perceive, but that it clearly must destroy. It is this doubling of opposites in the Comendador that marks him, in Girard's terminology, as "monstrous."[24] Yet this monstrosity is needed by the terrorized community, as its Other, both its tyrant and its victim.

No one will be surprised by the application of the term "tyrant" to the Comendador, as this term is repeated strategically by the play itself with more and more insistence as it reaches its apogee—"There's the tyrant and his accomplices! / Long live Fuente Ovejuna, death to the tyrants!" (1877–78). The term "victim," however, might appear more incongruous. Obviously on the level of diegesis the Comendador victimizes both the townspeople and, by betraying them, his feudal superiors. Nevertheless, when we consider the play on the more highly charged and abstract level of ritualized spectacle, where the question of conflicting and conflicted desire emerges (the internal desire of the play itself, as well as the desire that, emanating from the audience, is in some way satisfied by the play)[25] the structural necessity of Fernán Gómez as victim in and of the foundation myth the play traduces becomes evident. What I am suggesting is that on a deeper level, Fernán Gómez must be seen as a victim of the play, that is, of the ideology the play acts out.

In his important theoretical speculations on the origins of civilization (*Totem and Taboo, Moses and Monotheism*), Freud has left us with his own "foundation myth." This myth has proved seductive to both anthropologists and ethnographers in their attempts to explain the dynamics underlying the political organization of simple and complex human societies.[26] The myth of the primal horde ruled by a ruthless, self-enclosed, sexually dominant Ur-Father, although certainly not verifiably true, nevertheless echoes powerfully in the various founding narratives that societies invent to explain their own origins. That these myths are as illuding as they are revelatory goes without saying. What is important in the Freudian scenario is the fact that although the "brothers" of the primal horde rise up, kill, and ritually devour their tyrannical father, this cataclysmic act of violence, the acting out of their hatred, is immediately followed by an overwhelming sense of guilt — the sign that not only did they hate the father, but they loved and desired him, too.

The significant point is that the ambivalence of the brothers' hate/love of the father, the ambivalence of all children's relations to their parents, according to Freud, is especially manifest in those patriarchal cultures where this ambivalence is projected outward as the split, double images of the (good-bad) leader. This ambivalence toward the father appears in the Manichaean coupling of those opposites that represent him: God/Devil, King/Tyrant, and so on. In fact, de Certeau sees this ambivalent split as one of the essential underlying features of seventeenth-century Europe:

> First the importance of the ambivalence of God and the devil that
> Freud emphasizes seems to be confirmed through the multiple shapes
> of its persistence throughout the seventeenth century. Thus, in taking
> the place of a religious authority, the state (and in theory, "state
> policy") becomes a substitute (an ersatz) for God-the-Father, who
> was . . . "split up" by the wars of religion. But on the one hand, the
> initial ambivalence of God-the-Father is still expressed in every church
> through the vacillation of all religious experience between the divine
> and the diabolical, while on the other, it resurges as an ambiguity
> within the movement, which then causes this state policy to be read ei-
> ther as "divine right" or as the "policy of Hell."[27]

Bearing this ambivalent structure/desire in mind, it will be fruitful to return to the drama to see how this opposition is played out within the particular context of the sexual/political confines of *Fuenteovejuna*.

Throughout the first scenes of the play the Comendador is unques-
tionably firmly ensconced in his "traditional" (feudal) role as lord of Fuenteovejuna. He is a military leader, and we should not dismiss the fact that
his position is, through the elaborate rhetoric of Lope's description,
transformed into a shiny icon of feudal nobility, the desired object of his
vassals' ideals:

> Our lord, Fernán Gómez, rode at the Maestre's side
> on a powerful honey-colored horse with black legs
> and mane and a white muzzle. Over a Turkish coat
> of mail he wore a magnificent breast-and-back plate
> with orange fringes and resplendent with gold and pearls. . . .
> His red and white band flashed on his arm as he brandished
> an ash tree for a lance, making himself feared even in Granada.
> (485–500)[28]

The elaborate rhetorical descriptions of his person, his horse, his courage
in warfare, though perhaps meant to extol his lineage (to the contemporary, 1610, public) nevertheless clearly produce an image that is politically significant. The rhetoric creates Fernán Gómez as an image and
symbol of the leader, the "sovereign lord," of his vassals. Yet even here
this shining figure retains the ambivalence with which the Comendador
always exists in the drama: he is the beautiful image of a doomed caste.
The image is inextricably bound to his depravity, for we must not forget
that despite the luxuriant rhetoric he is waging war against the "rightful"
heirs to the throne, against his liege lords. Fernán Gómez marches forth
in all the rhetorical splendor of Lope's poetry as a traitor.

To this treacherous lord, the text opposes the less rhetorically invested, more sober representation of the "good lord," the Catholic Kings.
The "kings" (they are always referred to in the plural, *los reyes*) first enter
the scene of the drama at a moment of political and military crisis: the
troops of the Order of Calatrava have just taken Ciudad Real, a vulnerable strategic location in the ongoing military campaign against their rival, Alfonso, King of Portugal. This scene in which Fernando and Isabel
appear for the first time is doubly interesting. The image of "monarchy"
is one in which the political and the sexual are inextricably intertwined.
The king and queen are literally meant to "embody" the emergent concept of "absolutism": a union of the sexes that is also and concomitantly,
a political union. This image is nevertheless as deceptive as it is politically
and sexually necessary. Don Fernando and Doña Isabel exist as a bi-
cephalous monarch, a strange icon of the "king's two bodies," a single

unity comprised of two distinct persons. This unity is underlined by the insistent refrain "two who are as one" ("que para en uno son"), which runs as a leitmotiv through the text. It is a male-female unity, almost, I am tempted to say, an androgynous king/queen.[29]

> Long live fair Isabella
> And Ferdinand of Aragon
> (Two who are as one)
> He is made for her
> And she is meant for him.
> (2035–38)[30]

This image is alluring, and yet, as image, it uses sexuality to paper over the very real political difference it would not allow. The two kings are not actually the political unity their image would supply: Aragon and Castile remain separate legal states, each still ruled by its appropriate head, each still subject to the different reigning customs and laws that have defined them as different throughout their history. In 1476, "Spain" was fragmented rather than united. Nevertheless, the image of the kings projects back onto history a present (1609) desire, a desire that the "two be one," that is, absolute.

The two monarchs speak as one, although (and I shall return to this shortly) in the phallocentrism of the text Isabel always queries and defers, while Fernando commands, and in the end it is he who pronounces judgment. Their sexual harmony projects a proleptic image of the political harmony, the order that their reign will bestow on the war-torn nation. This political concord projects its security over the reality of the civil war that is rending the country, and whose bloody effects we have just heard Flores recount to the peasants:

> The city rushed to arms; the inhabitants
> apparently did not come out to fight but stayed within
> the city walls to defend their property.
> But in spite of the strong resistance the Maestre
> entered the city. He ordered the rebels and those
> who had flagrantly dishonored him to be beheaded,
> and the lower classes were gagged and whipped in public.
> (501–12)[31]

A sexual complementarity subtends the (illusory) political harmony the kings represent.[32] The two monarchs, in the couple they form, figure the perfect sexual symmetry that informs the political, that "naturalizes" it in a closed circle wherein the "proper" conjoining of male and female is presented as upholding, through an image of "natural" order, the entire political edifice the kings are trying to put into place. At the apex of the social/political order they represent the correct sexual alignment that is

the model for all organized social life. At the same time, as a political figure, they represent the sublimation of destructive passion in the socially
and religiously sanctioned ties of marriage. Thus, sexuality and politics,
confounded in the iconic images of the "kings," form a seamless, transparent web of contained, controlled, and naturalized communal existence.

At the bottom of the social ladder, the desire, courtship, and proposed
marriage of Frondoso and Laurencia reflect the image of sexual and political harmony incarnated in the kings at the top. The text underlines
this mirroring by using for both couples the same rhetorical refrain, "two
who are as one," to describe lawful (therefore, political) sexual union.
This union is the basis of community, ensuring its self-perpetuation. The
rhetorical mirroring creates an enclosure, a circular self-contained world
of sexual/political order, which, from the top of society to its bottom,
defines itself against the transgressive sexuality of the Comendador. We
might turn this around and say that what separates the play into unsym-
metrical parts — the utopian world of Fuenteovejuna and the kings, and
the dystopian world of the Comendador and declining feudality — is the
depiction of sexuality, or of "Eros," as itself ambivalent. On the one hand
is the erotic drive that unites, that conforms to social constraints, that accepts the Law (castration) and thus sublimation. On the other stands the
negative Eros, the Eros that transgresses, that destroys societal codes,
leaving in its path the loss of honor, social disintegration, and death.

What is most striking for a modern audience in Frondoso and Laurencia's courtship is that it is a totally public affair: the entire village is aware
of Frondoso's attraction to Laurencia, her disdain of men, and the frus-
trating stalemate to which their relation, at the beginning of the play, has
arrived:

> It seems that everyone in town is saying that you are running
> after me and I after you. And because you are the sort of
> fellow who struts about and shows off his clothes, which are more
> fashionable and expensive than other people's, all the girls and boys
> in the countryside think there must be something between us.
> They are all waiting for the day when Juan Chamorro will put
> down his flute and lead us to the altar.
> (728–42)[33]

Their sexuality is a communal desire: it is lived under the eyes of the
villagers, who approve it, sanction it, and desire its (legalized) consum-
mation. In the relation of desire uniting Frondoso to Laurencia it is not
so much the two young people who love each other, but the entire community, in its ethical, legal, political, and sexual predicates, that loves
them because it loves itself through them: it sees itself reaffirmed and perpetuated in that love.[34]

Frondoso and Laurencia's courtship is lived out under the gaze of the world. It is presented as "transparent," open, and legal. Frondoso's love is "contained," rather than transgressive. Whenever he speaks his desire it is always in legal, religious terms:

> You know that my only wish is to become your husband:
> is it fair then to reward my love in this way?
> (755–57)

> Come with me to the altar, and let us live
> like turtle doves, billing and cooing,
> after the church has blessed us.
> (767–71)[35]

In the sense that Frondoso's desire is entirely circumscribed within the law of his community, we are justified in describing it and him as both normative and prescriptive of socialized sexuality. Frondoso keeps his desire within the fixed bounds of societal law, just as he knows his social "place" within that law:

> I'm satisfied with my station in life.
> (851–52)[36]

The trouble in the play is, of course, that this "state" (the various signifying systems that have defined the world) and Frondoso's place in it are in a period of transition.

Fuenteovejuna exists as a utopian image of village: it is a bucolic fantasy, a literary topos, a locus amoenus.[37] The town and its inhabitants exist as a self-contained unit, closed off from the rest of the world. In the larger, exterior universe, evil is endemic: it is a world of warfare, change (e.g., the invention of the printing press), hypocrisy (see the amusing dialogues on "city speech" and its distortions of reality). The world of Fuenteovejuna, however, is presented as "pure," a bucolic never-never land where only stylized characters exist. They are all "good," all sympathetic literary-village "types"—the young lovers, Mengo the *gracioso*, the flirtatious but honest young women, the wise elders. (Curiously, this village is singularly lacking in older women, although it has several old men. Perhaps this is but another unconscious symptom of the text's patriarchal investment, for in that system old women are already coded as unacceptable: they are "ugly," "unnatural," "witches." In Spanish culture, they would seem to be subsumed under the image of the Celestinas, those purveyors of illicit sexuality, and for that reason banned from the universe of Fuenteovejuna.) Nevertheless, we know that in every Eden crawls a serpent.[38] What has been repressed in the representational universe returns to haunt and torment that universe in direct proportion to the energy exerted in its repression.

Depravity, when it appears, comes into the village from without, or rather, it enters the universe of the townspeople from that troubling, marginal space that separates and joins the closed world of Fuenteovejuna and the larger world of Castilian history. Fernán Gómez as the hinge in the universe of the play is its most mobile character, moving from court to country, from the highest noble relations to interaction with the lowliest peasant, from the world of war to the agrarian peace of the village. The Comendador represents an ambivalent, ill-defined presence in the world of Fuenteovejuna: he is both of the town, and not part of it; he resides there but is never really an integral part of the communal structure. The Comendador exists on the margins of village life, but, perversely, at its very center also. Hierarchically his position as feudal lord places him squarely at the top of the symbolic network of sociality: his role as lord situates him as the final authority, the despotic leader of communal existence. Many recent theorists of social organization have insisted on the real, or more importantly the mythic, function of the "leader" for social cohesion. In these theories, all directly or indirectly derived from Freud, the leader is always an ambivalent pole, attracting the libidinal desires of the populace by incarnating in a particularly strong and precise way the social ideals that govern society:

> The leader, the man . . . who proposes and represents the ideals of the group, who works, through his charisma, to siphon off the individual aspirations and fantasies, is the object put in the place of the Ego Ideal and (thus) induces the identifications of the faithful among themselves. He is also the ideal man one would have liked to have been and to whom all authority is delegated.[39]

At the same time, and in exactly inverse proportions, he can also serve as the pole of all the hostile, frustrated, and deadly desires of his people:

> The autocratic tyrants concentrate in themselves, to varying degrees, all the aspirations that normally are directed at the Ideal-Father. This is a particularly dangerous position because so many different hopes converge in one single individual. Success and victory greatly magnify him but make him more fragile too, when we consider the eventuality, the prediction, the expectation of defeat, both feared and yet hoped for because the constantly renewed exertion that is demanded eventually becomes intolerable, and this brings about and even hastens the debacle.[40]

That this leader is not necessarily or even usually, as twentieth-century history has amply shown, benevolent is intriguing. Only when we understand that the leader's charisma is in great part due to an alienating narcissism, both attractive and destructive, can we begin to perceive the workings of this apparent paradox.

The essence of this narcissism is its apparent independence from those worrisome fears of retribution, guilt, and desire that bind lesser mortals to their mundane fate. The charismatic leader, veiled in his narcissism, seems impervious to the outside, to society's dictates. Rather he acts out in his life the excesses — economic, linguistic, sexual — that others secretly desire.[41] The leader acts as the projection of those desires that are inadmissible in the individuals who compose the community. When these desires appear to exist unfettered in the leader or, in reverse fashion, when the leader appears to incarnate an unrestrained libidinal drive, he is placed in the envied yet dangerous position of irrational adoration. That this narcissistic position is intimately connected to death and serves as the vehicle of death, most notably the death of the charismatic leader, is evident in and from narcissism's origin, the myth of Narcissus.[42] What is important, of course, is the dialectical relation joining the leader to the community: the leader is the leader because he does or is permitted to do — to a certain varying, undefined degree — what is not permitted to the members of the community.

Therefore, it is precisely from the Comendador's structural position of societal ambivalence — both in and out of the community — that evil can be said to enter the village. Evil is figured as the unbridled, destructive sexuality that had been repressed in the representation of the socialized desire of Frondoso. The Comendador, whom we've seen opposed politically to the kings, is here opposed to Frondoso once more as a tyrant, but, in this widening of character, as a sexual tyrant. It is on the level of sexuality that the two strands of what has traditionally been seen as the opposing plots of the drama — the political plot of treason and the "social" plot of village tyranny — are actually intertwined.

Just as the Comendador in his opposition to the kings takes on the negative valence of political tyranny, his negative mirroring of Frondoso's masculine desire parasitizes the entire text. The first scene in the village is a dialogue between Laurencia and Pascuala whose purpose is to introduce the theme of Fernán Gómez's sexual aggressions. From the beginning we are made aware that the social order, here articulated in and through women, is besieged by the corrupt and corrosive force of unbridled sexuality, just as Ciudad Real, in another dimension, is under attack by the troops of the treasonous Order of Calatrava. We might say that Fernán Gómez in his aggressive pursuit of the women of Fuenteovejuna represents "sexuality" in its most pristine (that is, most unrepressed) form. He is, at least on this level of his characterization, an allegory, not far removed from those medieval allegorical representations of "luxuria." As sexuality, he is a force that recognizes no bounds ("Why are you trying to hide, / gallant maid? / Don't you know that my lynxlike desire / slips through walls . . . "), hurtles over obstacles in pursuit of its satisfaction, and refuses the "cutting no" of social interdiction that precisely defines and limits the acceptable forms sexuality can take in any given society. Pushed to its extreme, allowed to run unfettered, sexuality threatens communal life with disintegration. At the most fundamental level, the fantasy of unrestricted sexuality is the fantasy of chaos, the return to a primordial, powerful indifference in which all order, all life as it is known, ceases to exist. The text's insistence on the Comendador as "unbridled" sexuality (as opposed to communally regulated gender roles) concentrates on his character the fear of social collapse and further taints his already military personality with the colors of death.[43]

It is perhaps for this reason that Fernán Gómez's sexuality, as opposed to Frondoso's, is always marked as clandestine. It is relegated behind the closed doors of his commandery ("Step over the threshold, go, into the house") or to the equally hidden haunts of the surrounding forests. The Comendador's desire is aggressive yet furtive; it lurks in the dark shadows of those ambivalent mediating spaces where village life, the life of the known and the safe, imperceptibly fades off into the unknown, beyond the bounds of community into the surrounding "natural" terrain. We can thus better understand the underlying motivation for the constant rhetorical references to Fernán Gómez as a sexual predator, a hunter, and, to the different women he pursues, as prey:

> This is good luck.
> My chase of the timid fawn
> has led me to a lovely doe instead.
> (779–81)[44]

The words that are constantly used in the play to represent the Comendador's "desire" belong to the reifying vocabulary of the chase. Women are described as "beast," "hare," "doe," "meat" — prey to the Comendador as hunter. This insistence on sexuality as a hunt, although resonant with echoes of both classical mythology and the even more classic topos of the war between the sexes, carries, especially in the locus amoenus that is Fuenteovejuna, ever more threatening overtones.

The more Fernán Gómez represents the unfettered, desocializing aspects of the erotic drive, the more the text animalizes him, turning him into a "bloodthirsty beast . . . / poison that infests the whole countryside" (1148–50), a tiger ("you'd think he'd sucked his cruelty from a tiger"; 1183–84), and a tyrannical monster ("you mean Heliogabulus, / more wicked than a beast"; 1175–76). In the play these images of hunter and hunted circumscribe the sexuality of the Comendador as mortiferous. They display the negative, destructive, socially fragmenting aspects of desire that have been repressed in Frondoso's humble, socially invested courtship of Laurencia, and that return, overblown and menacing, in Fernán Gómez.

What compounds the negativity of the Comendador's destabilizing sexuality is the fact that his prey is almost invariably women who are already the "possession" of other men. In fact, I find it particularly significant that the text insists on repeatedly specifying this transgression:

> COMENDADOR: Did not Salustiana, the wife of Pedro Redondo,
> surrender to me—and Martín del Pozo's wife, too,
> only two days after her wedding?
> (799–804)

> COMENDADOR: And now—what news of Pascuala?
> FLORES: She says she's about to get married.
> (1059–60)

> COMENDADOR: What news from Inés?
> FRONDOSO: Which Inés?
> COMENDADOR: The wife of Antón.
> (1076)[45]

This repetition underlines the inextricable knot of sexuality and politics in the play. An insistence on the fact that the Comendador's sexuality invades those ties that, as we have seen in the image of the kings, are the very rock upon which the patriarchal social order of the play rests shows that the Comendador's sexual predation undermines that order precisely where sexuality, family, and honor intersect. Furthermore, the textual insistence of repeatedly articulating the infringement by Fernán Gómez upon other men's "pleasure" leads us to suspect that it is in this infringement that *his* pleasure resides. In other words, not only is Fernán Gómez's sexuality defined as destructive of the ties of sociality, it is also tinged with the hint of perversion. Fernán Gómez pleasures, perhaps can only pleasure, in the place of another man. His pursuit of women takes on the even more forbidden aspect of being the pursuit of men. To the crime of adultery, then, the text suggests another: the insistence on the Comendador's pleasuring in other men's wives underlines the hidden, repressed desire—the sexual disorder, the "unnaturalness" this pleasuring both hides and reveals. Through the women he seduces Fernán Gómez pleasures, also, in the men he cuckolds.

Gradually, as we proceed through the text, the trouble that is the Comendador invades ever more profoundly the communal existence of Fuenteovejuna. This invasion, the breakdown of communal order, is doubly marked as "political" and "sexual" tyranny. The Comendador's insulting rhetoric—he speaks too freely of the women in the town—

breaches, on the linguistic level, the same symbolic codes that his seduction sunders on the sexual level:

> COMENDADOR: She's determined to hurt me—while the wife of a nobleman here in town is dying for an opportunity to see me.
> ESTEBAN: Then she would do wrong—and you do yourself no good to talk so flippantly.
> COMENDADOR: My, my, what a circumspect peasant.
> (966-73)[46]

The final, irreparable transgression is also doubly political and sexual: the Comendador, in a fit of pique and anger, seizes Esteban's staff, symbol of this mayoral dignity, and beats him over the head with it. The symbolism of the staff (*vara*), the mayor's staff, needs no great elaboration in the further sexual imagery of the play. By disdainfully grabbing it from Esteban, and using it to humiliate him and his office, the Comendador effectively "unmans" the mayor, and thus the Law and Order he represents.

What we have been witnessing, what the play makes us concentrate our emotions and our own sexual-political investments upon, is the gradual unveiling of evil, tyranny: the "revelation" of the "other," the presence of evil in and among a "peaceful community." I have already suggested that on one profound level the text plays an interesting game of hide and seek with its readers/spectators: by insisting on the unambiguous distinction between the good and the bad, between the Comendador and the rest of the characters in the play, the play concentrates on him and on the hostility and aggression that he visits upon the town. On one level, this strong, unidimensional concentration of negativity on Fernán Gómez would seem to make him the only really interesting character in the play, would make him not only the internal hinge uniting and separating the two seemingly disparate plots of the drama but also the hinge connecting the internal dynamics of the represented universe with the "real" dynamics of the spectating audience. This centralizing positioning of Fernán Gómez by the text makes him the target of textual interest and of textual aggression. He is thus positioned as the recipient of the hostile, aggressive emotions of both the represented universe and ours as well.

Such a concentration of dramatic tension on one character would, however, seem to belie the commonly held critical position (already mentioned at the beginning of this chapter) that in Golden Age *comedia* "there are dramatic situations, but there is no intimate drama." *Fuenteovejuna* does not contradict the generalization: the "character" Fernán Gómez does not manifest any more verisimilar a psychology than any of the other characters in the play. He simply amasses a greater concentration of textual tension without this concentration's leading to what one could consider an intimate (i.e., "psychological") dramatic crisis. It is thus to the character in situ, as situation, that we must direct our attention in order to understand what on the simple level of plot appears as a truism: the Comendador is a "bad guy" and thus should and must be punished. If the play could be so simply reduced, it could just as simply be dismissed. The fact that it cannot be discarded, but that, on the contrary, is touted as the most powerful and popular ("nationalistic") work of Spain's most prolific playwright tells us that other forces are active in this character and in this drama that lift them out of the realm of the banal and project them into the sphere of the mythic.[47]

Our discussion of the communal crisis looming within the confines of life at Fuenteovejuna has necessarily left aside the other thread, the thread of history that is sparingly but pointedly woven into the play, completing its complex tapestry. "History," that is, the events of the "real" world surrounding and enveloping the village, appears to operate on another stage. Its presence makes itself felt in the utopian space of the village only by and through the presence of the Comendador. In a very real sense for the villagers of Fuenteovejuna, Fernán Gómez is their only link to the greater stage of the world: he is their history.

Fuenteovejuna represents, as I have said, history as a moment of passage. It is the passage from the world of the fragmented, feudal, dismembered Spain to the imposition of a unifying nascent absolutist monarchy. This passage is inscribed in the play in significant ways: on the first level we have two extended rhetorical passages that frame the "central" argument of the play, its more profound focusing on the internal strife of Fuenteovejuna. Both passages recount the battles for possession of Ciudad Real and in both the Comendador has a leading role. In the first he and his order are victorious. Their victory is a moment of historical indecision: by their investment of Ciudad Real they forestall the movement of history. Their triumph is a delaying tactic in the onward and (from the hindsight of the seventeenth-century public) inevitable triumph of the Catholic Kings. Nevertheless it is from this negative space of death and treason that the Comendador returns to his village and is received by his vassals as a hero. Their greeting of him, the poetry and song, the abundance of offerings — livestock, wine, and foodstuffs — mark his return to the village as a reentry into peace and life.

The second rhetorical passage traces the opposite movement. Recalled to defend the captured town against the counteroffensive of the army of the kings, the Comendador and his forces are defeated. The representatives of "progress" have triumphed on the greater stage of national history; their victory at Ciudad Real figures in the play their eventual triumph over all the tendencies of divisiveness in the peninsula, their reuniting of the country, and the eventual defeat of the system that has empowered the different feudal military orders. In the space of these two ornate rhetorical passages, Lope traces the (beginnings of the) demise of an entire world order, and the gradual putting into place of a new one.

The Comendador returns the second time to his village as a defeated man and as a defeated caste. He reenters the scene at the precise moment that the townspeople are celebrating that most highly invested of social rituals, the union of two young people in marriage, the promise and symbol of the community's renewal. The sexual union of Frondoso and Laurencia that the town is celebrating is also a political process, the celebration of the Law, the social codes that say "no" to unbridled sexuality and therefore say "no" to the Comendador. It is thus into this highly charged, communal celebration of the Law, of that which opposes community to narcissistic indulgence, that an already-weakened Fernán Gómez appears and, in one last aggression, attempts to impose his own, fragmenting desire. Interrupting the "marriage" (engagement) he puts an end to all rejoicing:

> Silence! You will all remain
> quietly where you are.
> (1570–71)[48]

Into this space of vitality and regeneration, Fernán Gómez appears as the specter of sterile tyranny. At the height of communal rejoicing Fernán Gómez returns, arrests Frondoso and Laurencia, and turns what was an affirmation of life into the triumph of death: "The wedding feast changed into a wake!" ("¡Volvióse en luto la boda!"). The general parasitizing and corruption of community by the Comendador's perversity — the irruption of evil in the utopian locus of community, the return of the repressed — throws the community into a final, desperate tailspin.

At this point of conjuncture, when death, regression, and backsliding politics threaten to engulf the town and its inhabitants entirely, Fuenteovejuna is forced out of its Edenic position and into history. In this transformation the town and its people become the symbolic representatives of an entire nation and that nation's rebirth. Before that rebirth can be brought to term, however, a final, decentering, desubjectifying descent into chaos, into the world of the "unnatural" must be invoked, bringing the town and its inhabitants into the vortex of their own disappearance. Only once this final battle between the forces of dispersion and those of unity has been engaged can the town, its inhabitants, and Spain emerge, having navigated the passage in the new order of ongoing Castilian history.

The final significant reversal, this return of the community to itself, is mediated by a woman. It is perhaps only "logical" (in the logic of the text, that is) that the instrument of rebellion be a woman, the most alienated object of the Comendador's aggression. After the dispersal of the wedding crowd, the arrest of Frondoso and Laurencia, and their imprisonment in Fernán Gómez's commandery, the men of the village are locked in impotent debate on how to remedy the situation; the surprise entrance of Laurencia and her impassioned speech finally set the village revolution in motion.

From the beginning, Laurencia has been an ambivalent cipher in the sexual politics of the drama. She is marked most significantly by her refusal of sexuality — of the heterosexuality imposed on women in a patriarchal culture. She rejects the respectful courtship of Frondoso and the aggressive desires of the Comendador. Both men, each representing, as we have seen, opposing valences of male desire, accuse her of being aloof, hard-hearted, and disdainful:

> FRONDOSO: Your disdain and beauty are so great,
> Laurencia, that when I see you and listen to you I fear they will kill
> me.
> (751–54)

> COMENDADOR: Such disdain, fair Laurencia, is an insult to the beauty
> heaven gave you.
> (786–89)[49]

Both accuse her of being "inhuman." Her refusal of their sexuality marks her as cruel, death-dealing, a new Amazon. Like an Amazon, her desire is kindled only by death. Only after Frondoso has put himself, in an uncannily pre-Hegelian move, in the place of death, has defied the Comendador, can she desire him:

> I used to hate men, Mengo, but since
> that day I've looked at them with different eyes.
> Frondoso acted so gallantly! But I'm afraid
> it may cost him his life.
> (1154–59)[50]

In a certain sense, by Frondoso's heroic action of exposing his own life to save her, he has elevated himself above the normal seductive strategies that Laurencia had foresworn at the beginning of the play. Frondoso's confrontation with death has placed him on a plane of the unique, and this uniqueness seduces Laurencia. What this means, however, is that once "seduced" her love becomes exclusive, totalizing, eternal. She returns more poignantly to still another cultural model of sexual fidelity/ enslavement: her love for her mate takes on the tone of a Roman matron. She becomes a new Lucretia, and her defensive anguish, her rage at the injustice that the Comendador inflicts upon her (them), is thus authorized to speak itself in the most rhetorically passionate, elaborate passage in the entire drama.

Laurencia's violent diatribe rhetorically replicates in one intense poetic passage the entire revolution in village life that we have been analyzing more prosaically. This one speech articulates the nefarious effects the Comendador has had on Fuenteovejuna: culture has been invaded and parasitized by "nature" (sexuality, evil) and the result has been the "denaturalization" of society. Through the use of the same animal imagery that we have already seen applied to the Comendador, and by him to the women he covets, the passage traces the decline of society into chaos. Laurencia, in her fury, accuses the men precisely of not being men. They are transformed into sheep, rabbits, and finally hens:

> Are you not good men? — Not fathers
> and relatives? Do not your hearts sink
> to see me so grievously betrayed?
> Oh, you are sheep; how well named
> the village of Fuente Ovejuna. . . .
> You were born timid rabbits;
> you are infidels, not Spaniards.
> Chicken-hearted, you permit other men
> to abuse your women.
> (1754–77)[51]

As the tone of her indignation mounts, the men descend in the animal order. In effect, what Laurencia, in a rather perverse reversal, is here giving voice to is her alienation, as a woman, in a male-ordered society. Having always rejected believing in the sexual order that governed this world, her outrage at being betrayed by it is all the greater after she has finally been seduced into love. She has been "seduced and abandoned" by an entire community. She has been left hanging, her interrupted marriage suspending her between two males: no longer quite the responsibility of her father, not yet the possession of a husband. It is from an undefined, untenable position, a "no-man's-land" that Laurencia wishes to be saved. Betrayed by a system that subjugates her, her female subjectivity no longer has an anchoring in the world. Her diatribe is a poignant plea for the men to be (act as) men, so that she can resituate herself in the community as a woman, even if that situation be a subjected one. But to be saved she must rouse the men from their prostration. The most effective way she finds for doing this is to taunt them sexually, to accuse them of not being men, but of being women:

> By the living God, I swear that your women
> will avenge those tyrants and stone you all,
> you spinning girls, you sodomites,
> you effeminate cowards. Tomorrow deck yourselves

in our bonnets and skirts, and beautify yourselves
with our cosmetics.
(1778–83)[52]

Her diatribe effectively describes the situation of impotence, the unmanning of the male villagers at the hands of the Comendador.

As the men are reduced to whimpering *castrati*, Laurencia's speech indicates another unnatural result of Fernán Gómez's tyranny: women have become monstrous. They are turned into Amazons, the "eternal terror of the world." The world has been turned on its head, all natural order (the order the text wants "naturalized") has been perverted: the men are feminized and the women turned into fierce warriors — "a spectacle of horror for the entire world." Laurencia's diatribe is descriptive of the situation, of the chaos wrought by the Comendador. It is also performative: once the speech has acted out the undoing of the world, once it has shown the pervasive presence of this unbridled political and sexual tyranny, once it has reduced the community from a "community of men" to a community of monsters, then the community can swell forth and kill the monster at the root of its perversion.

The men of the village rush out, roused to blind fury by Laurencia's speech. The women, under her command, follow. Their mob, a *turba*, is an uncontrollable, violent, passionate throng. They storm the Comendador's stronghold, killing him and ransacking his possessions. Fernán Gómez's body is dragged through the streets of the town. It is vilified and desecrated. The women cut off his ears, an obvious substitution for a ritual castration. As an ultimate outrage, the body is decapitated and the head paraded through village streets.[53]

The most striking feature of these scenes of revolt, as well as of Flores's narration of the rebellion, is the fury and collective violence of the mob. The happy philosopher-villagers have been turned into a beastly murderous throng that ransacks, burns, murders, and destroys ("Break them down, smash them in, burn, destroy!" — 1858). The textual insistence on the violence of the crowd (the revolt against and murder of the Comendador is repeated first as theatrical representation, then as theatrical narration when the kings are told of it) within the historical and mythic context we have been elaborating signals us that the theater is here acting out a ritualizing role. Centering on the mise-en-scène of the murder of the failed leader cannot but remind us of the importance of sacrifice in all those myths of social/political foundation.

René Girard's considerable work on the importance of violence and sacrifice as constituting the originary communal crime instituting and perpetuating societal cohesion has been influential in recent years in elaborating a seductive (and reductive) theory of the "imaginary" of social organization.[54] There are obvious applications of this theory to Lope's drama. Girard too sees the violence of sacrifice directed against a victim (always "innocent" in his scheme) who is made to embody the contradictions of the society itself, and whose death channels the indifferentiating violence in society into the patterns of societal "difference." Although I cannot do justice here to Girard's many perceptive insights, I would not like to fall into what is an essentially theological explanation of a political myth. We cannot lose sight of the fact that Lope's ritualizing drama rescripts a historical event in such a way as to render it mythic, that is, in our context, ideological, representing an acting out of political transformation and the "normalizing" of this transformation.

The elements we have been elaborating, the splitting of the image of the One, the absolutist ideal, into the opposing subject positions of Good and Bad Father have political resonances that are better elucidated, it seems to me, by a psychoanalytic rather than a Christological approach to communal myth. In *Fuenteovejuna* the entire thrust of the text has been to position the Comendador as evil, in that he represents a retrograde historical and political position, in the ongoing elaboration of the absolutist ideal. His destruction is thus necessary to complete the transformation of history around the newly empowered image of the Good Father, the Catholic Kings. In a profound sense what this means is that the play can both destroy and uphold the image of patriarchal culture by this passage in which the (old) king is killed in order for the new king to be born. In either case, what is upheld is the necessity for, and the political-libidinal subjugation to, the idea of the Father/Leader: the circle linking absolutism and patriarchy closes in on itself, creating a perfectly smooth whole, the order of the One. In this sense, it seems to me, the play works as an example of ideological mystification: through an emotional identification with the townspeople, on the diegetic line of representation, the play makes us accept what is essentially the same political scenario, only more abstract, more "modern." Rather than the local feudal leader, we now want, seek our protection from and our subjection to, the new leader — the symbolic leader of the new Spain:

> There are kings in Castile who are drawing up new
> rules to prevent disorder. And they will do wrong if,
> after the wars, they tolerate in the towns
> and country districts such powerful men wearing
> those huge crosses on their chests.
> Those crosses were meant for royal breasts,
> and only kings should wear them.
> (1620–27)[55]

The *immediate* textual transition from scenes of ritual violence and sacrifice to scenes of festive rejoicing is mediated, during the very moment of sacrifice, by the constant articulated opposition of the Comendador and the Catholic Kings ("Long live Fernando and Isabel, and down with tyrants! Long live Fuente Ovejuna! Long live King Fernando! Death to bad Christians and traitors!"). This mediation permits the communal rebirth in and through the new Father(s). It cannot but strike us as a powerful theatrical transition to pass from the bloody nighttime scenes of murder, dismemberment, and death into festive daytime rejoicing. This communal rebirth into the new political system echoes and reinscribes the merriment of the interrupted marriage.

All the sexual imagery that has marked the position of the kings, and the licit, public courtship of Frondoso and Laurencia, is once again employed to underline the reemergence of communal unity, the rebirth of Fuenteovejuna as a social and political entity. From the cauldron of dispersion, chaos, and monstrosity into which the Comendador's sexual and political perversion plunged the village, the town reemerges, purged and reborn. Fuenteovejuna (and by extension Spain) returns to order, the sexual political order represented by the kings:

> Long live fair Isabella
> and Ferdinand of Aragon
> (two who are as one).
> He is made for her
> And she is meant for him.
> May St. Michael guide them
> To Heaven by the hand.
> Long live Isabella and Ferdinand
> And death to the tyrants!
> (2035–42)[56]

What has transpired in the ritual sacrifice of the Bad Father, the expulsion of the "other within" (*malo cristiano*), is the birth of a new collectivity. The torturer's inquisition can do nothing but reinforce this newfound sense of purpose that was forged in strife. The entire scene serves to illustrate that, on the one hand, "each sacrificial spectacle is always a new point of departure, an origin," and, on the other, that the violence, the crime at the base of the sacrifice, becomes the shared guilt, the secret, that cements the community together as it attempts to excuse the crime that founds it.[57] For this reason the individual is lost in the collective: "Fuenteovejuna" becomes the symbolic object — the fixing of communal ideals — that replaces the dead leader. Even at the most intense moments of suffering, suffering that is meant to fragment and detach the individual from the community, the torturer fails to achieve the community's dispersion into articulate (separate) bodies. The only articulation possible is the reiteration of the "ideal" — "Fuenteovejuna" — that emerged as what saved the village from chaotic destruction.

The final apotheosis of the villagers' subjugation to the new ideal they have forged is strategically delayed until the very end of the drama. In the last scene we witness the final coming together of the people and their sovereign(s) in a mirroring that uncannily reflects Althusser's analysis of how ideology always "interpellates individuals as subjects."[58] The criticism of Althusser's definition of ideology has mainly been directed at what appears as a too dourly pessimistic view of human agency; in other words, what has been rejected in Althusser is the monolithic subjugating movement.[59] Although this rejection can be validated in relation to the modern bourgeois notion of the "subject," I wonder if in the more rigid caste system of seventeenth-century Spain, the system so exhaustively studied by Maravall and Diez-Borque, this explanation of ideological subjugation may be a helpful tool in understanding, first, the role of the sovereign, and then the role of the theater in the elaboration of absolutist ideology.

Althusser's version of subjective interpellation (which owes much to the Lacanian notion of the Other) is presented as a specular phenomenon:

> We observe that the structure of all ideology, interpellating individuals as subjects in the name of a Unique and Absolute Subject, is specular, i.e., a mirror-structure, and doubly specular: this mirror duplication is constitutive of ideology and ensures its functioning. Which means that all ideology is centred, that the Absolute Subject occupies the unique place of the Centre, and interpellates around it the infinity of individuals into subjects in a double mirror-connexion such that it subjects the subjects to the Subject, while giving them in the Subject in which each subject can contemplate its own image (present and future) the guarantee that this really concerns them and Him . . . [60]

In a certain sense the emphasis on the specularity of ideological interpellation reinforces its "imaginary" force. All images of the interpellating gesture are always only representations of a structure of subjugation that remains immanent.

The last act of the *comedia* is to place the protagonists in a situation of mutual contemplation, and through this contemplation to validate the system whose birth the entire drama has represented. The highest power of the state and its lowliest subjects are brought face to face in a wonderfully staged scene in which the rhetoric, while underlining their difference, sublimates this difference in a transcendence that is an apotheosis of the Absolute Subject:

> LAURENCIA: Are those the rulers? . . .
> ISABELLA: Are these the aggressors?
> (2386–90)[61]

This mutual questioning betrays, at one and the same time, a misprision that ironically announces the shock of Truth. "Are these beautiful [i.e., "sacred"] human beings the king(s)?" and "These humble [good] simple folk are the criminals?" — the questions imply the answer. In other words, the answer — the truth (yes these are the kings, yes these are the peasant rebels) — and the surprise that the questions express is further elevated to a sublime stasis of contemplation in which the kings, caught in the wide-eyed, admiring gaze of the peasants, are immediately sacralized — "By God, they're comely: / Bless them, St. Anthony." In this gaze they are removed from the realm of the merely temporal and clothed in the aura of the holy, as is befitting their divinely ordained position in the earthly corporate structure. Thus, once the Kings are endowed as both a divine and earthly Subject, the play can end with that Subject's recognition of its subjects, by and through its pardoning of them. Although the crime of the town is too troublesome for the entire order of invested privilege that the monarchy still represents, the play skirts the issue of rebellion by simply concluding with a pardon. The ending never pronounces on the villagers' guilt or innocence, for this is the centrally concealed conundrum of the *comedia* — the fact that although uncomfortable for the system the kings represent, the crime of Fuenteovejuna was necessary for that system. In a critical sense the crime gave birth, legitimating birth, to that system. The last words of the king, closing the circle, return the peasants to themselves, and their last words to him return them to their self-proclaimed subjugation to him:

> Sire, we want to be your vassals.
> You are our king and in your defense
> we have borne arms.
> (2434-37)[62]

Furthermore, the last lines of the play return the villagers to us, to our contemplation of them, to the mirroring that the play mediates between its underlying predicates, its ideological underpinnings, and those of the audience. It is in the "pleasure" of the spectacle, in the pleasure elicited in the spectating audience, that the play seduces that audience, that is, "to lead [it] aside, or away." The theater, as we said in the beginning of this chapter, is a perverse seduction in that it always responds to the desire of its audience, even if the audience cannot articulate that desire on a conscious level. In *Fuenteovejuna* the play's seduction lies in its playing with history, with the "real" in its rescription of history as a fiction, a myth of communal foundation. As myth, the play ritually reenacts the eternal now, the present of foundations, the founding of the first modern absolutist state of premodern Europe, and, at the same time, this perpetual reenactment is a continuous reinscription of the guilt that this foundation implies and that never can be eradicated. It is this "imaginary" guilt, this mere suspicion of paranoia, that, I would suggest, constitutes the pleasure of the spectator as essentially masochistic.[63] What we must question, of course, is our continued subjugation to a play, to a poiesis, that across centuries of change and of "liberation" is still able to seduce us into a subjugation of what we have, supposedly, rejected. The ideology of the "One," the absolutist corporate structure that the play represents, continues to haunt us as the totalizingly seductive myth of what we have sacrificed in the elaboration of our own fragmented "postmodern" reality. Our modern murder of the Father/ King and our continued nostalgic longing for him continue to produce the doubt, the "split within" the modern subject, that Lope's *Fuenteovejuna* first plotted at the dawn of modernity along the elegantly perverse boundaries where the fluid worlds of myth and history commingle in the illuding presence of the theater.

Chapter 3

La vida es sueño: Patriarchy's Sacrifice

Todo es desdichas y tragedias todo.
(All is turned to tragedy and disaster.)
       La vida es sueño, III, vi

The law always refers to the sword.
Foucault, *The History of Sexuality*

Of the two most cherished works of the Hispanic canon, works that, we are told, are both quintessentially Spanish and yet universal, one, Cervantes's *Don Quijote*, narrates the peregrinations of its eponymous hero across the length and breadth of the harsh landscape of central Spain, and the other, Calderón's *La vida es sueño*, unfolds in a never-never land that the play calls Poland.[1] At first glance this apparent contradiction between the foreign setting and the "national" character of the play should not strike us as any more incongruous than, for instance, Shakespeare's Venice, Corneille's Rome, or Racine's Greece. Nevertheless, despite the attempts of recent scholarship to establish a more genuinely historic rapport between the Spanish theatergoing public of the early seventeenth century and contemporary events in both Poland and the Duchy of Muscovy, the Poland of Calderón's tragicomedy seems to float free of any historical anchoring and to enter, unfettered, into the boundaryless realm (perhaps, its "universality") of European myth.[2]

In the same way that Lope's *Fuenteovejuna* projects the present conflicts of seventeenth-century Spanish society back into the past of Spanish history, Calderón's play clothes its own contradictions, its fears and doubts, in the costumes of another world. Instead of a voyage backward in time, however, the "othering" takes as its metaphor the voyage to a foreign land, a spatial rather than a temporal distancing. "Poland" exists, in the imaginary of seventeenth-century Spain, rather as Scythia functioned for the ancient Greeks: it is a land situated at the confines of civilization — at that strange and dangerous locus where nature and culture intermingle in a much more threatening way than they are ever allowed to do "at home." Poland, as it is presented in the play, is a divided land, a space separated into two opposed territories: the "rugged mountain" ("monte fragoso"), the crepuscular, deserted, no-man's-land where Segismundo's prison is located and where the civil war is fought, and the space of the court, home of the courtly but perversely seductive rhetoric of both "science" and sexual politics. These two contrasted loci are constantly fused, traversed by the comings and goings of the characters, the necessities of plot, and the twists of dramatic peripeteia.

As a metaphoric locus, "Poland" can be seen to spatialize the conflict of overlapping epistemic systems that, if we listen to Michel Foucault, is, at this moment, gradually shifting European culture away from the analogic system of the Renaissance and toward the space of classical representation. This overlapping of two different epistemic systems strategically situates the locus that is "Poland" within the dynamics of the "uncanny," as described by Freud. The significant feature of the "uncanny" is that the *heimliche* and the *unheimliche* are intimately interwoven in the same space, producing a universe of chaos and heterogeneity.[3]

It is out of the mist of this mixed, "indifferent" world that the monstrous issues onto the scene of Spanish drama and is offered up on that stage as both its offspring and its victim. The world of *La vida es sueño* is, I will argue in this chapter, a universe of impossible contradictions, a world in which internal conflicts can be resolved only by and through their projection onto "another scene" (an "andere Schauplatz"), a mythic scene in which the monstrous that is brought forth upon the stage of representation must, in an ambivalent ceremony of guilt and retribution, be sacrificed to the very society that produces what according to its own underlying codes of political and sexual propriety it cannot accept.

In our discussion of Lope de Vega we have seen how Spanish society of the late sixteenth and early seventeenth centuries was divided internally, fraught through with religious and metaphysical contradictions and facing the ever more acute effects of a military and economic decline whose consequences were only to worsen as the century progressed. The case of Spain was only a more critical example of the general European condition. Across the continent momentous political, religious, and economic changes situate the seventeenth century at a crossroads of epistemic change, as a charged moment of crisis whose effects were for many truly nightmarish.[4] The profound aspiration of European society (if one can speak in such humanistic terms of a vast network of exploding and imploding changes) has been defined by Michel de Certeau, one of the most astute exegetes of that period, as an imperious desire for and drive toward unity, for a totality of being that is dialectically informed by the actual and traumatic experience of heterogeneity. In a certain sense we must see the dream of unity expressed in so many political theorists, from Machiavelli on, as the wishful negation of fragmentation, the fantasized obverse of the real nightmare of seventeenth-century instability.[5]

Only when we understand how acutely the actual political situation of Europe (in which I include the epistemic changes, changes in economics, and changes in the economy of sexuality that Foucault so eloquently elaborates in his seminal studies) was experienced as a wrenching wound, a splitting and splintering of daily experience, can we begin to understand the seduction that the ideal of the absolute monarch, an ideal that is as much political as it is sexual, held for the political theorists of the day.[6] The dream of a unified nation, united under one God, one Prince, and one Law, is subtended by an appeal to the patriarchal family, in which the traditionally invested images of paternity — God the Father; the king, father of his people; and the father, head of the individual household — are seamlessly linked along a constantly evolving metaphoric axis.[7] These different aspects of the desire for the Father reflect each other and tautologically inform the utopian dream of an absolute (but beneficent) patriarchal monarchy. The seventeenth century, in its flight away from heterogeneity toward the order of the "One," in what Foucault has called the "great enclosure," reinforces the image of the Father at the same time that it begins, through its religious and economic practices, to encircle a sexuality that in its excessive drive is disruptive of unitary order.[8] The father as symbol of the repressive law of the absolute comes to represent, in highly ritualized terms, the priest upon whose altar individual desire is sacrificed to the ideal of a well-ordered state.

At the opening of the play, we are at the end of a reign — "Basilio . . . is no longer young" ("Basilio . . . se rinde al común desdén del tiempo") — and, therefore, at the as yet very murky beginnings of a new order. In a general sense the great, confused crisis in *La vida es sueño*, appearing at first only in chiaroscuro, but taking on ever more acute outlines as the play progresses, is a political crisis, but the political dysfunction is immediately described as a radical breakdown in the paternal order. As the play begins, and as it progresses, the political and the paternal are inextricably intertwined, and both are put to the rudest of tests: through the threat of the overthrow of the paternal order, the entire political network that the play both denies and affirms is brought to the brink of its undoing.

Inexorably this political crisis draws into its center the thematics of sexuality and monstrosity that, as we shall see, are inseparable from it. The initial indeterminacy, the fact that this moment of the transfer of political power is articulated as the death of an old order and the birth of a new, the rhetorical trope that most frequently appears in the lexicon of the text, the oxymoron, the trope that most acutely posits the impossibility of distinction composed as it is by the apposition of opposites, is authorized by and in turn authorizes the underlying instability of the political structures of the society the play puts on stage.

The transferential moment of sovereign authority is a fearful moment of societal trembling. The entire political order of the kingdom is thrown into disarray, at first seemingly because there is not one heir to the throne but two—Astolfo and his cousin Estrella—and then, we soon learn, three: Segismundo is added to the list of heirs. Segismundo's existence does more than just numerically complicate the political network of the kingdom. Basilio's announcement of the concealed prince instantly involves the play in an irresolvable dilemma in which the order of "nature" (that is, the biological transmission of sovereign authority from father to son in a patriarchal monarchy) is brought into conflict with the order of culture (represented by the "delegation" of political authority to either Astolfo or Estrella). It is precisely this immixture of the two orders that decenters the political basis of royal devolution, and therefore the paternal order on which society rests, and involves the play in its ever-deepening turmoil. This turmoil is reflected both on the thematic and rhetorical levels of the drama, but it is most forcefully underlined by the conflict in masculine devolution, that is, on the mythic substructure of the conflict between the father and the son, between the king and his heir. Here we can begin to talk of Calderón's rescripting of the Oedipus myth, but we must do so with several caveats.

Would it be too contrived to suggest that we take the play's title seriously, in a Freudian sense? *Life is a dream*, we are told, and immediately we realize that the play, that the theater functioning so similarly to the dream, enters the theatergoers' conscious in ways that so many critics have likened to the experience of dreaming.[9] In our attempt to interpret this dream that is a play, this play that like a dream fulfills some irrepresentable desire, we must therefore have recourse to the way this play/dream/desire uses the materials that are available to its cultural unconscious and refashions them, works them into the representable text of the drama. In *The Interpretation of Dreams* Freud reminds us that there is always a part of the dream that fades, like the mushroom's mycelium, into the ground from whence it springs and from which it is nourished, a part that remains invisible and thus intractable to analysis.[10] When we discuss the complex oedipal conflicts that the play does, I believe, re-script, we will have to delve beyond the most generally accepted parts of the myth, the myth that receives its most poignant realization in Sophocles' *Oedipus Tyrannos* as reread by Freud, in our attempt to see the common ground that sustains the archaic Greek legend and its Christian homologue, and that subtends the dramatic universe of Calderón.

It is a commonplace in Calderón criticism to speak of the oedipal rivalry in many of his plays, especially those that precede *La vida es sueño*, and to attempt to explain the prevalence of father/son rivalry by references to the biography of the playwright.[11] Although I find the possible relation between what is known of Calderón's life and his work intriguing, I do not believe that it is particularly revealing of the intense hold the play has over its audience. Rather than look for a grounding of referential authority in the narration of the author's life, I feel it is more fruitful to explore the textual unconscious and to map out those areas where the symptomatic moments of the text meet and are confined within the larger myths that subtend Western culture. For this reason it seems particularly relevant for any discussion of *La vida es sueño* to articulate in what way the supposed oedipal rivalry between the father and son fades back into a more general dynamics of guilt and retribution as this dynamics fuels the sexual/political systems of a changing cultural context.

In Calderón's version, the rescripting of Oedipus reaches beyond the most commonly accepted version of the myth, that of Sophocles' tragedy, to the more archaic conflict of generations and engendering. It is a conflict that has, since the dawn of Western civilization, been marked by the mise-en-scène of the father's mortiferous attack on the child, of the child sacrificed to paternal law. Let us not forget that before Oedipus murdered his father, that father tried to kill him. The initial attack by the father, his turning on his own child to save himself, cannot, however, be authorized, admitted into consciousness, except by a process of inversion. The fear of one's own aggressive tendencies is displaced onto the child. The hostility of the father, that is, the physically empowered but chronologically enfeebled adult (the very presence of the child implies the father's mortality, his necessary disappearance in the march of time, a march in which the child is always the victor), is inverted and perceived as a proleptic attack by the child on the father. This was, of course, the oracular message that frightened Laios into exposing his baby son to death on the mountainside, and it is also the fearsome fantasy of Calderón's king, Basilio:

> I retired into my study;
> And there and everywhere
> Found proof that Segismundo
> Would be a man without scruple,
> Impious as a king,

And as a prince, cruel.
I foresaw through him the kingdom,
By vice and treachery
Divided, torn
By civil war; foresaw
That, carried away by the fury
Of his rebellion,
He would rise up against me
And—I can scarcely tell it
For shame—I saw myself
Deposed, vanquished, prostrate,
And my white hairs brought low,
Spread at his feet like a carpet.
(I, vi)[12]

Basilio's prophecy, which simply transcribes his own fears of aging and decline onto a universal, if not to say cosmological, plane, is culturally reinforced by the allusions to the "natural" reaction, the universe's catastrophic response to Segismundo's birth:

Never had eclipse
So awful overshadowed
The sun, since, weeping blood,
It mourned the death of Christ! . . .
Darkness obscured the sky,
Earth quaked, and buildings trembled,
The clouds rained meteorites,
The rivers ran with blood.
(I, vi) [13]

I have quoted these well-known hyperboles because I think that we find here the essential nexus for perceiving the underlying dynamics—cultural, religious, and ultimately (as we shall see) sexual—of the play. In the same long narrative, the hidden oedipal fear, the father's fear of the child, is apposed to the images that perversely combine in one apocalyptic description of Segismundo's birth and Christ's death.[14] Thus, the tale of Oedipus's aborted immolation is suggestively linked to the Christian myth where the sacrifice of the child is "actually" carried out.[15] In the complex, baroque imagery of Basilio's speech the play underscores both the hold of a transhistorical, generational fear and its particular inscription within the pregnant mythology of Spanish Catholicism. It is, I would suggest, the impossibility (for human thought) of rationally grasping this most paradoxical basis of Christianity—the sacrifice of the Son/God, and his resurrection—that authorizes, that is the soil from which springs the entire declension of "life not life, death not death" so vitally important to post-Tridentine Spanish baroque metaphysics. This same, profoundly unfathomable paradox authorizes the entire rhetorical and metaphysical declension of the trope "reality/illusion (dream)" that has always cast its oxymoronic spell of baroque intrigue over the play. The rhetorical emphasis on oxymorons, their baroque *agudeza*, is, I feel, the particular Christian twist to the Oedipus myth that *La vida es sueño* both incorporates and enriches. This primal paradox is the origin and the end, the central conclusion from which the paradoxical possibility of the play's metaphysics arises, and to which it ultimately returns.

Basilio's speech only recounts, of course, in the present moment of drama, the sacrifice that has already been carried out and whose effects are only now being allowed into discourse. The effects of Basilio's speech, the speech of Segismundo's imprisonment, are changing the characters, and the audience, as they listen. At this moment we all become dramatis personae in this universal drama, active participants in the desire that the sacrifice, that this sacrificial theater, enacts for our pleasure and our guilt.[16] In a curiously paradoxical analysis Rosolato, following Freud's discussion in *Totem and Taboo*, hypothesizes that what is really at stake in all the myths of child sacrifice so essential to Western religion is the actual murderous drives against, that is, the attack on, the father.[17] What this type of analysis suggests to us is that we must look twice at any scenario that simplistically would oppose the father to the son, that would separate into two radical differences what is really a complicated dialectic, a dialectic of life and death, of love and hate, and of reality and illusion. Finally, it should also make us wary of establishing, on any but a hypothetical level, a radical ethical separation between good and evil, for in a patriarchal society, a society based on devolution of power from male to male, we must be aware that there is not only a heated animosity between generations of men, but their even more invested collusion in the symbolic structures of societal power.

What *La vida es sueño* does is to paper over this collusion and present the conflict of generations as absolute. What in fact could be more different than the presentations of Basilio and Segismundo? When we first encounter Segismundo, chained inside his dark, lugubrious prison, clothed only in animal pelts, two things immediately strike us. The first is that his rhetorical relation to the world is (perhaps understandably) interrogative: "What my crime is I have yet to learn. . . . why must I suffer more?" and "What justice, law, or reason can withhold / From man all nature's privilege and joy?" (¿Qué delito cometí? . . . ¿qué más os pude ofender / para castigarme más?"; "qué ley, justicia o razón / negar a los hombres sabe / privilegio tan suave / exención tan principal . . . "). Segismundo articulates himself as both guilty and innocent. Guilt, his guilt, an inexplicable, yet unavoidable state, preexists him, engulfs him, and defines him. Those who wish to read the play as a Catholic allegory would interpret Segismundo's questioning of the world and his place in it to be an expression of "original sin" — all who are born are born guilty:

> Nor do I question your strange justice, Heaven,
> But what my crime is I have yet to learn.
> Indeed Man's original sin is to be born,
> But, Heaven, beyond that common crime of birth,
> Tell me . . . In what else have I offended you?
> (I, ii)[18]

Nevertheless, what I find particularly significant is that the existence of guilt is posited by the rhetoric of interrogation. Segismundo's radical questioning of his state, of his place in the world, dialectically implies that he is guilty. His constant questioning of the world only underlines once again the impossible separation between fathers and sons, only points to their amorous/mortiferous bond. The father's fear of this child is not entirely unfounded, for the very presence of children is a threat to the illusion of sovereignty if only because the presence of the child is always a reminder of each father's own mortality, of the passage of time, and of death that is waiting. Children are guilty of, if nothing more but also nothing less, simply waiting — waiting to take the father's place, to take his power. This too is what is implied in Segismundo's interrogation: his horoscope only announces the fate of all fathers.

The second feature that strikes us is that to this display of dubitative intelligence is coupled a savage, bestial disposition. When he comes upon Rosaura and Clarín, who, unbeknownst to him, have entered his lair, his first reaction is murderous:

> Then I will kill you!
> For you have witnessed what no one must know, my weakness —
> I will tear you to pieces just for that — and my hands are not weak.
> (I, ii)[19]

Segismundo is thus marked from the beginning as guilty, mentally astute, and brutal. This combination of the human with the bestial authorizes his famous description of himself as "a human monster, man among beasts, beast among men" ("un hombre de las fieras y una fiera de los hombres"). He is a heterogeneous being, a "human monster." This is the first appearance in the text of the theme of monstrosity. We will be attentive to the ever-crescendoing echoes that this word, this theme, bears in the sacrificial dynamics of the play, and we should note that this monstrosity is intimately linked to a thematics of "sexuality," which also first emerges when Segismundo's strength is coded as particularly virile ("membrudos brazos"). These "powerful" arms, which would just as soon embrace as destroy this man/woman who is his victim, serve as an indicator of a troubling, aggressively unfettered sexuality.

Sexuality thus enters the play almost immediately, if surreptitiously, and it enters as an overinvested signifier of the child. Let us not forget that Rosaura, another child who has been forsaken by the father, also first enters the play as a victim of unsocialized sexuality. She has been seduced and abandoned by Astolfo, and in order to recoup her lost honor she forsakes Muscovy, ventures forth, and comes disguised as a man into Poland.

In its most elemental meaning, "sex" comes from the same Latin root as "cut," "split." A sexual being is one who is divided, cut into difference. As such, the introduction of sexuality, specifically focused on the two children Segismundo and Rosaura, highlights what the text perhaps ignores: that in a society whose drive is toward the order of the absolute, toward the order of the One, the child is always a dangerous, double being, a split, "sexed" being. S/he is the constant reminder of the impossibility of the "absolute ideal," because s/he is always the living proof of a mixed, heterogeneous nature. The child is always sexual by its very being, a being that is the product of two, not one, a being that in its very nature is divided. Thus it is especially revealing that the dynamics of social unrest and instability are made to repose in and on the two characters. Segismundo and Rosaura, who most successfully represent the excessive, heterogeneous drive of sexuality as an impossibility of being.

For this same reason, when we are first introduced to the father, Basilio, he is presented to us, before he ever makes an entrance on stage, as a "sexless" figure. Sexuality is precisely what Basilio has rejected.

> Basilio is no longer young,
> And more inclined to pass his time
> In study, than to contemplate
> A second marriage . . .
> (I, v)[20]

Because he has de-eroticized his relation to women, and eroticized his intellect, Basilio can assume the position of "king/magician" ("rey/mago").

> My scientific studies have earned for me
> The epithet by which the whole world knows me,
> "Basilio the Sage." The artist's brush and sculptor's chisel
> Have given me a universal fame
> As "Basilio the Great" . . .
> (I, vi)[21]

Basilio is proclaimed in a "universalizing" encomium as "sage" because of the sacrifice of his sexuality to his erudition. We should remember, however, that in this encomium the immolation of the child is not forgotten; it returns, if only obliquely, in the reference to Timantes ("the artist's brush"; "los pinceles de Timantes"), whose most famous painting was a representation of Agamemnon's sacrifice of his daughter Iphigenia.

As opposed to Segismundo, who is presented in his pure *Kreaturlichkeit*, Basilio is presented as "absolute mind." This total rejection of the body, of the body's attachment to the carnal, the base, allows Basilio to assume the place of the ideal patriarch: he subsumes in his being all attributes of ideal masculinity—"king, father, sage, elder" ("rey, padre, sabio, anciano"; I, vi)—and presents himself as a pure masculine immanence. He is the wise man, the pure scientist, who, precisely because he has gone beyond the body, has, if we wish to express it in more psychoanalytic terms, accepted the castrating gesture that allows him entrance into the symbolic systems that control his world, and thus into almost immediate contact with/as the Law. He can claim to be beyond time, beyond history, and thus beyond death:

> . . . You also know
> That I have made my special study the subtle mathematics
> By whose power I anticipate time, and make news stale;
> For those events which arrive from day to day
> Are already present in my tables of the coming centuries . . .
> (I, vi)[22]

Basilio's entire endeavor, his totalizing attempt to go beyond time and history, to be free of the contingency of his body, manifests the motivating fear of the father, the fear of death. He has banished death from his presence by sacrificing his son: he has sequestered Segismundo in the womb/tomb of his tower but now, as the play begins, death returns to the court by and through the illusion of intellectual omnipotence that allowed Basilio to exile it in the first place. Basilio's error is the sin of pride, the error of overestimating his own intelligence and of making of that intelligence the weapon that undoes him. At the same time, can we not also interpret Basilio's error to be, on another level, the failure of an entire episteme, the episteme that would "read" the heavens, the cosmos, as if it were a book? In a sense, Basilio's knowledge is not pure knowledge but local knowledge. His grasp on the world is a grasp on the analogic universe at the very moment that that form of knowledge is being challenged and displaced by a newly emerging scientific method.[23] All the indications of Basilio's knowledge situate him in the realm of the sorcerer's apprentice: he reads "natural phenomena" as if they were in immediate relation to a hidden universal truth. The entire "science" of Basilio is to be proved wrong, and the world order that this science supports is to be cast into turmoil. Before Mary Shelley's Frankenstein, Basilio is a prototype of a mad scientist, the scientist who wishes to control the real — death. In his desire to push beyond the limits of the known, he has created a monster, his son, who returns to haunt him, to remind him in the most blatant way of his hubris. Segismundo is brought back from death to kill the king and plunge the kingdom into the bloody violence of civil war. Only from this passage, through fragmentation and death, can a new monarch emerge and initiate a change in the order of things that Basilio's science is no longer able to master.

When we talk about the role of the father in *La vida es sueño*, we are only telling half the tale if we limit our discussion to Basilio. Basilio is only part of the composite picture of the father, which to be completed must include Clotaldo. Not only is Clotaldo Segismundo's surrogate father — to him is entrusted the care, the education, and the discipline of the cursed prince — he is the actual, although unknown and absent, father of Rosaura. While Basilio represents the sexless father whose intellect allows him to soar above common concerns and to glide effortlessly among pure principles, Clotaldo represents the father condemned to his sexual appetites, condemned to the realm of service to his king and to his body, and yet lost in the world he cannot master. Unlike Basilio, who interprets (erroneously) the "signs" of his world, Clotaldo remains lost in a fog. With the irruption of this man/woman, his child, into his universe, that world becomes a space of a confused and contradictory semiosis that Clotaldo no longer can decipher:

> What a bewildering maze! And not a clue for reason to hold on to!
> It is my honor that has been tainted! . . .
> Heaven may provide a solution,
> But it is hard to see how even Heaven can
> With nothing in the world but prodigies,
> The sky full of portents, and all in chaos.
> (I, viii)[24]

Rosaura's entry into Clotaldo's present is doubly traumatic: first, she appears to him, as she has to Segismundo, dressed as a man, and second, she comes into his presence as a criminal who has contravened the laws/limits set by the king:

> Fools, whoever you are who have trespassed here
> Against the king's decree that no intruder
> May enter this forbidden ground . . .
> (I, iii)[25]

Rosaura's irruption into her father's presence is a twofold infringement of the space of the law. It is first a contravention of the law of sexual difference, for despite the "romance" tradition that is often invoked to "naturalize" the fact that Rosaura enters the already ambivalently charged space of both Poland and the play disguised as a man, her sexually protean role in the drama tells us that this recourse to literary tradition is too convenient to bear the weight of Rosaura's excessive transgressions. Second, and more mundanely, Rosaura violates the king's secret. By entering into the space of Segismundo's prison she discovers the father's guilt. This double infraction of the law condemns her to death.

I am tempted to see this highly ambivalent act, whose ambivalence is textually and sexually underlined by the transvestism of Rosaura, as representing the return of Clotaldo's repressed — his betrayal of the laws of sociality and of marriage. Both of the fathers in this play have attempted to repress a sin/crime of their youth, and both are brought, at the same time, with the return of this repress, to what constitutes the two dramatic axes of the play. Each in his own way has sacrificed his child to save himself. It is, of course, this highly charged cultural transgression that the play's underlying ideology of patriarchy both authorizes and refuses. In an obvious sense, what the sacrifice of the child implies in the intimate intrication of parents and children under the law, is the coterminous loss of the father. By abandoning the child, the father also denies his own paternal role and therefore his place and function within a system of patriarchal devolution. Without the child's recognition of the symbolic function of the father there can be no "father" in the political sense of the term.[26] Once the father has eliminated the threat that the child posed to his own integrity, he, in a perverse sense, has also deprived himself of both his past and his future. For all intents and purposes, he has undone the symbolic infrastructure that made his own subjective position possible. Without the child, and that child's inscription into the socially symbolic networks that inform sociality, society is threatened with a return to chaos, to death. Culture, only so tenuously kept above the raging tide of the cosmological forces waiting to undo it, returns to the inarticulable dissolve of nature.

Although it certainly has not gone unnoticed, it is extremely curious that in a play whose central dramatic tension revolves around a conflict of generations, and thus the problem of familial engendering, there is a glaring absence at the very heart of this problem. Up to this point we have been focusing our attention on the male-centered dialectic, the mortiferous dialectic between father and child, but the absence of the mother cannot but strike us as a particularly telling textual void.[27] It is true that there are no "mothers" in this text that is so heavily dependent on the father. Segismundo's mother is mentioned only to be immediately evacuated from the text by her death. She is first ripped apart ("in a recurrent nightmare / [she] saw a human monster / that rent her body open"; "entre ideas y delirios / del sueño, vio que rompía / sus entrañas atrevido / un monstruo en forma de hombre") and then done away with ("my son was born / Segismundo; and, as a first foretaste of his nature, savage, even at his birth / he murdered his own mother"; "nació Segismundo, dando / de su condición indicios, / pues dio la muerte a su madre"). Rosaura's mother is mentioned only once when Rosaura, at the end of the play, is finally permitted to finish her heretofore constantly interrupted history: "my mother / was deceived by words of love, / and like them [other women] was deserted" ("mi madre, persuadida / a finezas amorosas, / fue infeliz como todas"). Although we must assume that Violante, Rosaura's double/mother, still lives in shame in far-off Muscovy, she is, in her distant exile, only a memory, a shadow, another absence.

What is interesting in these two fleeting references to the absent mother is the way these references are coded so as to embroider the mother into the textual fabric as a synonym for "nature." Clorilene is mentioned surrounded by images — her dream, her death — that all underline her as pertaining to the realm of birthing and death. The one word linking her two outstanding attributes is "blood":

> My Queen bore me a son
> At whose ill-omened birth
> The heavens rained down portents.
> While still he was shut away
> From the beautiful light of earth
> Within the womb entombed
> (They are much alike, death and birth)
> Many times his mother
> In a recurrent nightmare
> Saw a human monster
> That rent her body open
> And came bloodstained into the world
> Like a viper — his mother's murderer.
> (I, vi)[28]

The references to blood and death, compounded with the apocalyptic images of birthing and images of cosmic disorder, all contribute in circumscribing the mother in/as the place of nature. That this should be so apparent will not come as a surprise to any student of the play reading in the wake of contemporary feminist criticism. For many feminist critics, such as Irigaray or Clément and Cixous, the role of and constant appeal to blood and birthing is resonant of the fear of and repressed hostility to women in patriarchal cultures.[29] At the same time this fear is intimately linked to the association, through blood, the cyclic flowing of menstrual blood, to the woman as pertaining to the marginal space where culture and nature are as yet not split into difference, cannot be split into difference.[30] It is this resistance to (totalizing) appropriation by (masculinist) culture that makes the woman, especially the mother, such a heavily invested locus of cultural desire and fear.

Whereas Clorilene is strategically eliminated by a single textual gesture that both underscores her maternal role and returns her to the realm from which this role sprang (nature/death), Rosaura's mother Violante takes on that other traditional role of the dangerous, socially disruptive example of femininity — the whore, or more pointedly in this case, the bad, because sexual, woman. All we know of Violante is that she was beautiful and unlucky ("she was more beautiful than any, / but unhappy as all"; "fue como ninguna bella / y fue infeliz como todas"). Unlucky is perhaps too elliptical a term, for Violante's misfortune was to accede to her own sexual desire and to the desire of her seducer, and thus to break the societal codes restricting sexual conduct. Violante is a branded woman because society marks her as sexual, and she in turn underscores its hypocrisy, that is, its attempt to appropriate what is inherently other. Violante is dishonored precisely as the term "honor" is invested within an entire masculine code of propriety and property. Her sexuality, which is excessive and transgressive of the code of patriarchal appropriation, condemns her in that society whose codes have perversely seduced and abandoned her to the role of outcast, to the position of sexuality. Violante exists outside the bonds of marriage, which for her society signifies the far side of the social. She is cast out of the realm of respectability, and, as "sexuality" is situated on the extreme borders of the social contract, on those borders where the social disappears into the natural.

Both children in this drama appear as traumatically marked by the mother (for example, Rosaura says, "I was born, so like my mother / that I became her copy / not, indeed, in beauty but in actions and misfortune"), and this mark situates them as pertaining to the highly charged, ambivalent space where culture and nature intermingle. It is perhaps for this reason that Clotaldo, when talking of his own role in Segismundo's education, counterbalances his lessons with those of his "other," the only mother Segismundo has known, Mother Nature ("la madre naturaleza"):

> I went down, then, to Segismundo's prison
> We talked for a while of poetry and science
> (For he has studied in the divine school of the silent mountains and
>   skies [*la madre naturaleza*],
> And there learned his rhetoric from the birds and beasts).
> (II, i)[31]

The mother, though banished from the scene of the tragicomedy, returns in the mixed nature of the children, heterogeneous beings, products of both nature and culture and thus socially dangerous beings. They are dangerous for the political stability of the society that, suspi-

cious of them, condemns them to travel the long road out of heterogeneity and into the order of the One if they wish to be one with society.

Segismundo and Rosaura are condemned children, condemned by a
heterogeneity that inheres in them and that this world, striving for the
absolute, cannot tolerate. Their heterogeneity is both complementary
and different. It is to their mutual imbrication that we must now turn in
order to understand how the play resolves its own internal conflict in
terms consonant with the patriarchal ideology it both challenges and
upholds.

Let us recall that the play inscribes itself under the sign of heterogeneity by situating its opening at dusk: "The action begins at nightfall"
("La acción principia al anochecer"). The beginning is thus situated temporally as an indeterminate moment, both day and night, an impossible
moment where the separation of the world into difference is confounded
by the very principle of the "threshold," that is, as that which contains
and confounds dyadic opposition within itself, and by extension would
undermine any logocentric law based on the attempt to keep/impose a
difference that is constantly produced by certain underlying ideological
drives rather than given in any "natural" structure.[32] This ambivalent
temporal threshold is immediately resituated as a sexual one in the
presentation of Rosaura, who is a woman dressed as a man and who is
in the process of mediating another dyadic hierarchy — "high/low"
("Rosaura, dressed as a man, appears high up on the rock, and climbs
down to the plain"; "Rosaura, vestida de hombre, aparece en lo alto de
las peñas, y baja a lo llano"). Rosaura's transvestism has usually been
seen as merely a theatrical device, inherited from a long "romance" tradition.[33] Yet I feel that to appeal simply to a "tradition" never satisfactorily
explains the specific impact of its manifestation in a particular text.
Rosaura's appearance in drag at the beginning of the play evokes, I believe, an entire network of sexual indeterminacy that reflects an underlying fear of heterogeneity that is the basis of the dramatic action of the
play. From the very beginning, then, the politics of patriarchy is inextricably interwoven with the sexuality of the characters. This sexuality
is used as the most highly invested dynamic in which societal imperatives
to order and law are contrasted with individual desire.

Rosaura's transvestism is just one sign of her situation as culturally indefinable, a situation that tautologically returns to her as a being of sexual excess. Like her mother, Rosaura is marked by her sexuality. She has
been sexually active outside of marriage, outside, that is, of patriarchal
appropriation, and is therefore in a socially ambivalent position: she is
"dishonored" (i.e., she is unplaceable, cast out, an outlaw). For the moment, I will leave aside the equally interesting dilemma of her wanting
to recoup her honor, that is, her imperious desire to be "reinscribed"

within the social networks of power and sexuality that have played with her. We will return to this question, intimately connected with the "exchange" of women, their control in a patriarchal society, but now I direct our attention to Rosaura as we first meet her — a social outcast, and a sexually undecidable and enticing being. In her initial speech she refers to herself as male and female:

> For I must go on; in the dark, in despair [ciega y desesperada],
> With no path to follow but the way that lies before my feet,
> Down the rough entangled wilderness of this mountain
> Whose great brow now is frowning at the sun.
> An unkind welcome, Poland, you give the stranger [un extranjero],
> For at your frontier you demand his signature in blood . . .
> (I, i)[34]

Despite the appeal to any "tradition," there is something remarkable, something exciting, something that Calderón's text underlines in the fact that Rosaura confounds gender distinctions. By that confusion she is found to be eminently seductive. We must remember that it is as a man that Rosaura first seduces Segismundo:

> How your voice moves me!
> Your looks amaze me!
> Your pleading touches me —
> Tell me who you are! . . .
> Each time I look at you, I am filled with wonder —
> The more I look, the more desire
> To look and wonder more and more.
> (I, ii)[35]

And it is as a man that she confronts, unbeknownst to her, her father, Clotaldo. Neither of these two males with their very different experiences recognizes her as a woman. For the first scene, Rosaura is a foreigner ("extranjero"). We can only assume that even for the audience of the play, for an audience that has not read the didascalia, Rosaura would appear at the very least as a strikingly ambivalent character, a man/woman.

This indistinction is troublingly sexy, but becomes even more so when Rosaura reveals her "true" sexual identity, because — and this is perhaps even more revealing — whether Rosaura appears in drag or in women's clothes she is always presented as disguised. As a character Rosaura is marked by indeterminacy, as nonbeing. When we see her in act II she is playing the role of Astrea, Estrella's lady-in-waiting:

> My lady is saying
> That she is your niece —
> Her clever idea —
> Has assumed a new name,

And lives at the palace
As lady-in-waiting
To Princess Estrella.
(II, ii)[36]

In the first act she appears as a man, in the second as a woman. In either case this sexual indeterminacy, this mutability, of Rosaura points to yet another level of textual heterogeneity—the positing of, and, of course, the fear/desire of, a certain bisexuality. This "bisexuality" is particularly coded in the text within the same paradigm that declines "femininity," ambivalence, and ultimately monstrosity; in her final appearance Rosaura refers to herself as "being monstrous, both man and woman." This is also another key link that joins Rosaura to Segismundo along the same axis.

It might appear a perverse teasing of the text to claim that a part of Segismundo's "monstrosity" is his inherent bisexuality, but aside from the obvious fact that he desires Rosaura in both of her sexual avatars, as a man in the first scenes and as a woman in act II, there is another level to his sexual behavior that I think defines him as a mirror reversal of Rosaura in sexual difference. Segismundo's relation to the world is, as we have said, aggressive. That aggressivity manifests itself most forcefully in the play in two instances: first, when he kills, by throwing him from a window of the palace, the courtier who would rein in his uncourtly tendencies, and second, in the following scene where he attempts to rape Rosaura/Astrea. In these cases we have a nexus of aggressiveness turned toward representatives of both sexes. He is equally invasive of each, and if we consider, with Freud, that aggressivity is an inherent component of libidinal drive, it becomes clear that Segismundo's violence in the world is the obverse of the "tender" component of the libidinal drive: he equally aggresses both men and women, a clear sign of a nondifferentiated sexual appetite.[37]

This nondifferentiation, however, finally comes to rest most tellingly on Rosaura. That this should be the case in a text that purports to be a political allegory for a patriarchal society should not surprise us. We do not have to reread Joan Riviere's famous essay "Womanliness as Masquerade" to realize that in patriarchy femininity is definable only as a disguise, a masquerade the woman must don for the man.[38] Rosaura provides the most blatant, if perhaps unconscious, textual display of both the rhetoric and thematics of patriarchy's appropriation of femininity in the dynamics of the play. When she appears for the third time in the last act of the play she comes on stage garbed in her indeterminacy. Rushing to the battlefield to aid/demand aid of Segismundo, she is clothed, as she says, "monstrously":

Now both man and woman [monstruo de una especie y otra]
—By my dress a woman,
By my arms, a man.
(III, x)[39]

Rosaura's long speech in act III rhetorically counterbalances Basilio's speech in act I. These are the two most extensive speeches of the tragicomedy, and they act as a framing device for the entire sociopolitical crisis the play represents. The first is a monologue that represents the exhaustion of an entire epistemic tradition—the speech of Basilio's error in reading a world that is no longer legible because its grammar has inexorably mutated. Rosaura's speech at the end is equally revealing, as it illustrates by sexual example the impossibility of being that is her lot and the lot of Segismundo in a world that, for different but interconnected reasons, has betrayed them both. Her speech is also an apotropaic monologue of performative effects that indicate a change, a sea change perhaps, in the world of the drama.

When Rosaura appears on stage in the last act of the play, she arrives, we are told, on a swift horse. This horse is, in its heterogeneity, a monstrous being, and thus a metonymy for Rosaura, but also for the entire political situation of the universe of the play:

Upon the horse in question . . .
For he is a perfect model of the universe
In his own person.
His chest is a furnace, ocean foams are his mouth,
His body is earth,
The wind his breath—earth, air, fire, water,
An elemental monster!
(III, ix)[40]

Despite the extended commentary of Cilveti, Rosaura's steed clearly corresponds, rhetorically, to the "hipogrifo" upon which she first enters Poland, and both of these steeds, described in elaborately convoluted rhetoric, reproduce on the level of metaphor and on the level of metonymy the "monstrosity" that the ideology of the text is both attracted to and fears.[41] In her last appearance, Rosaura is dressed as a man/woman ("by my dress a woman, by my arms, a man"), and these arms are specified: "enter Rosaura with sword and dagger" ("sale Rosaura con baquero, espada y daga"). Her entire speech is, we might say, a constant oscillatory movement between these two ill-defined sexual genders, a back-and-forth rhetorical move between masculinity and femininity:

Three times you have seen me:
For three times I have come
In a new disguise.

> First you saw me as a man, . . .
> Then, the second time,
> As a woman you admired me, . . .
> This is the third time:
> Now, both man and woman . . .
> (III, x)[42]

This tirade is her attempt, I would suggest, to enunciate finally her being, an enunciation that has remained suspended from her initial contact with Segismundo, remained *en souffrance* from the beginning of the play. At the moment she was about to tell her story, and thus define herself to herself, to Segismundo, and to the audience, Clotaldo and his soldiers rush into the prison, aborting the narration of her being and leaving us suspended in midair with the enigmatic "I am . . . " ("Yo soy"). We have to wait until this last moment, until this extreme moment of crisis when the entire fate of the nation is hanging in the balance, to hear finally who she is.

But who is she? The long speech tells us she is her mother's daughter/double ("I was born, so like my mother / that I became her copy"). She is "woman," in the sense that she articulates herself as the product of and perpetuator of sexual excess. Her rhetorical self-fashioning disseminates her being across and through those cultural models of betrayed yet seductive femininity—Danae, Leda, Europa, all of whom show women as perversely sexual. All were seduced by their passion into "unnatural" couplings with Zeus; and these "unnatural" couplings, we might add, point to the sexual passion of women as precisely "natural," that is, not controlled by the confines of masculine, acculturated sexuality. Throughout this long narration of her history, her seduction and betrayal, of her story as the universal story of "woman," are woven those constant reminders that Rosaura is also a "man." She constantly interrupts the "narration" of her past, of a generic past, to refer to the present, a referral that is the almost-continuous fidgeting with, manipulation of, the only mark of the father that remains with her, the sword: "now the blade is sheathed, / but it shall be drawn" ("Enváinese aquí su hoja / que yo la desnudaré").

The entire speech, in its own vacillating stance between images of woman and images of masculinity, reproduces Rosaura's predicament. As a woman she is both within and without the law of the Father who has abandoned her. This ambiguous position, an undefinable position that is, I would like to suggest, the "hysterical position," a position of both/and rather than a position of clearly defined sexual roles, finally corresponds to the "I am . . . " of Rosaura.[43] As long as society refuses her a place, as long as she remains an outcast, she is clearly a hysteric, a man/woman, a (socially) dangerous monster—a position that has already been clearly defined by her father in his plea to her not to force him to take revenge on Astolfo. Clotaldo articulates her demand as essentially "spite," "folly," and "hysteria" ("despecho," "desatino," "frenesí"); she responds that it is "honor," "courage," and "rage" ("ciega pasión," "honor," "valor," "ira"). There is the same hysterical reversal and oscillation that her own speech reproduces. The speech ends not with a resolution of this "hysterical" indeterminacy but with a crescendoing affirmation of it:

> As a woman, here I beg you
> To defend and help me,
> And as a man I come
> To urge you on to conquest!
> As a woman, beg for pity,
> As a man, to serve you come,
> With my sword—but let me warn you
> If you make love to me
> As a woman, as a man
> I will kill you in defense
> Of my honor; in the conquest
> Of my good name, as a woman
> I plead, but as a man
> I will defend my honor!
> (III, x)[44]

Finally, the plea Rosaura addresses to Segismundo is a plea that he assume the place of the father, that he be the Law so that she might be free of her indeterminacy, for, although it might be her force and her seductive power, it is also her prison and her exile.

This is essentially, but in directly opposite terms, the entreaty that the rebel soldiers address to Segismundo. When the rebels burst into Segismundo's prison and demand that he assume his rightful place as heir to the throne ("you are our rightful prince; we will not recognize, admit or tolerate / any other leader. / We want no foreigner"; "Tu nuestro príncipe eres; / ni admitimos ni queremos / sino al señor natural / y no a príncipe extranjero"), they appeal to "nature" as the final unmediated grounding of their political culture. This appeal to nature, although immediately ironized in the text by their comic misprision—they have confused the jester Clarín for Segismundo—nevertheless turns the circle back on itself uniting politics and sexuality within the reaffirmed locus of a new male devolution. Segismundo is called upon by the populace, one more avatar of the monstrous ("the people, unchained and blind monster"; "Que el vulgo, monstruo despeñado y ciego"), to become the new leader, the king, to, in other words, assume the place of the (his) father. Segismundo is represented as corresponding to the desire of the people for a leader/prince who reaffirms the apparently seamless bond of cultural union — the prince and his subjects united in a perfect mirror-reflection of subjectivity.[45]

> And all the people know
> What he intends to do.
> They demand their natural king,
> And not a foreigner!
> (III, iii)[46]

The people want to be subjected to their natural, that is, native-born, ruler. They refuse the "foreign" other whom Basilio would impose on them, thus creating an unnatural state. It is to the expulsion of the foreign other that threatens the integrity of the state that Segismundo is summoned by his subjects. He is called to assume his place, the place of the father, of the Law, in just the same way that Rosaura demands that he come into that position and assume the consequences of the Law.

In a strange chiasmatic reversal, the "people," described as the last declension of the monstrous, appeal to "nature" in an attempt to reestablish political stability. It is curious, therefore, how semantically slippery and thus how ideologically rich the word and concept "nature" is in this play. The term is constantly invoked to foreground what is not natural — the polis — at the same time that it has been used in an entire chain of associations to designate what is "unnatural" — the sexual, the feminine, the monstrous, all that is chaotic and apocalyptic, constantly contaminating the vulnerable sphere of masculine culture.

Segismundo, raised in nature far from the court, far from the civilizing but ultimately sterile sexual/political coupling represented by the dysfunctional heterosexual couple Astolfo/Estrella, is natural precisely in that he shares in his excessive, uncontrollable, monstrous being the sexual aggressiveness that also marks Rosaura. In Rosaura's case, her aggressiveness manifests itself in her hyperbolic rhetoric as her assumption and affirmation of a masculinity that marks her as heterogeneously unplaceable in the political/sexual conventions of the court. Despite the passive aim of her aggressivity (to be married, and thus replaced within the parameters of appropriated femininity), Rosaura's decidedly active assumption of her own cause casts her into male garb, dresses her as male.

Segismundo joins Rosaura in the realm of sexual indeterminacy precisely where the text constantly appeals to his aggressive, untamed, too-beastly "nature." This nature that the horoscope defines as violently destructive of polity structurally situates Segismundo as outside the law, outside the containment of culture. This "outside" metonymically joins the declension "nature," "sexuality," "monstrosity," and femininity that links, I would suggest, Segismundo to Rosaura, that appears as the feminine in him. Thus together, joined in their too-violent passionate hold on the world, Segismundo and Rosaura meet as a strange heterogeneous beast, a new androgynous couple, where each communes with the other, is attracted to the other, in that overlapping space where each is, within the limits of a patriarchal society, monstrous.

Finally, it is this textual insistence on situating the children as excessive, and thus dangerous, that we can interpret as the children's refusal of the law of the Father. We might turn this around and say that it is the law of the (inadequate) father who has abandoned the children. This abandonment, a symptom of the breakdown of a well-run society, is represented in the play as the collapse of the political: Poland is plunged into civil war. On one side of the conflict stand those representatives of the old, enfeebled order (Basilio, Clotaldo, Astolfo) and on the other the monstrous conglomerate (Segismundo, Rosaura, the people).

What is intriguing about the rhetoric of this war is that it echoes the mythic description of Basilio's horoscope. The war is the acting out of that horoscope:

> . . . the riots spreading in the streets and squares
> You will see your kingdom afloat on scarlet waves
> Dyed with the purple of its own blood.
> How lamentably all is turned to tragedy and disaster!
> Your empire is in its death-throes — violent,
> All sights are terrible, all sounds apall.
> The sun is outraged and the wind infected.
> Every stone marks a grave-plot, every flower
> Grows for some funeral wreath; and not a house
> But now has become a vault and sepulchre;
> And all your soldiers are corpses walking to the battlefield!
> (III, vii)[47]

Thus the society of the play is plunged into the chaos that was predicted by the horoscope and that Basilio's (mis)reading attempted to prevent. At this point the play leaves its already none-too-firm grounding in a historical/political "reality" and enters more figuratively, more definitively, into the realm of myth, that realm where narration attempts to mediate the impossible, contradictory demands of reality. In this sense, *La vida es sueño* is mythic: it represents in dramatic form the impossible quest to make sense (unity) out of chaos.

The battle of the civil war recasts in an ever-renewed light the myth of Oedipus, and, beyond that particular agon, a more archaic conflict, the generational conflict of the Titans. In that myth the children of Gaia, inspired by their "mother-earth" (the "earth," but in a fuller sense the "natural" world), scaled the heights of Mount Olympus to castrate and cast down their father Uranus, and choose a new Father/leader from among the younger generation.[48] In a sense what this myth recounts is the impossible conflict, in patriarchal culture, between generations, a conflict that is always mediated by a symbolic sacrifice figured as the imposition of the cutting law of difference, of "castration." Now we know that "castration" in either Freudian or Lacanian terms signifies the child's entrance into society, into, that is, those symbolically signifying systems that define him or her as a "sexed" being, a being of Law and language. This symbolic inscription also signifies the continuity of generations, linked through their common acceptance of the Law, through the sacrifice of what in their "nature" is inherently inimical to social cohesion.

The play opened with the already-there of immolation: Basilio's sacrifice of his son, represented by the banishment of Segismundo from the world of culture and his imprisonment in the hostile tower. Rather than destroy the son and save the father, this sacrifice comes back to haunt the father. It returns to torment him in exact proportion by making the son's recognition of the father, as a representative of law, and therefore society, impossible. Segismundo refuses to recognize Basilio as king or father. His rhetorical boasting of omnipotence and his actual aggressions at court—the murder of the valet and his attempted rape of Rosaura/ Astrea—are dramatic demonstrations that he will not accept the law of "no," the law of societal restraints. Not only does his behavior demonstrate the nonresolved "nature" that still inheres in him, he also clearly articulates a refusal of the law: "In what is unjust, kings should not be obeyed" ("En lo que no es justa ley / no ha de obedecer al Rey"). This rejection of filial obeisance throws the entire ideological substructure of the play into disarray.[49] What the play is suggesting, in ways that are quite possibly unavailable to itself, is the unthinkable of seventeenth-century political theory: the putting into question of the law of the father/ruler, a questioning that is posed as the threat, the constantly present menace of patricide/regicide, the revolt against the father/king. This threat to patriarchal monarchy is particularly overdetermined by the text's rhetorical conflation of the name of the father, Basilio, with the etymological echoes of kingship (*basileus*) that are heard in it.

If the play were to end with the civil war and the triumph of Segismundo over his father, it would perhaps be seen as one of the most radically disconcerting plays of the seventeenth century. That the play does not end on the triumph of Segismundo but rather on his victory and the reconciliation of father and son shows us that, as "myth," the play is constantly mediating conflicting social realities that perhaps can never be adequately resolved on the level of reality, but only on the level of desire, that is, in/as a dream.

How is this reconciliation brought about, and what are its consequences? I would suggest that primarily the play narrates both the degradation and the reaffirmation of a new structure of patriarchal monarchy.

It will only seem that I am repeating the obvious to insist that in a highly patriarchal society the relation between sovereignty in its political forms (monarchy) and its metaphysical imperatives (the relation between God and the world) turns, as Freud suggests, equally on the elevation and sublimation of the figure of the father and his destruction.[50] Calderón's tragicomedy does this by returning us to that basic, hidden structure of male immolation that we have already suggested is the modus operandi of all those originary sacrifices that pertain in Western monotheisms. In those attacks by the father upon the son we have seen that what is really at stake is the unavowable attack on the father. The father is attacked surreptitiously in and through his double, his replacement.[51] What these repetitive mythic narrations also underline is the inherent impossibility for any real separation of the father/son. Both are reversible images of the other, situated within the same dynamics of power in a system of male devolution. The devolution of power from male to male implies their mutual imbrication, their necessary collusion in any political system based on a genealogy of males. A sacrifice is necessary to mark the "origins" of this bond, and as usual what must be sacrificed in this world of patriarchal monarchy is the other that inheres in the male characters: the feminine that must be circumscribed and appropriated by masculinist culture.

When Segismundo's forces triumph over Basilio's supporters the prophecy of the horoscope seems vindicated:

> Prince, you are looking for me, I believe—
> Here I am. [*kneeling*] Let my white hairs be your carpet,
> Set your foot on my neck, trample my crown,
> My dignity pull down,
> Humble to the dust my self-esteem, take vengeance upon my honor.
> After all my strivings to avert this hour
> Let Fate fulfill its law, Heaven's word be kept!
> (III, xiv)[52]

Nevertheless, it is at this moment of maximum dramatic intensity, the moment when we expect the unthinkable—the son's murder of the father—that the remarkable occurs: Segismundo, having accepted the precariousness and illusoriness of reality, instead of killing the father puts himself in his place. An inversion occurs, which, to my mind, despite its probable dramatic intention of bathos, more significantly underlines through rhetoric the powerful forces of ideology that are here at work. In the beginning of the play, as part of his cruel experiment, Basilio claims to put Segismundo in his place, on his throne—"I will place him upon my throne, / Under our royal canopy; in fact, he shall reign, / with full authority, in my place" ("Yo he de ponerle . . . en mi dosel, en mi silla, / y, en fin, en el lugar mío"). At the end, Segismundo puts himself in the same (rhetorical) position as his father:

> Rise, Sire — give me your hands;
> Heaven has proved to you how wrong were the ways
> You took for your revenge; I submit to your judgment.
> (III, xiv)[53]

Both the father and the son have placed themselves in the position of the other, which is the position of sacrificial victim. Each has exposed his self to the vengeance of the other, each has humbled himself, but neither has died. Rather, what we have in this recognition of a mutual reciprocity, of the always-possible inversion of father/son, is a reaffirmation of the circle of masculine solidarity in the political structures that empower them both.

Segismundo begins his walk out of bestiality and into the Law by this first acceptance of the Father. He sacrifices to his father, and thus to himself, that aggressive, bestial part of himself that attached him to "nature," to the ambivalent, chaotic force of the mountain fortress, to sexuality, and to Rosaura. He renounces the "immediate," the gratification of the body for the community of masculine law. For this sacrifice to be complete Segismundo must take one more key step in the recognition of the law by participating in what I would call a self-imposed castration — he must renounce his lust/love for Rosaura:

> Rosaura is in my power; my soul worships her beauty;
> Why should I not capture this moment, let love break all the laws . . .
>   for if this world is a dream
> Who for its vain glory would forfeit the divine? . . .
> Rosaura is without honor: it befits a prince
> To bestow honor, not to destroy it.
> (III, ix)[54]

During the course of this inner debate between lust and honor, between, that is, individual desire and social responsibility, Segismundo renounces the bestial in him, denies his passion, and accepts the social structures that engage him in a network of "honor." That "honor," a vast system of complicated social, sexual, and political ties, is less to the point for us than the fact that this represents Segismundo's acceptance of a loss of pleasure in order to gain entry into this symbolic network, to enter into patriarchal society.

By renouncing Rosaura, Segismundo renounces the primacy of the bestial in himself, renounces his personal pleasure, for social restriction. By accepting "castration," the law of the "no," Segismundo sacrifices Rosaura and coterminously extirpates from his being that part that "was" Rosaura — the natural, the sexual. Segismundo sacrifices precisely what made him a heterogeneous being, a monster, by immolating to society his passion for Rosaura.

Despite Segismundo's sacrifice, however, Rosaura remains an unresolved and imperious threat to the social order of patriarchy. She still remains that "loose cannon," an ambivalent, sexually excessive, monstrous presence that confounds her father's wishes, Astolfo's political ambitions, the entire political order that is only shakingly being restructured by the reconciliation of father and son. In order for the world of the play to reestablish its equilibrium, it must not allow this newly strengthened political structure to be vulnerable to its own fractious other. To the sacrifice of his own pleasure, his renouncing of Rosaura, Segismundo further reaffirms patriarchal culture in two ways. On the one hand he reaffirms the importance of the tower, that is, that locus on the frontiers of nature/culture that symbolizes the necessity for any society to define and isolate its "other." By condemning to perpetual imprisonment the soldier who liberated him but by so doing defined himself a "traitor" to the ideal of patriarchal monarchy, Segismundo affirms this ideal's ideological imperative yet also creates its own undermining. The tower reappears at the end of the play, as at the beginning and middle, to accentuate the ritual necessity of victimization, the drive for any totalizing society to exclude from its midst what it dialectically has produced as its other. This appears to us an inherent injustice, an ingratitude on Segismundo's part, but that is precisely the point: gratitude is a sign of the personal that is here sacrificed to the higher demands of *raison d'Etat*.

On the other hand, and more important for the ideological dynamics of the play, Segismundo restores Rosaura's "honor" to her. This restoration of honor is accomplished by that most highly invested of all patriarchal acts, which according to Lévi-Strauss is an originary act of all (masculinist) culture: Segismundo places Rosaura in circulation, uses her as all male-dominated cultures use women, as an "object" of exchange that seals alliances between men. Rosaura is "exchanged," she is put into circulation, circulates between Segismundo and Astolfo as well as between Astolfo and Clotaldo. This sexual exchange between men affirms their mutual debt to each other as it affirms the very principle of exogamy that institutes and affirms all systems of male devolution.[55] We might say, therefore, that the play's "happy" ending—the ending that recognizes both the reconciliation of the Father and son, as well as the reestablishment of a political union among men based on the sexual barter of the object of desire and that object's containment within the sexual political codes that appropriate it—returns us by way of these exchanges to the original myth with which we began, that of Oedipus. Nevertheless, we should remark the shift that has been mediated by the play, by its "tragedy" and by its "comedy." For if the play begins by rescripting the hidden origin of the Oedipus myth, the conflict and sacrifice of the father/son, it ends with the resolution of this conflict, the institution of exogamy: the acceptance of "castration" and the law, figured as the exchange and control of the desired female/other among the (political) rivals/brothers. From this newly affirmed configuration a new social order emerges; we might call it the "modern" social order, finding its first tentative representations on the stages of early modern Europe. These first preliminary adumbrations are destined for a bright future, for it is from within this structure that the oedipal myth that Freud has made the central myth of our modernity emerges. It issues here in *La vida es sueño* in a particularly tantalizing form, almost, we might say, full blown, with all the seductive power of the dream and all of its dangers, too.

Chapter 4

Playing Dead:
Corneille's Canon and Absolute Tragedy

During the sixteenth and seventeenth centuries, something disturbing took place in the depths of the unconscious: there, at the center of the imaginary, love and death drew so closely together as to become indistinguishable.

Ariès, *L'homme devant la mort*

. . . for the absolute is of an entirely different order than life.

Jankélévitch, *La Mort*

The annals of dramaturgy generally acknowledge that in the space of less than ten years (1636–44) Pierre Corneille radically altered the focus and direction of French tragedy. Despite the obvious debts to his French and Spanish predecessors and despite an entire century of Italian neoclassicist theorizing, when *Le Cid* was first produced in Paris at the end of 1636 the emergence of a new and vigorous talent was immediately apparent.[1] Breaking dramatically with the past, Corneille began by imposing a novel theatrical subjectivity on the stage of European representation. This subjectivity, which was finding at the same moment its philosophical predicates in Descartes, is inseparable from the evolving political and social contradictions that were shifting Europe away from the realm of an outmoded feudality and along the path of an emerging "absolutist" political system.[2]

Although he could not rival his Spanish colleagues' prodigious output, during his long and active life Corneille wrote many plays — comedies, tragicomedies, tragedies, pastorals, and other *divertissements* — in a career that spanned the reigns of Louis XIII and Louis XIV. Despite his large

and varied output, however, posterity has kept only four of these plays
(*Le Cid*, *Horace*, *Cinna*, and *Polyeucte*), all written between the years 1636
and 1644, as the most representative, the "masterpieces," of Corneille's
neoclassical revolution.[3]

The question of what in these plays constitutes this new "subjectivity,"
its parameters and limits, is complicated and vexed. For the purposes of
this chapter I would simply like to propose that Corneille's protagonists
represent in a way particular to them and novel to their epoch the social
and sexual contradictions inherent in the crisis of political and epistemic
change. Let us not forget that the political (in its most obvious sense)
drive of the period in the countries discussed in this book is the ever more
concentrated and focused disposition of a centralizing, totalizing bureaucratic government, whose actual displacement of corporatist traditions is
being theorized by those enumerable treatises defining in metaphysical
justifications both the "divine right" of rulers and thus the concept of an
"absolutist" monarchy.[4] In these appeals, as we have seen in the case of
Spain in chapters 2 and 3, there is an imperious drive to banish division,
alterity, and all that smacks of heterogeneity for the order, the peace, and
the stasis of the central, unitary monarchy, for the order of the One. In
France, of course, the imposition of the absolute monarchy is the work
both of Richelieu, cardinal and prime minister of Louis XIII, and of
Louis XIV. The writings of Richelieu (his *Testament Politique*, for example) and of Louis XIV (*Mémoires*) underline the horror that political
leaders felt for social heterogeneity and the concomitant desire for a centralized, ordered, stable monarchy grouped around the person of the
sun/king.[5] That the drive to centralize the French monarchy was met
with diverse forms of resistance — religious, corporatist, feudal, and so
on — is obvious to any student of the period's history. From the turmoil
of the popular and nobiliary uprisings against the encroaching imposition of the monarchy, new social structures emerged in the period from
1630 to 1660. The swift and brutal repression of peasant uprisings (as in
Corneille's hometown of Rouen) and the equally spectacular execution
of recalcitrant nobles underline the fact that central to an "absolutist"
drive, congruent with it, is the threat, the always-there, of death. As
Louis Marin reminds us, absolutism, the desire for the noncontingent,
is inseparably connected with an imperious death drive.[6]

Cornelian theater has often been studied as a reflection of the social
and political turmoil of its time, and it will come as no surprise to us that
Corneille's most successful tragedies represent the conflict between these
different drives in his protagonists' inner struggles.[7] In other words, what
Corneille first radically figures in his dramatic conflict is the contradictions between a protagonist who wishes to be absolute — that is, in conformity to an ambient ideological drive, which of course results in the crea-

tion of the famous Cornelian "Moi" — and at the same time the contradictory "split within," the internal fracture that makes Corneille's characters "dramatis personae" as they struggle with what inheres in them that is irreconcilable with the exigencies of the absolute monarchy, their amorous and mortiferous desire. For the first time on the French stage, the confrontation with the other is not so much, to paraphrase Vernant, the murderous duel with the "other person" (foreigner, i.e., Othello) but rather with "what is other in the person."[8]

In Corneille we are presented with what I would like to call the coming into being of the "absolute" subject. This absolute subjectivity is intimately inscribed within the overriding dichotomy that rules the Cornelian universe: death/transcendence, or, if we wish, death/immortality. This dichotomy, in different inflections, is present as the central debate in all of the four canonical tragedies as they elaborate the outlines of a new subjectivity. It is a debate in which the finitude of the individual subject is defined in relation to its aspirations to eternity. In this controversy the subject becomes what we know as the "modern" interiorized, "self-conscious" subject by incorporating in self-interrogation the question of limits, posed in these plays as the problem of mortality. All of Corneille's great plays, in one way or another, constantly pose the question of limits, of death and of the possibility of transcending this ultimate frontier, at the center of their passional/political drama.[9] In this sense they are "absolute" tragedies, absolute because of the ways in which each of them takes up the question of the subject subjected to its own negation, a negation internal to it and from which it attempts to be freed. The way this dialectic is embodied in the protagonists of Corneille's dramaturgy is, I would suggest, radically different from the projection of characters that preceded it. Corneille's particular genius for "embodying" this new subjectivity in the protagonists of his theater is what accounts, I would suggest, for their status in the French canon and for their continuing interest and passion today.

When we familiarize ourselves with Corneille's four canonical dramas, we cannot help but remark the enormous structural importance coupling plays in the elaboration of Cornelian subjectivity, which radically separates him from the other dramatists of his day. It strikes me that nowhere else does the dramatic tension of the play depend so heavily and so forcefully on an almost uncanny sexual symmetry as in Corneille. Despite the fact that his plays, like those of Racine or Shakespeare, bear the name of an eponymous hero, and despite the fact that these names are relentlessly masculine, the tension and conflict of Corneille's plays are inseparable from a sexual division, an opposition of male and female characters whose importance for the dramatic conflict of the play is primordial. Surely there are passionate and engaging "couples" in the works of Racine and Shakespeare, as well as in those of Calderón and Lope de Vega, but the tragic of these plays remains attached, exclusively and poignantly, to the protagonist, whether Phèdre, Segismundo, Othello, or Hamlet. The amorous counterparts of the protagonists are always marked with a lesser sign of the tragic, always pale in comparison with them. This is not, I would suggest, the fate of the Cornelian couple — could we imagine an interest in Le Cid without Chimène, in Horace without Camille, in Cinna without Emilie, or in Polyeucte without Pauline? (These couplings are not exclusive, of course, and there are other poignant possibilities, such as Camille and Curiace or Pauline and Sévère.) This difference, this compelling importance of the "couple" in Corneille, focuses our attention on the importance of an institutionalized sexuality, that is, a sexuality that is a "social production."

In a recent book, *Making Sex: Body and Gender from the Greeks to Freud*, the cultural historian Thomas Laqueur argues that until the eighteenth century European civilization was, ideologically speaking, a "one-sex" civilization.[10] He suggests that because of an inherited tradition of patriarchy in which what is male and what is female were distinctions of value rather than distinctions of kind, sexuality was studied as a system of greater or lesser attributes of the same (male) sex. Female genitalia were observed, studied, and described as simply "inverted" male genitalia, internal to the body because woman, a less perfect creation of nature, was incapable of producing the proper refined and refining "heat" that in the male system propelled the sexual organs out of the body. Women, being of an inferior nature, retained the "same organs" inside their bodies.[11] In a very real sense this model of sexuality, as Laqueur analyzes it, is perversely tautological; biology mirrors ideology, which in turn forms the parameters inside of which "sex" is seen. What this seeing reveals, of course, is a universe of male prerogative and power, a political universe that subsumes into and as itself the realms of biology, reproduction, and desire. The predominance of the one-sex model reproduced what Western civilization had said to itself from Aristotle onward: man is the model of all things.[12] Laqueur's hypothesis strikes me as valid, on one level, for understanding the dramatic intensity of Cornelian theater with its insistence on symmetrical coupling, for in this coupling the difference between men and women is the difference of the mirror, but also the way this mirrorlike reflection is coded, ideologically, as positive or negative. Women are marked as different from men because they are more given to the body; they are "men's bodies." What this means is that in this universe where sexual difference is a difference of power the attributes that distinguish men from women are metaphysical attributes transcoded into "physical" symptoms: women are marked as "softer," their bodies are bodies in "flux," bodies of tears and blood, bodies that are not one, while men are marked by bodies that are never referred to as such but exist only as an ideal, a unitary ideal, of political dominance.

Where Corneille seems to mark a first step out of this model is in his tragedy's insistence that sexuality is absolutely inseparable from the political. Corneille's couples, though they are assuredly "essentialized" (that is, masculinity and femininity are seen as givens of a natural order), are nevertheless freed from any concern with biology. Sexuality in Corneille can never be assimilated to reproduction. For all the importance the family and coupling plays in Cornelian dramaturgy, the couples he presents in dyadic sexual opposition, in symmetrical pairing, are sterile. Caught up in their own passionate claims for a subjectivity that would situate them beyond the realm of contingent reality, their sexuality is a purely abstract production, informed by the way they attempt to control the social and political forces that impinge on their own imperious desires. They are "political" in the same sense that they are sexual. At the same time, and this strikes me as potentially more perverse, this insistence on sexuality, on a combative aggressive sexuality, reveals within the particular context of Cornelian tragedy (where the couples are more often than not engaged in and representative of larger forces of social and metaphysical contradiction, forces that are locked into tragic, alienating conflict) a novel introduction of the nefarious other. This most elusive and occult of others haunts the universe of Corneille as an object of both desire and fear, and seems utterly inseparable from the erotic impulse that serves as its vehicle, death.

It might first appear an enormous banality to claim that "death" is the central obsessive presence in the four canonical dramas. After all, in one important sense, the presence of death, or at least the "horizon of death," tautologically defines these plays as "tragedies."[13] However, and this strikes me as more pertinent, Corneille's protagonists seem to live in the shadow of some eventual death not so much as something that will eventually envelope them in its obscurity, depriving them of the light and thus of their presence in the world, but as something intimately internal to them. It exists as an essential division that inheres in his heroes and to which, in an orchestrated but voluptuous abandonment, they succumb.

When Freud published *Beyond the Pleasure Principle* in 1920, besides dramatically reshifting his topology of the human psyche, he introduced what was to become the most heatedly opposed innovation in his evolving elaboration of the unconscious, the concept of a death drive that actively but silently works to return the human organism to a state of nirvana-like indifference. One of the most disturbing aspects of this newly defined "instinct" was its hypothetical nature: it is an instinct that can never be isolated in and of itself, but can be approached only asymptotically through the workings of its obverse, the pleasure principle. Freud tells us that the two instincts that he originally presents as dualistic are not to be envisioned as an opposition but rather as a conjunction.[14] The instincts of life (in essence the sexual instincts) and those of death seem to work, he says, together:

> Another striking fact is that the life instincts have so much more contact with our internal perception—emerging as breakers of the peace and constantly producing tensions whose release is felt as pleasure—while the death instincts seem to do their work unobtrusively. The pleasure principle seems actually to serve the death instincts.[15]

Recent psychoanalytic theory has followed Freud's speculations about the inextricably interwoven nexus of death/sexuality. We might say that for contemporary followers of Freud, sexuality is inseparable from death, from, that is, death as a metaphor for a precipitate fall into loss, into absence. Only at the "moment" of this fall into "difference," into the psychic space of castration, does a sense of the self as an individuated entity, as an "I," emerge.[16] Through an initial traumatic apprehension of difference, that is, separation, the individual infant is cast into a subject/object dialectic, and from this dialectic the individual, subjected to death, emerges as a subject, a subject of language (the "I" of difference) and of sexuality.

The fact that human beings are, to use Bataille's terminology, "discontinuous beings"[17] means that in our quest for the absolute, for the reunion with the object(s) of our passion that would suture our initial wound, we are condemned to a spiraling of desire in which the other that is death and the other that is the promised plenitude are inextricably confounded in the same fantasy of absolute alterity and absolute identity. What this confusion also implies, and this is particularly resonant with political overtones for the entire seventeenth century, is that death becomes coded as the absolute of human experience, the horizon beyond which no human thought and no human yearning can go, except perhaps in a projection of a mystical union with God. But in this case, the confusion of the ultimate object of mystical love and the absolute limit of humanness increases once again in their mutual imbrication.[18] The radical consequences of Western speculations on and about death are evident not only throughout the history of philosophy (and more intensely from Hegel onward) but, more to our point, in any of the passionate couplings such as we find in Corneille. Another revolutionary consequence of Freud's theorizing the collusion of the instincts of death (which later psychoanalysis has termed "Thanatos") and of Eros is the realization that the difference that is precipitated out of the self as sexuality, the projection of difference as a sexual (male-female) split, is but one of the different modalities taken by an internal splitting, the death inherent in the subject itself, a "difference within," which unbeknownst to the subject is the origin of the very conditions of his or her being as "subject."[19]

Corneille and his pre-Freudian world were ignorant of the theories and language of psychoanalysis, but this does not mean that they were not aware of the essential dynamics of human behavior that Freud was to theorize three centuries later. They only had to cast an eye over the corpus of Greek myths transmitted to them in either their original form or their Latinized versions to be told, in more poetic fables, the same thing. What, for instance, does the myth of Pandora (or Eve) teach us but that sexuality and death enter the world simultaneously? Before the creation of Pandora humans (men) did not die, they simply fell into a long and peaceful sleep. Only by the gods' introduction of woman (that is, for a phallocentric culture, of difference, of the woman-as-other) did sexuality and death enter the universe of mortals. "Death and women," to quote Vernant again, "arose in concert together."[20]

The recourse to a common vocabulary (terms such as Eros and Thanatos) and to a common mythological corpus can, on the one hand, be seen to link, across the centuries, the Greeks to Corneille and Corneille to Freud. On the other hand, we will have to explore the ways the individual links in this chain function, the particular twists at one of the key moments of epistemic change in the West—the period separating and joining the world of the Renaissance and the emerging world of neoclassical aesthetics, the moment of Corneille's theatrical triumph—to see how this moment forms an independent but heavily invested loop in the genealogical chain of Western patriarchal culture.

In order to establish Corneille's place in this metaphysical chain and before entering into a detailed discussion of how this place is circumscribed in the four canonical plays, I would like to outline what at first might appear too dangerous an analogy, a sphere of communality of thought in which the two extreme limits of this chain—its origins in Greek thought and a certain terminus in Freud's—intermingle. To do this I will start at the end of the chain with Freud and his thinking about death and instincts.

Any discussion of the Freudian death instinct must consider the general theory of the instincts and their manifestations that Freud first presented in a series of metapsychological essays published in 1915. "Instincts and Their Vicissitudes," "Repression," and "The Unconscious" all deal in greater or lesser degrees with the particularly quirky aspects of instincts: the impossibility of ever seizing an instinct in its "essence"; their ability to manifest themselves in reversals of their aims; and their tendency to split into positive and negative (active and passive) manifestations. One of the most startling of Freud's pronouncements was his statement that instincts are never available as such to our conscious (or even unconscious) apprehension. They are knowable only as a representation: "an instinct can never become an object of consciousness — only the idea (*Vorstellung*) that represents an instinct can. Even in the unconscious, moreover, an instinct cannot be represented otherwise than by an idea."[21] What this means is that in any attempt to circumscribe an instinctual drive we must be aware of the difference between an instinct and the aim of an instinct. According to Freud only the aim is capable of variation, and taking as his examples the classic descriptions of sadomasochism and voyeurism-exhibitionism, this variation is most commonly a reversal into its opposite (to look/to be looked at, to torture/to be tortured).[22] Furthermore, on the level of representation, the instinct can undergo a splitting. Part of the instinct that may be too negatively threatening to the ego is, because of the process of repression, forever lost in the unconscious, while another acceptable part appears in conscious representation as an idealization.[23] Instincts, including the death instinct, can be split: their manifestations can appear in negative reversal or in sympathetic mimesis. When tracking the path of the invisible instinct, therefore, we must look for its traces, which appear most frequently in binary opposition. This opposition is not the sign of two, but rather a single imperious drive. The aim of the instinct can be either passive or active, terms that (at first) Freud associated with "masculine" and "feminine," and whose manifestation can take on positive or negative ideational content depending on the ideological weight a given society attributes to its sexualized manifestations.

Curiously, the Greeks also tended to represent the forces of death as split into gendered representatives.[24] They had not a single but at least a binary conception of death, which corresponded to their own conscious, patriarchal, anxieties. Although psychoanalysis borrows the term "Thanatos" as a universalized concept indicating the death drive, the Greeks distinguished ("split") their discussion of death into (at least) two figures that were already sexually weighted. Thanatos, Vernant tells us, was a masculine figure that does not seem to incarnate, for the Greeks, the "terrible destructive force that descends on human beings to destroy them." Rather, Thanatos represents an already-idealized, ethereal, I am tempted to say "sublimated," ideal of death not as bodily demise, but as an ethical/political ideal. Thanatos leads men to a "state other than life, that new condition to which funeral rites offer men access and from which none can escape."[25] Vernant further develops this idea by which the Greeks seemed to transform the reality of bodily decay into the elaboration of a political vision:

> Thanatos . . . is a social strategy that attempts to domesticate death, civilize it — that is, to deny it as such by transforming the dead . . .

into the very past of the city, a past made continuously present to the group through the mechanism of collective memory.[26]

The horrible *Kreaturlichkeit* aspect of death, the death that signifies bodily rot, is the attribute of another deity, or pair of deities, both female — Gorgo and Ker:

> In its fearful aspect, as a power of terror expressing the unspeakable and unthinkable — that which is radically "other" — death is a feminine figure who takes on its horror: the monstrous face of Gorgo . . . And it is another feminine figure Ker — black, grim, evil, horrible, execrable — who represents death as a maleficent force that sweeps down on humans to destroy them.[27]

Thanatos and Ker, masculine and feminine versions of the unrepresentable, already indicate at the dawn of Western civilization a splitting of an instinct and its coded representation. This representation is coded in the values of a patriarchal culture so that what is fearful, bodily, and material is associated with a female deity, and what is ethereal, idealized, and political is associated with the male.

In his classic study of Western European conceptions of death and dying, *L'homme devant la mort*, Philippe Ariès offers the hypothesis that the period separating the end of the sixteenth and the beginning of the seventeenth centuries saw a radical shift in the way death was portrayed, both in iconography and in literature, that would tend to corroborate, on another level, the early hypothesis of Foucault, who saw this intermediary period, generally called the "baroque," as one of the major transitional moments in the history of Western epistemology.[28] Ariès suggests that the major difference in the way Western civilization represented death changed from one imaginary depiction, the macabre, which had dominated iconography from the late fourteenth through the late sixteenth centuries with its emphasis on the *Kreaturlichkeit*, the depiction of the body in death as the body in corruption and decay, to the more "classical" funerary monuments of the seventeenth century.[29] Colbert's monument by Coysevox in St. Eustache comes to mind. In this monument Colbert is represented kneeling in the position of a supplicant; his robustness and his courtly robes make us wonder if he is praying to the Heavenly Father for the forgiveness of his sins, or simply asking a favor of his royal patron, Louis XIV.

This change from an emphasis on the body, on its corruption, its disintegration, on the imaginary delectation of our own materiality, to an idealized, etherealized representation of death as but a more nobly abstract projection of human (and divine) perfection corresponds to an entire scientific and spiritual revolution in human knowledge in which the body, while becoming more and more a focus of study, an "object," is separated from the essential part of our humanness, the "soul," the "spirit." This split, though reinforcing a traditional division, underlines the more metaphysical conception of human existence that is surely more conducive to the economic and social models that are evolving in early capitalist Europe.[30] To this complex move in the circumscribing of human subjectivity corresponds, it seems to me, the transformation and imposition, first in France and then in the rest of Europe, of the ethical and aesthetic parameters of neoclassicism that Corneille was the first to embody in his theater.

That neoclassicism first imposes itself in the theater, and that its triumph dates from Le Cid's spectacular debut on the Parisian stage in 1636, signals that we must turn our sights to Corneille if we are to understand the complex workings of ideology, of the ideology of subjectivity as it necessarily revolves around the complicated and vexed knot that sexuality, death, and politics forms at the heart of this new representation of the tragic that appears and imposes itself on the cultural life of France in Corneille's four canonical masterpieces.[31] Following Terry Eagleton's arguments, it is in literature that we are most subtly able to trace the workings of the often ambivalent and evanescent imperatives of ideological contradictions.[32]

For the purposes of our present concerns I propose that we begin by considering the four canonical plays as a unit. I would like to delimit the major phantasmic structures, the desire(s) informing the Cornelian universe, before examining each of the plays individually in order to demonstrate how each declines in ever more refined scenarios the ambivalences we find in the general delineation of the canon.

I will only be restating the obvious when I say that Corneille is the most "political" of dramatists. His plays, eschewing the temptations of mythology, are firmly grounded in historical anecdote, and each anecdote is a tale of crisis, a story of a trembling moment of history in which the fate of nations, empires, and entire world orders hangs in the balance.[33] The historical moment Corneille chooses for his tragedies is always a "dramatic," fraught moment, a moment of history becoming, a moment of passage, a threshold where what has been vanishes into what must be. Corneille's historical tragedies, from Le Cid to Polyeucte, are situated at the point where ideologies collide. In Le Cid, we are at the court of the first king of Castile, Ferdinand, whose rule is only shakily imposed; it is threatened from without by the ever-present menace of the Moors — the exterior other — and from within by the feudal horde, represented by Don Gomez. Horace presents us with what we might call a historicized foundation myth: we are called upon to witness the founding moment of Rome's nascent hegemony, the battle that forever establishes Rome as a separate identity and sets her on the road to empire. *Cinna* takes place in the uneasy aftermath of Rome's civil wars and traces the establishment of a divine-right "monarchy" that is called upon to replace the exhausted remnants of the "Republic." Finally, *Polyeucte* makes us witness to the prostration of the Roman Empire, threatened by external enemies (the Persians) and by internal division (the Christians). The tragedy successfully traduces the end of the pagan world and Christianity's (eventual) political triumph.

Despite the varied historical moments that Corneille chose for his dramas, we can detect a certain permanent anxiety at the heart of the dramatic tension of each play beyond their merely evenemential differences. In each drama the political situation, that is, the represented "real," is inscribed within a bipolar oscillation. On the one hand is the constant, often dreamlike evocation of a nefarious yet strangely jubilant chaos — images of disintegration, total social breakdown, and death that form the backdrop (I am tempted to say "the primal scene") haunting all the characters of the play. On the other hand, in its aspirations and heroic resolution, is the equally present vision of a proleptic moment of utopian plenitude, an absolute quietude of permanence, peace, stasis.

Perhaps the most harrowing example of the first instance is found in *Cinna*, when Cinna evokes for his fellow conspirators the past — their common past, their deadly past — that lives on in each of them and from which they cannot be freed:

> Then, with a long recital of the woes
> Undergone in our childhood by our fathers,
> Reviving both their memories and their hatred,
> I doubled in their hearts their thirst for vengeance.
> I drew for them pictures of those sad battles
> When Rome with her own hands tore out her vitals . . .
> I painted these men to them, emulating
> Each other in their boasted massacres,
> The whole of Rome bathed in her children's blood,
> Some of the victims slain in public places,
> Others cut down amid their household gods,
> The wicked led to crime by its rewards,
> The husband in his bed killed by his wife,
> The son all reeking with his father's gore
> And carrying in his hand his father's head,
> And asking for payment . . .
> (*Cinna* I, iii)[34]

To this terrifying scene of an entire society turned against itself, of the breakdown of the most "sacred" and most heavily invested of social units, the family (a scenario joined to the originary myth of chaos — Oedipus and his family), corresponds the desire for another world, a world of no change, no corruption, of eternal harmony:

> . . . they aspire,
> If truth be told, only to transient blessings
> Which cares will vex and dangers will attend.
> Death takes these from us; Fortune sports with them—
> Today a throne, a dunghill on the morrow—
> And their bright splendor rouseth so much envy,
> Few of your Caesars have enjoyed them long.
> I have ambition, but 'tis nobler, fairer.
> Those honors perish; I seek immortal honors,
> A bliss assured, eternal, infinite,
> Above the reach of envy and of fate.
> (*Polyeucte* IV, iii)[35]

And:

> Your blessings are inconstant never,
> And death, to crown my soul's endeavor,
> Serves but as a kindly door
> To bring us to that blessed shore
> Where we shall find comfort forever.
> (*Polyeucte* IV, ii)[36]

I would suggest that it is within the limits of this same fantasy of death—a fantasy marked by a negative (death as chaos, dispersion, tumult) and a positive (death as harmony, union, stasis) pole—that Corneille situates the dramatic crises of his couples. It is a sign of his extraordinary talent as a playwright that he knew how to bring the greater political crisis that serves as the frame for his tragedies into the very center of the passional conflict that tears apart his protagonists. He does this in and through that other pervasive presence of Cornelian tragedy, the paterfamilias, that imperious, monolithic presence that serves as the hinge by which the public and the private, the family and the state, interweave in a seamless and deadly web.

We must not forget that although Cornelian tragedy is always "political" it evolves within the confines of the family. The imbrication of the family and the polis is never questioned in this world that ignores any separation of private and public spaces. In Corneille the family doubles the state. It should not surprise us that in this highly patriarchal society (but, we should also mention, a society that has been shaken to its foundations with more than three-quarters of a century of civil and religious strife) the figure of the Cornelian father serves as the arbitrator of social law and individual desire. We might suggest that this representation of the Cornelian father serves as the "nodal point" in which and through which the individual and the state are joined in a seamless, but not sim-

ple, conflictual system of debt and retribution. The presence of the father
(the oedipal father, father of the primal horde, and father of interdictory
fantasies), be it actual (*Le Cid*) or metaphysical (*Polyeucte*), looms over the
fate of the couple as the interdicting instance that renders their passion
both inimical to the state and to themselves. His presence, a prohibitive
"no," tinges their ardor with the tantalizing taboo of transgression. The
political in Corneille thus comes inverted into his couples' passionate desire as a dialogue of oedipal duty and sexuality that renders his heroes
tragic to the exact degree that they are in opposition to the father whom
they both fear and love. At the same time, their agonistic dialogue never
lets us forget that these heroes are dramatic precisely because their ardent
beings are inseparable from the political conflict that threatens the very
structures of their world with death.

What most strikes us in Corneille's first theatrical triumph, *Le Cid*, the
play that with Racine's *Phèdre* remains the classic example of seventeenth-
century French theater, is the uncanny reflexivity of the two young
lovers, Rodrigue and Chimène. From the very first lines of the play their
love is presented as mutual, self-enclosed, and totalizing. Its force is first
revealed in the initial dialogue between Chimène and her *gouvernante*, Elvire, a conversation that also reveals the hidden anxiety of this love, the
place and desire of the father:

> CHIMÈNE: How now,
>   Elvire, what must I expect? What fate
>   Is to be mine? What did my father say
>   To thee?
> ELVIRE: Things which should very much delight thee.
>   He admires Rodrigue no less than thou
>   Dost love him.
> CHIMÈNE: My good fortune is so great
>   That I distrust it. Can I really credit
>   Such words?
> ELVIRE: He goes yet further; he approves
>   Of Rodrigue's wooing and will soon command thee
>   To plight thy troth with him.
> (*Le Cid* I, i)[37]

From the outset of the Cornelian canon we are given its essential ingredients: the desire of the two lovers, precipitated into anxiety by the mediating presence of the father. In *Le Cid*, which, in its political dimension,
traces the social evolution of a society away from an outmoded, regressive feudalism toward a "modern" progressive centralized state, the role
of the father by which and through which this evolution is figured is strategically split.

The play offers us two fathers who are uncanny doubles of each other, and two lovers who are also presented as essentially mirror images, in sexual reversal. It is from the image of the other, the double-lover, that the hero must break free in order to be able to allow society a way out of the repetition of feudality and into the progression of history.

Although Don Diègue and Don Gomez are presented as rivals for the honor their king is to bestow upon only one of them, and although this rivalry will radically sunder them, on the more profound level of the text's investment in an ideology of masculinity the two fathers are merely an image of the "same" presented at different stages of a temporal progression. Not only are the two fathers identical, but Rodrigue too, the young, untried male, is inseparable from them. "Thou art today what I was formerly," Don Diègue tells the count. This statement merely echoes the latter's "Thou hast been valiant; I am valiant now." Finally, Rodrigue is greeted by his father after his duel with the count with an outpouring of paternal narcissism:

> My valor hath no reason to disavow
> Thine own. Thou hast well imitated it,
> And thy brave daring maketh live again
> In thee the heroes of my race. From them
> Thou art descended, and thou art my son.
> Thy sword's first blow hath equalled all I smote . . .
> (*Le Cid* III, iv)[38]

The insistence on "today" ("aujourd'hui") introduces into the basic sameness of these men the anxiety of time, which is the anxiety of death. These masculine characters representing "the three ages of man"— youth, virility, old age—figure both a permanent masculine essence that devolves from father to son along the lines of both biological and symbolic systems, and the insecurity inherent in the social system that produces those laws and that is, nevertheless, unsure of being able to reproduce them continually.[39]

This insecurity becomes most insistent when confronted with temporal reality. For example, we see the emphasis on "aujourd'hui" in the heated confrontation of the two fathers, or in the more direct apostrophe to time in Don Diègue's famous monologue:

> O fury! O despair! Hateful old age!
> Have I, then, lived so long only for this
> Disgrace? In toil of war have I grown grey,
> To see my laurels wither in one day?
> (*Le Cid* I, iv)[40]

In the system of male devolution whose insecurities the play is both obfuscating and uncovering, the enemy, the silent, nefarious enemy, is internal. It is the body-in-time, the body condemned to its own undoing:

> And does the arm at which all Spain has marvelled,
> My arm, which has so often saved this realm,
> So often given new strength to its king's throne,
> Betray my cause now and avail me none?
> O cruel remembrance of my vanished glory!
> A whole life's effort canceled in one moment!
> (*Le Cid* I, iv)[41]

This treacherous body, incapable of remaining at the apex of its virility, incapable of being a *corps glorieux* but rather destined to indignity, must be eliminated if the hero is to exist. The first task of the hero is to eradicate the body and thus to stop time, and the first body Rodrigue does away with is the body of the Father.

This confrontation with the Father elevates *Le Cid* from the realm of the historical quotidian and replaces it in the mythic, in both the traditional sense of the word and its more ideologically laden, psychoanalytic evocations.[42] Don Gomez is presented by the play as the "bad father." On the level of metapsychology he is cast in the image of the Freudian chief of the "primal horde." He is the undisputed leader ("his exceptional bravery will not allow any rival in his stead") because he is the most powerful warrior. The depiction of him "covered with blood and dirt" clothes him in imaginary scenes of brutality and carnage. He also possesses the right to *jouissance*; he controls the object of desire of the younger males and decides which of them will be given his daughter as a sexual prize:

> The lofty spirit which thy words reveal
> Has from thy face been long apparent to me.
> The future hero of Castile, naught less,
> I saw in thee, and joyfully my heart
> Destined for thee my daughter's hand.
> (*Le Cid* II, ii)[43]

It would be banal to suggest that Rodrigue's conflict with the count is simply an "oedipal" rivalry between an older and a younger man, although it is obviously this, too. The count is "bad" not only in relation to the object of the young male's desire, he is also — and this is where the play pivots back from the dynamics of personal desire into conflicts of historical evolution — politically retrograde.

In the mythic-historical evolution that the play traduces, the count represents not only the "primal father," in relation to Rodrigue, but the leader of the "primal horde," the unstable group of feudal nobles. This anxious feudal class, as we have already noticed in the Spanish plays we have analyzed, is threatened with disempowerment by the nascent centralized monarchy. The conflict between these two forces, the conservative nature of the former and the "progressive" albeit precarious nature of the latter, is underlined by Corneille in his *examen* where he tells us that "don Ferdinand was the first king of Castile—those who were Castile's masters before him only bore the title of 'count.' He was perhaps not absolute enough master of the grandees of his kingdom . . . "[44] The count's hubris, his refusal to humble himself to the orders of the king, and his veiled threats, although bestowing on him a certain aura of noble resoluteness, mark him as the victim the play must sacrifice on the altar of the absolute:

> THE COUNT: Sir, to preserve all that I value most,
>   A little disobedience is no crime;
>   Yet were it e'er so heinous, my great service
>   Now to the realm would more than cancel it.
> DON ARIAS: However great and glorious are one's exploits,
>   A king is never in his subject's debt. . . .
> THE COUNT: I can outlive a single day's displeasure.
>   Let all the realm be armed for my destruction;
>   If I should perish, the whole state will perish.
> (*Le Cid* II, i)[45]

The direct attack on the Father, not to mention his murder, is, as we know, the unthinkable taboo of a highly patriarchal culture.[46] Certainly in most cases the object of the murderous drive is never the father, but his substitute, the child. In *Le Cid*, the dead count reappears, hydralike, in all the substitute fathers, including his own, that Rodrigue must now affront. The murder of the father would be an impossible act if there were not the double other Father, who embodies the values of the emerging social order in his own person. Don Diègue, Rodrigue's father, is the first of those stern, morally incorruptible, politically "correct" patriarchs who populate the Cornelian universe. They are marked most notably (as we have seen in Calderón's Basilio) by a certain desexualized masculinity, freed from the fetters of desire, which incarnates in its moral rigidity the Law of absolute denial. It is a law marked most perversely by the father's willingness to sacrifice his child to those ideals—honor, duty, family, state—he represents. When the king, at the end of the play, is loath to have Rodrigue risk his life in a politically useless duel, Don Diègue, having ordered his son first into battle against the count, then against the Moors, indignantly steps in and countermands the king's leniency:

> What, sire! for him alone annul the laws
> Which all thy Court so oft have seen observed?
> What will thy people think or envy say
> If he takes shelter under this exemption
> And makes of it a pretext not to go
> Where men of honor seek a valiant death?
> (*Le Cid* IV, v)[47]

Although most probably unaware of the profound acuity of his desperate statement "What tears and misery our fathers cost us!" ("Que de maux et de pleurs nous coûteront nos pères!"; III, iv), which he utters at the exact center of the play, Rodrigue does situate the entire passional and dramatic center of his and the play's predicament around this passage, the never-completed passage that the children in this play must navigate out of the mortiferous desire of the father(s) and into a new, noncontingent heroic realm.

The murder of Chimène's father has transformed both of the lovers by radically altering their relation to each other. What was presented at the beginning of the play as an adolescent love has been changed by death into a passionate politicosexual imbroglio. It would not be an exaggeration to say that death — the attack on the father, the father internalized as guilt and duty — has converted a banal example of puppy love into a passionately tragic drama. At the same time this personal, passional conflict once again reinserts the individual into the larger political crisis. Chimène is moved by her father's death into his retrograde political position: she must defend a feudal tradition of personal vendetta. She single-mindedly pursues Rodrigue despite the fact that he has now become vital for the historical survival of the state:

> Now, Rodrigue is our country's sole support,
> The hope and idol of an adoring people,
> Castile's defense, the terror of the Moor. . . .
> Thou seekest in his death the nation's ruin.
> (*Le Cid* IV, ii)[48]

The dead father is now an internalized obstacle to their love, making this love transgressive of the social and political order. To love Rodrigue is to forget her sense of self, as that sense is inscribed in a familial-political structure. It is the temptation of the loss of self that is, I would suggest, passionate. Chimène feels herself divided in front of a vortex in which her political position is at odds with her desire. We must understand that this "political" position is figured by the play as retrograde, as that which must be sacrificed in order for the society that the play represents to progress. Thus it is dramatically opportune that Chimène's passion for Rodrigue grows stronger (" 'Love' is too weak a word to use, Elvire. / I worship him. My adoration of him / Joins battle with a daughter's natural feelings. / I find my lover in my enemy") in direct proportion to Rodrigue's acceptance of the dictates of his own father's moral and political code — the dictates of death. In this way the play figures in the transgressive passion of the two lovers the passage from one political schema to another, a passage mediated by and through the Law of the Father.

The two lovers are cast as mirrorlike reflections of each other. This reflection is underlined by the stichomythia of act III, scene v, the famous scene of amorous/deadly confrontation in Chimène's house. This pathetic rhetorical duel places each lover in front of the other in order to reduce their difference, their sexual and political difference, to the merest hairbreadth of separation, the separation of a past participle:

> CHIMÈNE: Rodrigue, who would have thought? . . .
> RODRIGUE: Chimène, who would have said? . . .
> (*Le Cid* III, v)[49]

The difference between desire ("croire") and reality ("dire") opposes the one to the other in a sexual chiasmus. The chiasmus, however narrow, remains unbridgeable, joining and separating the two lovers in a brutal struggle to the death. On the success or failure of their passion the political future of Spain—the chaos of the feudal horde or the order of the monarchy—hangs in the balance.

The battle is played out in *Le Cid* between those forces of masculinity and femininity represented by the two lovers. It should be obvious that these forces are not univocal nor are they solely identifiable with the biological sexes of the protagonists. Rather, it is around the obstacle of the dead Father that both of the protagonists must confront the other in them, the other body, the other sex.

At the beginning of the play the young lovers are both marked by their "indifference"—each is lost in the other, each is the double of the other. This effect of doubling, which we know since Freud's essay on the uncanny, is troubling because the double is seen as a hostile threat to the ego, and thus is always perceived as a harbinger of death.[50] From the beginning, then, the two lovers, as mirror images of each other in sexual reversal, can be seen as if already proleptically marked by and through their relation to death. Only with the actual intrusion of death are they radically altered. When Rodrigue is confronted with his father's ultimatum, the absolute ultimatum, "Die or Kill" ("Meurs ou tue . . . "), he enters into a dark night of the soul (his "stances"), beginning the meditation as a divided being ("Within my breast how wild a storm! / My honor is at stake, my love at stake. / If I avenge my sire, two hearts I break").[51] At the end of the stances, he has worked out of this division and has freed himself of the ambivalence that inhered in him. In the world of the absolute to which the theater of Corneille tends, "division," be it moral, sexual, or political, is always negatively coded. It is the mark of weakness, confusion, and lack of "integrity." In this patriarchal system that desires the security of totality, "division" is given the coded shadow of the feminine. Thus, I would suggest that Rodrigue, as he works through the stances, works out of division and into the realm of the masculine one.[52] He does this most symptomatically by ridding himself of the division in himself, a division most specifically attached to physical desire, to the body's desire. In accepting the law of his (the) father, Rodrigue accepts, in a sense, castration, the "no" to the body, the "no" to pleasure. He rids himself of the feminine in him; he rids himself of Chimène. We might go one step further and suggest that what the sacrifice to masculinity entails is the immolation of physical desire for political glory, the elimination of the "body" for a transcendental ideal. Rodrigue sacrifices his body's desire, he sacrifices the "body" to death, to the immaterial imperative that places him squarely in the space of paternal Law — the space of absolute transcendence of the self in an ideal of filial, that is, political, duty:

> . . . My father's claim
> Stands first, not fealty to my heart's adored.
> Whether I die of grief or by the sword,
> I will not bring upon our ancient name
> Disgrace. Already do I blush that I
> Did not to vengeance fly . . .
> (*Le Cid* I, vi)[53]

By choosing death Rodrigue renounces the body. The more Chimène ventures into the realm of vendetta, however, the more she appears marked by the body: first the body of her dead father, then the body of Rodrigue.

> My father, sire, is dead. Mine eyes have seen
> His blood in great streams pouring from his side.
> That blood which has so oft kept safe thy walls, . . .
> His wound gaped wide and, to incite me more,
> His blood wrote in the dust my duty for me.
> (*Le Cid* II, viii)[54]

Although on one level she maintains her vendetta against Rodrigue, each time he moves (through and for her) closer into the realm of the heroic, each time he affronts death, she suffers in her body the affronts she imposes on his. Chimène is obsessed with Rodrigue's body. Always in her thoughts, it betrays her desire:

> CHIMÈNE (to Elvire after the battle with the Moors): Is Rodrigue wounded?
> ELVIRE: As to that, I know not . . .
> Thou turnest pale. Take heart again.
> (*Le Cid* IV, i)[55]

> DON FERNAND: Though Rodrigue overcame our foes,
> He just now died before us, from their blows.
> (To Don Diègue) See how already she is drained of color!

DON DIÈGUE: But look: she swoons, and in that swoon supplies
   The proof, sire, of a love that hath no bounds!
   (*Le Cid* IV, v)[56]

In the final analysis, and we will see this confirmed in the plays that follow *Le Cid*, what seems to separate men from women, masculinity from femininity, in Corneille's drama is that masculinity is synonymous with a renunciation of the body and thus, as the body is never allowed to intrude into the space of men, with a utopian idea of death as "Thanatos." Death becomes a political ideal. The mark of women, however, is the mark of the body. Women are never allowed to articulate death in any way other than in terms that show them remaining in the realm of the physical. This, of course, should not surprise us, for Corneille's plays represent, in not unambivalent terms, a dominant patriarchal culture, and in that culture not only are women seen as less given to sublimation than men, more connected to the body, but, in more radical terms, for phallocentric society women are the body.[57] Chimène's attachment to and identification with the body, and at the same time her "heroic" stance as revenger of her father, place her in a divided, "hysterical" space of being both/and, both male and female in the Cornelian world. She remains divided, a split being, sundered between desire and duty, between Rodrigue and her father:

   I find my lover in my enemy,
   And am aware that notwithstanding all
   Mine anger Rodrigue still within my breast
   Contends against my father.
   (*Le Cid* III, iii)[58]

Every time the play forces the question of Rodrigue's body on Chimène, a split appears in her that refigures the divide between the "real presence" (physical, bodily) of the hero and his metaphysical impulse toward sublimation. The split manifests itself in her own bodily reaction (fainting, turning pale, and so on). We might say that what the "stances" have accomplished for Rodrigue — the sacrifice of his body for his honor, the suture that has transformed him into Le Cid — is constantly undone in Chimène's perception of him. Chimène constantly reenacts the split, the division between a physical and a metaphysical presence, underlining once again the tragic aspect of this tragicomedy: the couple exists as metaphor for the impossibility of freeing oneself from the other that is internal, that splits our being. The only possible liberation is death.

Because the deaths of the protagonists have been excluded from this play, and because as a couple Rodrigue and Chimène have been reduced by the internal logic of two conflicting patriarchal injunctions, the only hope for a resolution depends on a change imposed (on Chimène) from without. The change (in this very patriarchal play) is necessarily brought about by the metamorphosis of the male protagonist, who, as he moves from the realm of the immanent to the empyrean of the transcendent, sheds the skin of Rodrigue to drape himself in the robes of legend: he becomes "Le Cid," a name, a being, bestowed on him by the vox populi ("Thou never would'st conceive how all admire him / And make the heavens echo, with one voice, / With this young warrior's glorious achievements"). As Rodrigue moves ever more intimately into the space of transcendent death he becomes one with the dead Father to whom both he and Chimène are indebted. After the battle with the Moors, Rodrigue no longer exists. In the place of the adolescent boy stands "the Cid," a new hero. It is he who now replaces, militarily and politically, Chimène's dead father: "In him alone . . . thy father lives again" ("Que ton père en lui seul se voit ressuscité"). Through his heroism, Rodrigue has died to this world, but this "death" has changed Chimène ("Rodrigue is dead at last, and by his death I have been changed"), allowing her (or forcing her) into a new space, the space of a desired/refused marriage.

This play that ends on an ambivalent note also ends on a scandalous one. The scandal of the play, the cause of so much outrage among the *doctes*, was in great part the scandal of Chimène, the fact that she consents to marriage with the murderer of her father. (But does she? The play is mute in this regard, only history speaks.)[59] More scandalous perhaps than the seventeenth century could admit, however, is not so much that Chimène consents to what is after all the onward movement of history, a movement put in place by the Cid, but that she opts to join him, be joined with him, in the eroticized place of death.

It is *Horace*, however, the first fully successful "neoclassical" tragedy of the Cornelian canon, that materializes this "eroticized" place as the space of family, thus creating as the frame of tragedy a locus of desire and death reduced to its most quintessential oedipal ingredients. *Horace* is a transitional play in which a strong textual blood-lust vies with an equally strong impulse toward sublimation. The tragedy tries to be both a ritual of familial, incestuous murder and, by one and the same (killing) stroke, a sacred act of political foundations. *Horace* is the only drama of Corneille's four masterpieces whose tragedy turns resolutely around the problem of death. Killing is the central conundrum of the play, be it the "glorious" military deaths of the three Curiaces and the two Horatii, or the inglorious, sullying murder of Camille.

This splitting of death along political/familial (sexual) lines reveals a tension in the tragedy that retraces through a sexual division the same conflict between self and other that we have already noticed in *Le Cid*. The two central actions of the play, the duel of the Curiaces-Horatii, and the murder of Camille, delineate the two conceptions of death, one mas-

culine and the other feminine, one politically expedient, the other politically retrograde, that attempt to reconcile a dichotomy that the play reinforces even as it attempts to suppress it.

More than any other of the Cornelian tragedies, *Horace* underlines the
fictitious nature of the other and its absolute necessity in the development
of the nation-state. What could be more artificial than the "political"
difference that separates Rome and Alba? What could be more artificial
and yet decidedly imperative? The legend of the Horatii has been analyzed in diverse ways as a foundation myth, a myth based precisely on
the elision of "nondifference" and on the creation of an impossible difference.[60] On the political level, *Horace* represents a war of *frères ennemis*. As
articulated repeatedly throughout the play, but most insistently in the
mouths of the female characters (and those male characters the play
marks as "feminine"), we are presented with two countries that are actually one "people":

> Neighbors are we; our daughters are your wives,
> And marriage links us with so many ties
> That few among our sons are not your grandsons.
> We are one blood, one people, in two cities.
> (*Horace* I, iii)[61]

The rhetorical affirmation of familial ties takes us back beyond
brothers, grandchildren, and brothers-in-law to an even more primordial, more insistent bond. Alba, we are told, is the origin, the matrix of
Rome:

> . . . Ungrateful city,
> Remember that unto its royal seed
> Thou owest thy name, thy walls, and thy first laws.
> Alba is thy source. Stop and bethink thee
> That with the sword thou stabbest thy mother's breast.
> (*Horace* I, i)[62]

The image of the child plunging a sword into the mother's breast, powerful enough in itself, is even more chilling when we recall that this is the
only mention in all of the four canonical plays of any, even metaphorical,
"mothers." Corneille's universe, a world totally representative of an impossible familial/political structure, is glaringly "motherless." Maternity
is mentioned just once in the canon, and only as it is being annihilated.

This insistent "sameness," this one blood, one origin, one people,
echoes throughout the play only to be denied, repressed, by the line of
demarcation, the political demarcation of the two armies facing one another on the field of battle. This line of difference is carried into the center
of the tragic conflict, into the center of the family, where once again the
antithesis Roman-Alban is both blurred and redrawn. Not surprisingly

it is redrawn along the lines of sexual division, a division internal to the male and female characters, all of whom (with the exception of Horace) appear as divided, split beings, whose very essence seems incapable of being situated in one or another of the camps. They refuse or are incapable of the absolute locus that only Horace can occupy. The split that is externalized on the battlefield is internalized in the male-female dichotomy and it is inseparable from the economy of the family. The family is thus cast in the role of repeating endlessly, and against its own intimate desires, the bloody necessity of the political. This imposition of difference, the creation of an "other," that the play articulates as both a fiction and a reality marks *Horace*, it seems to me, rather than *Cinna*, as Corneille's most subversively "political" tragedy.

The word that "insists" the most conspicuously in this drama is, not surprisingly, blood ("sang"). It circulates throughout the text, as it does in all of Corneille's work, as a strategic mediator of opposition. It is perhaps the one word whose ambivalent meanings, both metaphoric and metonymic, allow it to weave across the abyss of Cornelian sexual division a complex fabric in which opposition is papered over in the indeterminacy of rhetoric. In a sense "blood" is appropriated by the male rhetoric of sublimation, where it stands in for "family," "race," "genealogy," and even "history," all the terms that are used to transcend the merely contingent individual male condemned to disappear in the ignominy of death ["I know my own blood better than that, he knows where his duty lies" ("Je connais mieux mon sang, il sait mieux son devoir"; *Horace* III, vi); and "Come to me, my child, come, my own flesh and blood" ("Viens, mon fils, viens, mon sang"; *Le Cid* I, v)]. In the mouths of the female characters, it retains its most *Kreaturlichkeit* of meanings, meanings that are also ambivalent: blood as a living, fragile substance, whose presence or absence signals the creation of life or its end, death ["Begin at once what you must do; / To spill his blood, begin with his sister, / And with his own wife begin the first mortal thrust" ("Ne différez donc plus ce que vous devez faire; / Commencez par sa soeur à répandre son sang, / Commencez par sa femme à lui percer le flanc"; *Horace* II, vi)].

For Horace, the most eloquent spokesman for the absolute imperative, death is never articulated in any way that is not already a sublimation. Death is a political sacrifice of the self to the state by which one becomes one with that state. It is an "immolation," a "sacrifice." It is the passage in and through "Thanatos" that assures the self's eternal perpetuation, its immortality, as an indelible mark of its *gloire*:

> To meet in mortal combat for one's country
> An enemy and face some stranger's blows,
> Is but an act of any man of courage.
> Thousands have done it, thousands more could do it.

> Death for one's country is a death so glorious,
> So beautiful, that untold numbers seek it.
> But to attempt to kill, for public weal,
> A man one loves, to fight one's other self,
> To assail the cause of those that, to defend it,
> Have chosen a warrior who is the brother
> Of one's own wife and also is the lover
> Of one's own sister — to break all these ties
> And in one's country's service draw one's sword
> To take a life that one would give his own
> To save — such strength of will is ours alone.
> (*Horace* II, iii)[63]

What Horace is here extolling is precisely death as an absolute: absolute because it sunders the warrior whom it caresses from all those ties, those purely human, contingent ties, the ties of the body, of family, and exposes him alone to his own transformed destiny. We should be particularly attuned to the weight that a word such as "vertu" — with both its Latin ("virs") and Machiavellian ("virtù") echoes — has for the paramount discourse of the heroic, that is, masculine, ethos of the tragedy. In a previous rhetorical ejaculation, Horace has already voiced his narcissistic attraction to death:

> But though this combat means my death, the glory
> Of being chosen swells my heart with pride.
> (*Horace* II, i)[64]

Death is articulated as the sublimated object of an erotic desire, and here, in the character of Horace, who "swells" up at the thought of death/glory, we find adumbrated one of the first of that long line of male protagonists who, from Corneille to Genet, tend to corroborate Freud's pessimistic statement that "love cannot be much younger than the lust to kill."[65] In *Horace*, just as family ties are de-eroticized, death, that is, sacrifice to the state, becomes eroticized as a longed-for and glorious "object" of desire. Does not Horace himself make this strange chiasmatic confusion, in which sexuality and death (spouse/combat) are so closely approximated as to be one?

> Rome hath made choice of me; I ask no questions.
> With eagerness no less than that I felt
> To wed thy sister, I shall face her brother.
> (*Horace* II, iii)[66]

As the most absolute example of the heroic male in Corneille, Horace is meant to represent one side of the sexual division that separates the world into two essentialized camps, masculinity and femininity. This division, although symmetrical, is not, of course, equal. The sphere of the women, the world of the body, of a liquefying body (a body of tears and of blood, an "open" body from which and into which things come and go, a body in flux) that threatens the male world with its corruption, with its femininity, is coded as a negative, excessive other. The only response a man can have to the demands of this other that attracts and threatens him is flight:

> What are ye doing here, my children — hearkening
> To love and wasting time with women still?
> Soon to shed blood, do ye now heed their tears?
> Fly hence, and leave them to bewail their woe. . . .
> Only by flight can one avoid such influence.
> (*Horace* II, vii)[67]

The elder Horace is right, of course. He knows that these young men are still subject to the *surprise des sens*, to their own body. They have not as yet gone through the purifying flame of immolation. They remain on the near side of the absolute. This is the side of the body, the side of the women, who are condemned to an eternal oscillation between the two camps, the two invented, male-produced armies, male-produced political realities. The women can never come down on one side of the divide, because — more so than the men — this divide is lived not as external happenstance but as an interior, wrenching reality:

> I am a Roman, for Horace is.
> I became one when I became his wife.
> Yet marriage bonds would be but chains of slavery
> If they forbade me to recall my birthplace.
> Alba, where first I breathed the breath of life,
> Mine own dear city and my earliest love, . . .
> Rome, if thou deemest me a traitor to thee
> In feeling thus, make choice of enemies
> Whom I can hate. When from thy walls I see
> Thine army and their foes', in one my husband
> And in the other my three brothers, how
> Without impiety can I find words
> For prayers and ask of heaven thy success?
> (*Horace* I, i)[68]

Sabine is divided. She is torn between those ties of the body, the bonds of family and marriage, that Horace so zealously wishes to sunder. This difference makes the man, the hero, the spokesman for a new, absolute imperium, the imperium of death, and situates the women in the retrograde position of being unable to sublimate the demands of the body into a "progressive" idealization. When Sabine, or Camille, contemplates the duel that is going to take place, the duel to the death that is to decide the fate of two nations (but one people), unlike the men they can never transport themselves into the abstract imperium of *raison d'Etat*. They can see only the blood and gore of torn and battered bodies:

> I feel my sad heart pierced by all the blows
> Which rob me of a brother or a husband,
> And thinking of their death, which I envision,
> I think not in what cause but by whose hand
> They die, and when I shall behold the victors
> Exalted presently, I shall consider
> Only at the expense of whose dear blood.
> (*Horace* III, i)[69]

The insistent weight of sameness is brought down to its most suffocating confinement in the couple that takes up and carries to its extreme the conundrum of sexual difference we first saw articulated in *Le Cid*. Despite the fact that the play incorporates a classic technique for relaying the tragic conflict through two couples, one married (Sabine-Horace) and one not (Camille-Curiace), on the level of ritual, of both the sacred and psychoanalytical ritual of desire and death, it is the couple Horace-Camille that forms the epicenter of the tragic in this drama. The couple Horace-Camille carries to its most extreme the impossible sameness that cannot exist without the sundering imposition of difference, the weight of the tragic. "Le vieil Horace," the father, a further avatar of those unsexed *pontifs*, representatives of the Law of repression,[70] tells us of the primordial oneness of the sibling couple:

> Show him thou art his sister, formed by heaven
> In the same womb and of the selfsame blood.
> (*Horace* IV, iii)[71]

"Même flanc / même sang": the rhyme accentuates the identity of the two. On the one hand it is an obfuscating periphrasis for the "mother" who is absent from the play. It echoes in significant ways, establishing an analogy between the "private" protagonists, Horace and Camille, and the "public" division Rome-Alba. Just as the sameness of Rome and Alba is underlined by an appeal to the maternal, so too is Horace and Camille's identity underscored. It is the absent maternal presence that in metaphor attaches the public to the private, making them one. On the other hand, the siblings are presented as "twins," that compellingly chilling (for all primitive cultures) double in sexual reversal. This same/other configuration, because it represents the threat to the self's dissolution, always carries along with it as part and parcel of its fascination its immixture in its own annihilation.

Just as occurred in the confrontation Rodrigue-Chimène in *Le Cid*, *Horace* concentrates its entire tragic thrust on and in the couple who represents the most extreme forms of identity and difference. We might say that the tragedy forms its tragic precisely around the production of sexual difference in its most heated convolution with death. Horace, when he returns triumphant from his battle with the Curiaces, reappears in the space of neoclassical representation, besmeared with the blood of the vanquished. He returns from the locus of death still marked by an immersion into a furious bloodletting that places him in an ambivalent posture: his physical reality is at odds with his idealizing rhetoric. His body, its immersion into death, has reasserted its materiality, a reassertion that symptomatically erupts into his rhetoric. His first speech when he reappears on stage is autoreferential, and he attributes to himself not the masculine, phallic unity he was before going off to battle, but an amalgamation of different body parts, most particularly of "arms," the arms that killed:

> Sister, behold the arm that hath avenged
> Our brothers' deaths, the arm that hath reversed
> The course of hostile fate, that hath subjected
> Alba to us; behold, in short, the arm
> Which hath alone decided on this day
> The fortunes of two cities.
> (*Horace* IV, v)[72]

Horace is met by a weeping Camille ("Accept my tears . . . "). The ensuing dialogue, a tense stichomythia, builds upon this division between a tearful, vengeful woman and a man who is stridently attempting to reestablish his hold on a world of sublimated ideality. He needs his double/other to reflect back to him an image of unity, of reconfigured and transcendental masculinity. Instead, what he receives is precisely the reflection of the other as death, a female image of decomposition, disintegration, and confusion. Camille's emotional outburst crescendos into another version of the chaotic "primal scene," the threatening vortex that, as we have seen, haunts the world of male control and order:

> Rome, which I hate, the source of all my pain!
> Rome, for whose sake thou hast my lover slain!
> Rome, which thou worshippest, which gave thee birth!
> Rome, which I hate for holding great thy worth!
> May all her neighbor states, to undermine
> Her power e'er stronger, in one league combine;
> And if all Italy is not enough,
> Let East and West take arms against her, both—
> A hundred peoples, from earth's farthest plains,
> Cross, to destroy her, seas and mountain chains!
> May civil strife devour her, overthrow
> Her walls, and lay her open to the foe!
> May heaven's wrath, kindled by my prayers, send down

A rain of fire on that accursed town!
May I with mine own eyes see the storm fall,
Her homes aflame, thy laurels dust, withal —
See the last Roman heave his final sigh!
Let me cause this, and I with joy shall die.
(*Horace* IV, v)[73]

Camille's invective is a highly charged — we might almost say "ecstatic" (in the sense of "standing out") — moment, a moment of intense narcissistic pleasure where, freed from the fetters of family and politics, she indulges in pure difference: difference from Horace and from Rome. The threat of this difference is too menacing for the political stability only recently and shakily established, too menacing for all that Horace has sacrificed to and for, too menacing for his own sense of himself as male and noncontingent, not to be cut down brutally. Horace meets Camille's orgiastic rhetoric with the phallic violence of the sword he had called upon his sister to adore: "Look on these spoils, / These tokens of my glorious deeds; accord / The honor which thou owest my victory" ("Vois ces marques d'honneur, ces témoins de ma gloire, / Et rends ce que tu dois à l'heure de ma victoire").

To Camille's moment of ecstasy, to her one orgasmic moment outside of those patriarchal bonds that would confine her, responds Horace's act of violence that forever excludes him from the domain of the heroic. Horace's crime is a crime of passion, of masculine self-destruction. Camille has led him into the space of excess and there he is lost. The play is aware, of course, of the impasse into which its "hero" has been led. It uses an entire act in an attempt to rehabilitate him without, however, successfully accomplishing anything other than a "political," that is, non-dramatic, and finally uncomfortable compromise with the other that has erupted into its midst. Horace, more than anyone else, knows that he has sullied his honor, has lost his chance to be ever-congruent with the ideal he has fixed for himself. He claims that only death can transport him beyond the realm of the contingent and into the empyrean of immortal glory:

Hence, to preserve my glory and to leave
Behind me an illustrious memory,
My death today is necessary. Rather
It should have followed close upon my victory
For I have even now outlived my honor.
A man like me deems his fair fame is sullied
When he incurs the slightest risk of shame. . . .
Let me, O great king, with this conquering sword
Slay myself for my own sake, not my sister's.
(*Horace* V, ii)[74]

What Horace articulates here is simply the Greek desire for a heroic "Thanatos." He wants what he can no longer have — the unsullied eternity of immortal glory. He wants to go down through the generations as the hero who saved (and founded) Rome. But it is too late. He has been tarnished, dragged down by Camille, his double/other, from the heights of his heroism into the quagmire of the quotidian. It will not be too much for an entire act, an act of masculine *mauvaise foi*, to save what little he has left, his life, and that only for the prosaic safety of the state.

Corneille himself was uncomfortable with the last act, the most "legalistic" act in his theater:

> The fifth act is one more reason why this tragedy has not sufficiently pleased some people. It is almost entirely composed of courtroom speeches, and this is really not the place for long addresses and harangues. These are bearable at the beginning of a play where the action hasn't as yet gathered all its momentum; but the fifth act should be more action and less talk.[75]

It strikes me, however, that the fifth act must be an act of legalistic rhetoric in order to calm the enchafed action, the explosive action of Camille's murder. The entire act is a crescendo of male voices called upon to efface the threat of female difference. In a series of courtroom debates Horace's crime is underlined for the horror it was, defended as a result of his exemplary patriotism, and finally papered over as a political necessity:

> In every country many worthy subjects
> Show by goodwill alone their loyalty.
> All men can love their sovereign, but not all
> Can by heroic deeds preserve their realms.
> The skill and might to make secure a throne
> Are gifts which heaven bestows on very few;
> 'Tis in such subjects that a king's strength lies;
> And such as they are hence above all laws
> Let law be silent, then; let Rome not heed
> In thee what she ignored in Romulus.
> (*Horace* V, iii)[76]

The king, Tulle, announces his verdict, an exculpation based on political necessity. Thanks to Horace he is now king of two states; Rome has begun her march to hegemony. A new world order has been born. Curiously, however, his analogy between the even more ancient foundation of Rome, the fratricidal battle between Romulus and Remus, and the fratricidal murder of Camille by Horace, a murder/end that is, as he says, a "birth" ("naissance"), witnesses the return of the maternal presence so forcefully suppressed by the rest of the tragedy. All foundation myths conceal a bloody, "sacred" crime, the violence of birth/death that is their origin. In *Horace* what has been evinced from the stage of the nation/state is the excessive female other. By the tragedy's final words, Camille is returned to the realm of the same that she, in life, refused:

> Since in the same day the same patriot zeal
> Cut short her lover's life and hers as well,
> Lo, now: let this same day which saw them die
> See them in one same grave together lie.
> (*Horace* V, iii)[77]

But this new nation of the "same" (the echoes of "même") inscribes by its attempted appeasement the troubling other, the other of the grave, that will return (as all that is repressed does) to haunt it from the center of its originary fantasy.

This violent scene of chaotic self-destruction that triggers the tragic denouement of *Horace* reappears as the primal nightmare that fuels hatred and fear and leads to the assassination conspiracy in *Cinna*. It seems that Corneille actually worked on these two "Roman" tragedies simultaneously, but *Horace* is marked by bloodletting, the tragedy of duels and fratricide, and *Cinna* is the only one of the four canonical tragedies to turn resolutely away from death. This refusal of death (Auguste's clemency) has led critics and skeptics to define *Cinna* as Corneille's most "political" tragedy.[78] In this sense, "political" would seem to function as the antithesis of "death," as its other, yet it appears to me that it would be a mistake to oppose these two terms, for in no other of Corneille's plays is death so omnipresent, as fantasy and desire, and in no other play is this fantasy and desire so intimately intertwined in the nefarious love that joins the two protagonists Cinna and Emilie together in a political plot. This extraordinary collusion of love as death led Serge Doubrovsky to describe so appropriately the political/amorous journey of Cinna and Emilie as "the couple's descent to hell."[79]

Just as the murder of Camille marked an originary moment, a "birth," of a new Roman state, *Cinna* too situates the origin of its drama in the death of the "Republic." From Emilie's first words we learn that death serves as the midwife for all her anxiety, all her resentment, all her mortiferous love: "Ye restless longings for a noble vengeance / Which were begotten by my father's death" ("Impatients désires d'une illustre vengeance / Dont la mort de mon père a formé la naissance"). As in *Le Cid*, but in a more convoluted development, the dead father presides over, is the primum mobile of both the political and amorous desires of the heroes. Emilie seems to be a new incarnation of the vengeful, headstrong Chimène, but more than Chimène, perhaps because we cannot see the immediacy of her grief, perhaps because she strikes us as too obsessively single-minded, Emilie appears as a much more threatening, much more destructive presence. From her first incantatory lines Emilie stands before us as totally inscribed within a circle of blood and destruction:

> When I behold Auguste in his glory
> And ye recall to my sad memory how,
> Murdered in cold blood by his hand, my father
> Served as the first step to the throne on which
> I see him sitting—when ye raise before me
> The bloody picture of his fury's victim,
> The cause of all my hatred—I surrender
> Myself to your fierce frenzies, and I deem
> For that death he deserves a thousand deaths.
> (*Cinna* I, i)[80]

Guez de Balzac was undoubtedly right when he described Emilie as "a divine and adorable Fury" ("la sainte et adorable furie").[81] The Furies, assimilated to the Greek Erinyes, are daughters of Nyx (like Gorgo and Ker), infernal, death-dealing primitive deities whose major function is to punish those who commit crimes against the "transgressions of natural order, and especially of offenses which touch the foundation of human society."[82] In other words, beyond the gallant tone of Balzac's comparison the mythological reference reminds us of the beating wings of madness and death that Emilie incarnates.

The couple Emilie forms with Cinna is perhaps the most chillingly disturbing example of "lovers" in the entire Cornelian canon. The two protagonists are locked into a desiring structure that is absolutely inseparable from death: in order for Cinna to obtain Emilie's hand he must kill.

> Though I love Cinna, though my soul adores him,
> If he would win me, he must slay Auguste.
> He cannot gain my hand save at the price
> Of his head.
> (*Cinna* I, ii)[83]

> . . . That he must needs
> Acquit him of his promise, and that he
> Can afterward choose either death or me.
> (*Cinna* IV, v)[84]

Cinna is trapped by his lust and by his word: "But I am bound by three things: my rash oath, / Emilie's hate, the memory of her father" ("Mais je dépends de vous, ô serment téméraire! / O haine d'Aemilie! ô souvenir d'un père!" III, iii). In order to obtain the object of his desire, Cinna, like Rodrigue, must situate himself in the place of the dead father. He must, in other words, confront the father (Auguste, who, after eliminating both of their biological fathers, has stood in as a surrogate father for the orphans), confront his own conflicted feelings of hatred and love, and, by

killing him, win his sexual prize. Cinna, as the head of the conspiracy
to assassinate Auguste, must be seen as a leader of the primal horde of
brothers, whom, Freud theorized, want to kill off their feared (and loved)
Ur-vater, to take his place, to take his women.

Although we might see a resemblance between Cinna's dilemma and
that of Rodrigue, there is a more serious contradiction in the "political"
aspect of their passion. Rodrigue is seen as the masculine avatar of historical progression, who triumphs over the interior (and exterior) other, a
threat to absolutism's hegemony, but Cinna remains attached to an outmoded, regressive history, a history of cyclical vendetta, of social instability and death. Cinna incarnates, within the couple he forms with
Emilie, the "political" other inimical to absolutism's progress.

Politically Cinna espouses the cause of empire (of absolutism), but this
espousal is in direct contradiction to his passion for Emilie, who sees herself as not only the avenger of her father's death, but also the defender
of Republican Rome. Auguste's assassination is confused in her mind as
both a private and a public matter. With his elimination, Emilie sees herself as the heroine of Roman liberty:

> Let us unite the pleasure of a parent's
> Avengement with the glory that one gains
> By punishing a tyrant. Let us cause it
> To be proclaimed throughout all Italy:
> "Emilie hath achieved Rome's liberty."
> (*Cinna* I, ii)[85]

Emilie and Cinna repeat, as characters, the inseparable dialectic of
sadomasochism. Emilie tortures Cinna in/as his object of desire:

> Remember that love's flame burns in us both,
> And that Emilie as well as glory
> Is thy reward, and that thou owest me
> Thy heart, and that my favors wait for thee . . .
> (*Cinna* I, iii)[86]

Cinna can conceive of his passion for Emilie only as a tyranny that she
exercises over him. In their relation he is the more passive, suffering partner. In her thrall, his desire for her is fueled by the mortal danger she
holds over his head. Hers is, he says, a more pernicious, more exacting,
and, we must assume, more exciting tyranny than the political autocracy
of Auguste:

> Well, then, I must do all as thou desirest.
> Rome must be freed, thy father be avenged,
> Against a tyrant righteous blows be launched.
> But know that less than thou art is Auguste
> A tyrant. If he robs us at his pleasure

> Of our possessions, wives, and lives, he hath not
> Up to this time constrained our consciences;
> But the inhuman power thy beauty wields
> Does violence even to our thoughts and wills.
> (*Cinna* III, iv)[87]

Cinna and Emilie can desire only in the space of death. Emilie is blinded by the urgency of her need for revenge. What is more troubling is that this urgency is not particular about its victim: "Whoe'er shall die — Auguste be it or Cinna — / I owe this victim to my father's spirit" ("Quoi qu'il en soit, qu'Auguste ou Cinna périsse, / Aux mânes paternels je dois ce sacrifice"). There is a strange collusion in Emilie's desire for a sacrificial victim, a collusion in which the difference between Cinna and Auguste, between surrogate father and lover, is blurred. Cinna, for his part, seems torn between his desire for Emilie, which he masquerades in political rhetoric, and his attachment to Auguste. His own inner conflict expresses itself in his wish to die for her and yet, perversely, to live on in his sacrifice: "Ah, grant that though I die I still may live in thee" ("Ah! souffrez que tout mort je vive encore en vous").

This dialectic of love in/as death would not be particularly interesting if it were not totally inscribed within a larger political framework. Cinna and Emilie's deathly passion was born of a common trauma, the turmoil of the Roman civil wars. All the characters in this play are the products of this tumultuous past. The past, the dead, are constantly evoked and are, in a strange and morbid sense, present in the lives and passions of all the characters. History in *Cinna* is a history of murder, destitution, and rapine. It clings to all the characters in the play as a death that will not die. In a very real sense, *Cinna* is one of the most convincing portrayals of the power of one's ancestors, of the dead who continue to vampirize the living with their strange absence/presence: it is the tragedy of the "undead." Against this background, the haunting memory of these wars, a memory that always resurfaces in the speeches of the protagonists as a nightmare of chaos, destruction, and loss, the present political debate between the Republic and the empire takes place. This nightmare forming the political "past" informs the entire present of the tragedy. In this past death reigns supreme. Death and social disintegration are inseparable from any discussion of "Republican Rome," and it is precisely in order to conjure away this threat of death that inheres in Roman history that Cinna pleads with Auguste not to abdicate the throne:

> Sire, to save Rome, she needs must be united
> Under a noble chief, obeyed by all.
> If still thou wouldst be gracious to her, take
> From her the means henceforth of all division. . . .
> If thou resignest that empire, thou wilt plunge it

Again into those evils whence it scarcely
Yet hath recovered, and another war
Will drain it, sire, of the little blood still left it.
(*Cinna* II, i)[88]

Each of the conspirators is a victim of the civil wars and none can separate personal amorous passion from the desire to seek revenge on Au-
gustus Caesar. There is a chiasmus functioning in the drama in which
each of the protagonists deludes himself or herself into believing that he
or she is acting out of patriotism by plotting against the emperor. All
want to return to the past, the past of republican Rome. This desire to
repeat the past, to re-create a free "republican" Rome (see Emilie's narcissistic fantasy, "Emilie hath achieved Rome's liberty"), can only be
regarded as retrograde. The conspirators who are allied to Cinna and
whom he describes as "patriots" are portrayed by Auguste as a band of
rabble ("a rabble covered with debts and crimes"). Although they think
of themselves as defenders of Roman liberty they are actually portrayed,
in the context of the play, as historical backsliders. They represent an
outmoded political system, a system condemned to replay a constant series of murders, vendettas, and assassinations:

No one is frightened by another's doom.
Dead Salvidienus evoked Lepidus.
Then came Murena: Caepio followed him.
The tortures that robbed both these twain of life
Chilled with no fear the fury of Egnatius,
Whose place now Cinna fills unflinchingly.
(*Cinna* IV, iii)[89]

The past is a parade of victims, of the dead, who seem in an "unnatural"
fashion to give birth to new victims and more death. The past of Roman
history is presented as a death machine. This past, this death, haunts
Emilie, haunts Cinna, and haunts Auguste. The emperor, victor of the
bloody civil wars, is obsessed both by the cost of his own triumph and
by its fragility:

I wished for empire, and I have achieved it;
But wishing for it, I knew not what it was.
In its possession I have found no charms,
But fearful cares, endless anxieties,
A thousand secret foes, death everywhere,
No pleasures unalloyed, and never peace.
(*Cinna* II, i)[90]

The play represents the coming into being of the absolute subject and
does this by first presenting us with characters who are internally divided
by their history into a "then" (of Republican Rome) and a "now" (of sta-

bility, flourishing economy, and peace of Augustan tyranny). Emilie is torn between her "love" for Cinna and her desire for revenge, which in a perverse fashion is also a desire for Auguste, a desire that is revealed fleetingly in the strange confession, tinged with sexual overtones, that she makes to her confidant: "I would accept from him the place of Livie / As offering surer means to seek his death" ("Je recevrais de lui la place de Livie / Comme un moyen plus sûr d'attenter à sa vie"). Cinna is wrenched between his passion for Emilie and his "love" for Auguste ("He would love Caesar, if he weren't already in love" ("Il aimerait César, s'il n'était amoureux"). Finally, Maxime, Cinna's friend and coconspirator who betrays the assassination plot to Auguste, is split between his lust for Emilie and his attraction to Cinna: "It is my friend I love in thee — thy lover" ("C'est votre amant en vous, c'est mon ami que j'aime"). All these characters, the emperor included, are represented as divided, politically and sexually, against themselves. Each desires aloud a political platform and yet knows, sotto voce, that his or her "real" desire is inimical to the greater political well-being of the state.

When Auguste first discovers the plot to assassinate him, a plot instigated by his closest advisers and "friends," his initial reaction is self-flagellation:

> Octavius do not wait for some new Brutus.
> Die; rob him of the glory of thy fall.
> Die; thou wouldst basely, vainly seek to live
> If such a multitude of brave men vow thy death . . .
> Die, since beyond cure is this ill case. Die lastly
> Because thou must slay everyone or perish.
> (*Cinna*, IV, ii)[91]

The repeated echoes of "Die," "Die," reveal that on the most basic level Auguste/Octave is at this point still within the realm of the contingent, the realm of his battles and crimes as Octave. Although he may be emperor, he is not "absolute." Only at the end of his tortured monologue are the real stakes of his past and his present revealed to him:

> O Romans! O revenge! O sovereign power!
> O bitter struggle in my wavering heart,
> Which flies from every alternative
> At once that it proposes to itself!
> Prescribe some policy for a hapless ruler.
> Which course ought I to shun, and which to follow?
> Oh, either let me die or let me reign!
> (*Cinna* IV, ii)[92]

The contrast "perish/reign" is, it seems to me, particularly evocative. Although this is an opposition that is not normally an absolute one, we must nevertheless assume that in this verse, by the very weight of its rhetoric, as the punctum of Auguste's long and wrenching monologue, the opposition "périr-regner" takes on absolute status. The absolute negative of death ("perish") casts its shadow over "reign," conferring on it the role of death's opposite. Because the ultimate verse of this impassioned speech brings all the weight of rhetoric and poetry to fall on "reign" in its opposition to "perish," this one word, the sense of "reign," must here be understood as the absolute contradiction of death: to reign is to live, to be — and, we might add, in front of death's eternal negation "reign" here can only mean to be forever, to be immortal. Octave's wish, therefore, a desire that cannot be articulated except in a periphrasis, is to reign, to be, to be immortal, or, in other words, to be absolute.

Trapped as they are in their flirtation with death, all the characters are precipitated, as the play reaches its climax, into a dizzying dance of self-immolation. After their plot has been discovered, each of the three plotters confesses guilt to the emperor/father and each wishes to expiate this guilt in death:

> CINNA: . . . Fate is to thee
> As kind as it is cruel to me. I know
> What I have done; I know what thou must do.
> Thou needs must make of me a dread example.
> (*Cinna* V, i)
> EMILIE: I now have come to offer to thee, sir,
> A victim — not to save him by accusing
> Myself of guilt. His death is naturally
> The consequence of his attempt, and every
> Excuse in crimes of State is unavailing.
> To die with him and join again my father
> Is all that brings me here; 'tis my one hope.
> (*Cinna* V, ii)
> MAXIME: . . . Thou seest
> The outcome of my shameful trickery.
> Yet if some favor is my due because
> Of my disclosures, let Euphorbus die
> Amid the cruelest torments, and let me
> Perish before the eyes of these two lovers.
> (*Cinna* V, iii)[93]

Each of the lovers/conspirators demands of Auguste what he alone can give — death. By so doing they all implicitly recognize what up until now they have refused to see: Auguste is the sole arbitrator of their destinies. He has become the absolute other and as such, to their demand for death, a desire that would allow them to become one with their past, to return to the embrace of their ancestors' ghosts, and thus simply to reinscribe in the new present of Rome its old fratricidal tradition, Auguste just says "no." He spares them, returns them to life, but to a life that is here lived as an epiphanous moment in which they are reborn as new subjects and in which he is reborn, immortal. His "clemency" is a stroke of political genius because it is the founding, transcendental moment in which an old political system, the system of clanic rivalries, vendetta, and social turmoil, a political system situated under the sign of triumphant death, is replaced. In its stead we have a new father, a father/emperor who by rejecting death transcends it and becomes the ruler he desired to be in that rule's absolute otherness to death. The tragedy ends not only with the conspirators' pardon, but with the further "favors" of the emperor: Maxime is made governor of Sicily, and Cinna is given Emilie as his bride. Emilie receives a husband who is at once a new "father" and more: "In giving back to thee alive a husband, / I give back more to thee than any father" ("Te rendant en époux, je te rends plus qu'un père"). The most important transformation, however, is obviously Auguste's. The play's end sees him situated exactly where he wanted to be; he has become the master of his subject's minds and hearts. He has triumphed over Emilie in the sense that he has replaced her as both the political and erotic object of all subjects:

> Sire, let the virtue in my heart reborn
> Pledge thee a faith which I have once forsworn
> But which is now so constant, so unwavering,
> That were the heavens to fall, 'twould not be shaken.
> (*Cinna* V, iii)[94]

This absolute mastery is confirmed and given ontological status in Livie's ecstatic oracle:

> For thou hast learned the way to rule men's hearts.
> Rome with a joy both keen and deep consigns
> Unto thy hands the empire of the world.
> Thy kingly virtues make it very plain
> That happiness for her requires thy reign.
> Her mind from ancient terror wholly free,
> She now desireth naught but monarchy.
> She rears to thee already shrines and altars;
> Heaven find a place for thee among the immortals . . .
> (*Cinna* V, iii)[95]

The "tragedy" ends not with death but with an apotheosis. There is a complete abandonment of the body, of the physical desire that fueled political rebellion, for the political worship of a new imperial body—the *corps glorieux* of transcendent monarchy. In Livie's ecstasy Auguste ascends to the heavens, to his place among the immortals. He also remains in Rome to be worshiped by his new subjects as the sole master of their lives and fates. It is a mastery to which the three conspirators acquiesce with a joy (let us not forget that *joie* and *jouissance* have the same origin) that signals the end to their murderous passion. At the same time it underlines the birth of a new political structure that wipes out the vestiges of the past and allows a new "state" to be born:

> Heaven hath resolved that thou shalt be supreme.
> To prove it, sire, I am myself sufficient.
> I proudly dare lay claim to such distinction;
> Since heaven doth change my heart, it surely wishes
> To change Rome, too.
> (*Cinna* V, iii)[96]

With changed hearts and a transformed state *Cinna* ends. The intertwined workings of death and desire have brought about a transcendence that was unthinkable when the tragedy began. But, in this elaboration of a world order situated beyond death and beyond desire in the transfiguration of the emperor, Corneille's Roman world has still to meet and confront its most significant other—the Christian God of *Polyeucte*, a noncontingent deity in comparison to which the gods of the Roman firmament, Auguste included, are all condemned to eternal oblivion.

Polyeucte (1642), the last of Corneille's canonical tragedies, is (as its subtitle, "A Christian Tragedy," indicates) a drama of martyrdom, of death and transfiguration. It is both structurally similar to the preceding tragedies and yet different. The drama is situated, like all Cornelian tragedy, at a particularly charged moment of historical change. We are once again transported to ancient Rome, but this time to the far outpost of the empire, to distant Armenia. Here, at the very limits of "Rome," the first cracks in the empire, the incursions of the "barbarian" others, are being felt with greater and greater intensity. These foreign tribes, as we know, will eventually infiltrate the empire to its very heart and overturn it. For the moment, however, this "external" other remains only a menacing threat, distant thunder on the Roman horizon. Far more dangerous than the outside appears a fault interior to the Roman state—Christianity. Inexorably the empire is being undermined from within, split in its very body (its imperial corporate structure, in which emperors are gods) by this new sect that, refusing the traditional deities and values of Rome, worships a new and dangerous God. Upon this unstable terrain, attacked from without and from within, *Polyeucte* evolves in an atmosphere of anxiety and doubt. At the opening of the play, we are presented with the most dramatic of scenarios as both the "throne and the altar" are threatened.

Curiously, this anxiety and doubt that in the preceding plays had always been expressed by the female protagonists is here placed in the mouth of Polyeucte. *Polyeucte* is the only one of the four great tragedies to begin with the male protagonist on stage; *Le Cid*, *Horace*, and *Cinna* all begin with women. In the previous plays, anxiety, that unspecified dread of impending disaster, had been presented first by the women and only later, if ever, relayed to the men. In a strategic reversal, Polyeucte is the *porte-parole* of an anxiety that, although it takes the form of simply repeating the anxiety of a woman, cannot be separated from his own. Polyeucte tells his friend and religious mentor Néarque that he would prefer to delay his baptism because his new wife has had an alarming dream. We might say there is a relaying of anxiety here by which Pauline's nightmare becomes the excuse for Polyeucte's anxiety. What he is anxious about is, not surprisingly, women, that is, his own desire, his sexual desire for Pauline.

To Néarque's uncompromising demand that he ignore Pauline and hasten to baptism, Polyeucte responds:

> Thou knowest not what it means to have a wife.
> Thou knowest not her hold upon one's heart
> When, after she hath long enchanted us,
> The marriage torches have at last been lit.
> (*Polyeucte* I, i)[97]

Polyeucte situates its action on the far side of that ever-tantalizing promise that the three previous dramas never see realized — marriage. *Polyeucte* presents us with the already-there of marriage, the already-there of sexual union, whose realization in the other plays had only been a distant, flickering mirage. It was a mirage that led the protagonists of those plays forward, but here, on the contrary, it is an obstacle to the hero's further perfection.

Sexuality, therefore, as a burning physical reality, holds Polyeucte in its thrall. Yet Corneille never allows sexuality to be separated from its threatening, destructive aspect. The play opens with the relaying of female anxiety by the hero and does so by incorporating Pauline's nightmare in Polyeucte's speech. In this dream she is frightened by the scene of her husband's proleptic (martyrdom) murder:

> Pauline, unreasonably filled with woe,
> Dreads and expects e'en now to see my death,
> Of which she dreamed. Sore weeping, she opposes
> The purpose that I formed, and tries to keep me
> From issuing from the palace.
> (*Polyeucte* I, i)[98]

The play begins with a reshuffling of the cards and a confusion of what we had come to expect from the other plays. Here sexuality and death are immediately presented as the intertwined conundrum that presides over the anxious universe of *Polyeucte*. But they are presented inverted, if only structurally speaking, by being placed in the mouth of the male protagonist. What has not changed, but in fact has been reinforced, is the association in this male-centered world that sexuality (the body, the body's desire) and death are intimately connected with the woman (Pauline). To this association is further added the new "spiritual" element, Christianity's "truth," which is opposed to pagan illusion and is also tainted with both the political and sexual in ways that simply prolong into this new epoch of history the patriarchal values that have regimented gender distinctions in the old idolatrous universe.

If we listen to Néarque's response to Polyeucte's anxious delaying, we hear the refrain that has since the Greeks placed women along the same metaphoric axis as matter. Women are, Néarque tells him, but an illusion, an illusion that obfuscates spiritual "reality" and thus condemns man to the false security of earthly pleasures. There is a slippage in the rhetoric of his rebuttal in which women are compared first with "false illusions" and then, surreptitiously, to the satanic. The flesh and the devil are one:

> Thus doth the foe of all mankind beguile thee.
> When force avails him not, he useth craft.
> Jealous of righteous aims, which he would foil,
> If he cannot suppress them he diverts them.
> Thine he will thwart with hindrance after hindrance,
> Today with tears, each day with something new;
> And this dream, filled with black imaginings,
> Is but his first device wherewith to stay thee.
> He uses prayers and threats and all things else;
> Ever he strikes and never doth he tire;
> He deems that he can do at last whatever
> He cannot do yet, and that anyone
> Who will delay is half o'ercome already.
> Frustrate his first attack. Let Pauline weep.
> God wants no heart which worldly things possess.
> (*Polyeucte* I, i)[99]

If Polyeucte is thus presented torn between his desire for Pauline and his desire for God, Pauline, in the chiasmus she forms with him, is split between her "love" for Polyeucte and her passion for Sévère. She is torn between "duty" and desire. The "love" she experiences for her husband is the product of her abnegation, the sacrifice of her desire to filial duty:

> . . . When I reached this land
> I met Polyeucte and in his sight was pleasing,
> And as he is the foremost of your nobles
> My father was delighted when he wooed me . . .

> He sanctioned
> Polyeucte's love and plighted me to him;
> And I—when I thus found myself betrothed,
> I gave, as duty bade me, unto him
> Who was to be my husband that affection
> Which my heart's wish had given to the other.
> (*Polyeucte* I, iii)[100]

The other in question is the "dead" other, her lost love Sévère. Each of the two protagonists is therefore caught between desire and sublimation, immanence and transcendence, the body (death) and the spirit. In this new sexual symmetry that *Polyeucte* adumbrates, the two protagonists bear unequal metaphysical valences, however: Polyeucte, the male, is weighted more toward the spiritual, and Pauline, as touching as her plight may be, as sympathetic as she as character may be for the audience, is made to bear the burden of materiality. She remains for the men a mortiferous presence.

In a certain sense we might say that the entire tragedy of *Polyeucte* is confined to a dialectics of sexuality and death. We move from the death of Sévère to the martyrdom of Polyeucte. Both of these deaths are mediated by the object of sexual desire, Pauline, and both are not, in the final instance, "true" deaths: Sévère returns from his reported demise on the battlefields of the empire ("Sévère is not dead"; "Sévère n'est point mort") and Polyeucte's martyrdom assures him of eternal life with God.

Pauline is situated as the troubling focal point of all the males in the play. Pauline, Pauline as body, temporarily retains Polyeucte in the realm of hesitation and doubt. Sévère travels back from death in the (deluded) hope that Pauline will at last consent to be his:

> What pleasure or confusion doth my coming
> Beget in her? Can every hope be mine
> From this glad meeting? For I would rather die
> Than wrongly use the emperor's favoring letters
> To win her hand.
> (*Polyeucte* II, i)[101]

His return, which Pauline's dream had enigmatically predicted, is the cause for the increasing anxiety of the third male character, Pauline's father Félix. Once again, it is in and as an object of exchange, an object of sexual exchange between men, that Pauline serves as the connecting link between the intimate sexual drama of the play and its larger political frame. As we know, this exchange of women between men, however sublimated it might be, forms one of the most archaic of communal bonds and is said to "initiate" politics.[102] Pauline is presented as the link between the personal and the political and yet the victim of this collusion, too. She is victimized by the entire order of patriarchy that she has internalized and which has informed her desire precisely as a conflict between paternal law and its other.

Pauline articulates her entire sense of herself as a product of filial duty:

> But since my duty decreed otherwise,
> Whatever man my father chose for me—
> E'en had'st thou joined the splendors of a crown
> To the attractions which thine own worth gave thee,
> Had'st thou been here, and had I hated him—
> I would have sighed, but I would have obeyed.
> (*Polyeucte*, II, ii)[103]

Pauline is repeating what all of Corneille's heroines, from Chimène to Emilie, have already stated: their being as woman is defined in direct proportion to the sacrifice of their own desire to the law of the Father. What each also demonstrates, at the cost of her life, is that this Law is inimical to them; they cannot survive its dictates.

Pauline too is betrayed by the law that both defines and limits her. She is abandoned by her husband and her father, by the two legal representatives of male authority between which women are exchanged and from which exchange they acquire the only "social" value and power available to them. She is betrayed by her husband ("What have I done thee, cruel man, to be treated thus?") and she is betrayed by her father:

> Ah father, though his crime be hard to pardon,
> If he is mad thou art not. . . .
> A father does not cease to be a father,
> And so I still dare cling to some slight hope.
> (*Polyeucte* V, iii)[104]

But Félix, the Roman governor of Armenia, is portrayed as a weak-willed, sycophantic courtier who can think only of his own advancement in a system of political patronage that is as unpredictable as it is vain. Too threatened by what he imagines to be Sévère's vengeful resentment, he cannot come to his daughter's defense. Rather, in the political power game in which he constantly sees himself as a defenseless player, he must sacrifice his daughter to save himself. He is therefore the living embodiment of all that Polyeucte in his spiritual quest turns against. Félix is the prime representative of worldly *nugae*, of instability, of change, of chaos, that Polyeucte rejects:

> . . . yet they aspire,
> If truth be told, only to transient blessings
> Which cares will vex and dangers will attend.
> Death takes these from us; Fortune sports with them—

Today a throne, a dunghill on the morrow
(*Polyeucte* IV, iii)[105]

Félix, presented as indecisive and fluctuating, has no moral or ethical integrity. He exists in this tragedy as an example of an effeminate male. As representative of the falsehood of earthly political ambition, he is thus allied to the "physical" trap that is Pauline. For Polyeucte, the father-daughter couple of Félix/Pauline is what must be rejected in order to find the true peace of immutability:

I have ambition, but 'tis nobler, fairer.
Those honors perish; I seek immortal honors,
A bliss assured, eternal, infinite,
Above the reach of envy and of fate.
(*Polyeucte* IV, iii)[106]

Polyeucte simply reiterates here, at the end of Corneille's last canonical play, the same intimate desire that has presided over the entire Cornelian endeavor. He wants the absolute, the absolute transcendence of all that is unstable, chaotic, threatening in life, for the immutable peace of eternity. In the preceding tragedies that transcendence has been only shakily achieved by those plays' heroes. They achieve a relative form of glory, of "Thanatos," by radically separating themselves from the feminine, the "body" that inhered in them, and by constructing themselves as "integral" males, by becoming one with an ideal that fused them, beyond death, to the state.

Polyeucte carries this desire for transcendence to its greatest height. Polyeucte leaves behind the world of the mutable, the world of vainglorious politics and sexual desire, for the absolute empyrean of God:

The God of Polyeucte and of Néarque
Is the almighty king of heaven and earth,
The one and only self-existent Being,
Sole master of our fate, the great First Cause
And sovereign end of all.
(*Polyeucte* III, ii)[107]

His example frees Pauline, his female-other, from her trap in the patriarchal system that has betrayed her. When she comes back from "witnessing" her husband's martyrdom, when she returns from the experience of extreme limits to which her husband's obstinacy and her father's cowardice have pushed her, she is transformed. This transformation is expressed as an "ecstatic" rhetorical outburst, allying her across the plays to the other female protagonists (Chimène, Camille, Emilie) who have been dupe to and betrayed by their own devotion to a patriarchal system that trades in women:

In death my husband left his light to me.
His blood, in which thy executioners bathed me,
Hath now unsealed mine eyes and opened them.
I see, I know, I believe: I am
Released from error. . . .
Lead, lead me to your gods,
Whom I abhor. They broke but one of them;
I will break all the rest. I shall be seen
Defying there all that ye hold in dread—
Those powerless thunderbolts wherewith ye arm them—
In God's cause flouting the authority
Which birth imposed on me, and for one time
Failing in my obedience to thee!
(*Polyeucte* V, v) [108]

Pauline's ecstasy places her outside of the political system of Rome while simultaneously breaking her "filiation" to her father (one is obviously the reflection of the other). Pauline's movement outside of Roman patriarchy is, of course, too threatening for the patriarchal parameters of French neoclassicism. As we have seen, Corneille's entire canonical production has been a delicate balancing act in which patriarchy and its other—a too-threatening femininity—had been transcribed into a metaphysics of death and immortality. *Polyeucte* continues this dialectic by finally situating the hero's triumph in the empyrean of Christian immortality. Although the hero is transported to and becomes one with his absolute ideal, the heroine, his other/double, remains behind. Despite her conversion to Christianity, Pauline is not transported to heaven. She becomes (in this tragedy) neither a glorified martyr nor a saint. To her is left the more mundane role of witness, universal witness to her husband's glory. Her husband has triumphed over her, over Pauline as woman, as body, over his own desire, but Pauline has, in a sense, been subjected to his triumph. She is left behind with her father Félix, whose eyes have also been opened by Polyeucte to the truth of Christianity. Abandoning his own ways, his conversion recuperates his daughter's, bringing her back from her stance outside of law ("How joyfully I find again my father!"). Father and daughter are reunited and form a curiously "sexless" couple in the new world of Christian truth. It remains for them, in this new world, to bear witness bravely to the miracle in which they have shared and which they now go forth and "universalize":

We others now should bless our happy lot.
Let us give burial to our martyrs, kiss
Their sacred bodies first, consign them straightway
To worthy sepulchers, and then acclaim

With glad cries everywhere God's holy name.
(*Polyeucte* V, vi) [109]

This witnessing both adores the body and disposes of it. Unlike Camille's body confined in the "same" grave as Curiace's, these are male "holy" bodies, bodies that are and are not bodies. Saintly they are incorruptible. Etherealized, at last, the body can now be an object of worship, a transmuted, sublimated object of desire. Death is finally both venerated and repressed. Corneille's canonical cycle ends, therefore, with many things changed but with the reinscription of the same dialectic that impelled it forward from the start. With *Polyeucte*'s elevation of the absolute desire to the realm of a spiritual and political ideal, Corneille seems at last to have achieved the imposition of the ambient sociopolitical climate as a permanent ethical and aesthetic ideal on the French stage. In the course of the next century, French neoclassical drama would become the model for dramaturgy across Europe. The internal impetus of this drama, however, a sexual dualism that presides over this tragic universe, continues to play out the battles of patriarchy, the struggles of life against death, of Eros and Thanatos, in ways that perversely exclude the nefarious other from the world of the absolute and also reinscribe it as the sexual desire/anxiety that betrays absolutism's intimate attraction to death.

Chapter 5

Racine's *Bérénice*
and the Allegory of Absolutism

Partout du désépoir je rencontre l'image
Je ne vois que des pleurs, et je n'entends parler
Que de trouble, d'horreurs, de sang prêt à couler.

(Everywhere looms the image of despair.
I see naught else but tears, hear only talk
Of anguish, horrors, blood about to flow.)
Bérénice, V, vii)

Narcissism is in its very essence totalitarian and minorities are not tolerated under
its rule.

Grunberger, *Le Narcissisme*

Is *Bérénice* Racine's most radical tragedy? This question may at first appear egregious, especially when we cast an eye over the tragic arena of the Racinian universe only to shudder at the perverse sadomasochism of *Britannicus*, to be transfixed by the incandescent passion of *Phèdre*, or to remain frozen in horror by the matricidal fury of *Athalie*. In the Racinian world of monstrosity, perversion, and sacrifice, *Bérénice*'s rejection of blood and death, its turning away from what for many is the "truly tragic," and thus its relinquishing, at a crucial moment not only in Racine's literary itinerary but in the elaboration of the absolutist edifice of Louis XIV, of the intense, perhaps masochistic, pleasure of the dramatic spectacle, would seem indeed to condemn it to being but a timid reflection of its dramatic siblings. Placed as it is under the pall of "une tristesse majestueuse," *Bérénice* seems destined to a melancholia that can only "faire triste figure" when compared to the fury and passion of the other great tragedies of Racine.

At first glance, *Bérénice* does seem to be the "odd play out" in the Racinian canon. This difference, however, strikes me in several ways as uncan-

nily "modern," an example of "experimental" theater, whose originality
is precisely undercut by the (unsuccessful) critical attempts to fit it into
an overarching scenario, into a generic description of the Racinian
world. This totalizing exegetical drive, which is compounded by the strategically limited number of plays in the Racinian corpus, obfuscates what
does not fit, thematically, into the critical endeavor while diverting our
attention from what, less blatantly but in a sense with more subtle perversity, underpins the spectacular ideological ambivalence of the more violently tragic plays.[1]

Racine, of course, was aware of the critical difference his new tragedy
inflected. In the preface to the play, a preface rich in telling detail, Racine
returns to Aristotle (without mentioning a specific source) to defend this
"tragic-less" tragedy.[2] *Bérénice*, he tells us, does without blood, does without death. It is this tragedy "without" that is, nevertheless, capable of
pleasuring its audience:

> It is not essential for there to be blood and corpses in a tragedy. It is
> enough if the action is elevated, the characters heroic, the passions
> aroused, and if all the play breathes that majestic sadness which is the
> whole pleasure of tragedy.[3]

What Racine is defending here is not simply a tragedy without the
tragic, that is, without death, but more radically, I would suggest, a
tragedy without the body. By one and the same stroke Racine not only
redefines the locus of theatrical tragedy, and thus of theatrical pleasure,
he politically prefigures (the inextricable interrelation between the space
of theatrical pleasure, and the locus of political subjugation, their commingling) the future of the absolutist state. This state and its subjects will
gradually evolve, as Foucault has suggested, away from the subjugation
of the individual body and toward the internalization, the creation of a
"mental space," an interiorized sense of self based not exclusively on
physical difference, but on metaphysical angst. This uncernable metaphysical state mediated by and through a reinscription and a redefinition
of a generalized sense of guilt and loss becomes the new "center" of subjugation and subjectivization; it is the mark of the modern.[4]

By eliminating death as a necessity for his tragedy, Racine shifts the
locus of tragic intensity from a culpable body, a body that is the site of
sin, and places it in a noncernable "other space." The tragic scenario
shifts from the palpable, the tactile, the manipulable, from the thing, the
body itself, and becomes rather a purely undefinable, ungraspable, absence: a no/thing, a *rien*. It is precisely this "no/thing" that Racine tells
us, in his preface, that *Bérénice* represents. Furthermore, this representation of absence, of nothing, is, he states, the highest form of art, the form
that in *Bérénice* he is presenting to an unsuspecting and perhaps uncom-

prehending audience. That audience, accustomed as it is not only to his previous dramatic endeavors but to an entire tradition of "corporeal" tragedies, possibly cannot understand that the highest artistic achievements consist in elaborating a work of art around "nothing." Nevertheless, those tears the audience sheds are the forceful reminder that if it doesn't "understand" theoretically, it does comprehend an intuitive truth that is powerfully effective.[5]

In a strangely proleptic way, Racine, as he elaborates the most abstract tragedy of the French seventeenth century, prefigures by two hundred years that craftsman of nineteenth-century bourgeois angst, Flaubert, who claimed that *Madame Bovary* was a novel about "nothing" ("un livre sur rien"). Across two hundred years, in an uncanny echoing, *rien* reverberates in an eerily closed network of literary practice where, despite differences in genre, in society, and in political structures, the ambiguous *rien* both underlines and (as we shall see) undermines two of the most intense examples of subjective positioning in the French canon. Both the tragedy about nothing and the novel about nothing are oddly consonant in the way in which they incorporate the absence that is at their center and concentrate it in the textual bind of their eponymous heroines. In both *Bérénice* and *Madame Bovary* the nothing that they represent, the nothing at the center of their two very different tragedies, is the woman who gives her name to the tragic, at the same time that this tragic effaces and eliminates her from the textual universe. In the eradication of this nothing, this nothing that is and is not the female protagonist, Racine's new tragedy enters onto the stage of the emerging mythology of absolutism garbed in the tragic veils of "une tristesse majestueuse." This majestic sadness that hangs as a pall over the universe of *Bérénice* and that induces, Racine tells us, in the audience the particularly plangent pleasure of "tears," seems to mime its own loss, the loss of its tragic center, the loss of a tragic that the play can only allegorize as a representation of melancholic dispossession.[6]

Rather than a "tragedy" at all, most of the students of the play tend to agree, implicitly at least, with Voltaire's dismissive quip that what we really have is an "elegy."[7] For more contemporary scholars (such as Roland Barthes) *Bérénice*'s tragic difference would quite simply signal "the death of the theater."[8] For more than three hundred years, then, starting with Racine himself, the words "sadness," "elegy," and "death" reverberate in crescendoing echoes about this play, whose most revolutionary break with the tragic tradition is possibly its direct ejection of death from the scene of tragedy. The death that is absent from the play seems, nevertheless, to make constant metaphoric intrusions in the text itself where the single most prevalent adjective — "fatal" — resounds from one end of the tragedy to the other, thus incorporating in the drama itself the mortiferous atmosphere to which Racine, Voltaire, and Barthes all respond.[9]

In the place of actual (represented) death we are given a world that, although beyond death, is nevertheless entirely inscribed within the space of an impossible loss, within a continuous mourning for a loss that it could articulate only with the greatest difficulty. We know, of course, since Freud, that all melancholia, rather than representing the loss of a particular "object," represents something indefinable that has been lost in the object.[10] The questions we must ask as we approach this tragedy of loss, of melancholia, are: What are the ideological investments of this tragedy in loss? How and in what ways are the thematics of the tragedy and the politics of the period interwoven? Finally, rather than attempt to decipher the psychological state of the protagonists, we must look beyond this representation, must see this representation as but the allegory of a more profound loss that the play, rather like the *Trauerspiel* in Benjamin's analysis, mourns in ways that are perhaps forever incomprehensible to itself but that nevertheless succeed (the proof of the tears, the only sign, and an exterior one at that, of the body's presence) in establishing a mortiferous bond with its audience.[11]

Georges Couton has spoken of the importance of allegory and allegorical thought for the French seventeenth century:

> Allegory is one of the most obvious forms of thought and expression in the seventeenth century: one thinks and one speaks in models, exempla, emblems, and figures. The heroes, the characters of Fable, of History, of literature, offer themselves as models, as precedents for the living and lend their names, which remind us of their vital choices and of their lives.[12]

If we accept as the broadest definition of allegory the rhetorical device by which a thing, an event, a belief is represented under the guise of another, it will perhaps be easier for us to understand the importance that an unreliable historical anecdote has taken in those discussions that attempt to circumscribe the "origin," not only of this drama but of Corneille's *Tite et Bérénice* as well.

According to "la petite histoire," Henriette d'Angleterre supposedly suggested to both Racine and Corneille that they use the historical disguise of Titus's dismissal of his longtime love, Berenice, Queen of Palestine, to represent an episode in Louis XIV's amorous career. As legend has it, Louis, when a young man, fell passionately in love with Marie Mancini, niece of his cardinal prime minister Mazarin. Despite their ardor, higher demands of state worked inexorably against the match. A more politically motivated marriage awaited Louis, a marriage upon which the possibility of a generalized European peace depended. Thus, despite his love, despite himself, and despite Marie ("invitus, invitam"), the affair ended with her leaving the court for an arranged marriage to a Savoyard nobleman.

The anecdotal importance of this youthful affair is of only passing historical interest to scholars of the play. The veracity of its supposed influence remains a subject of some debate among literary historians. On the one hand Raymond Picard accumulates impressive evidence for eliminating it or, at best, accepting its hypothetical possibility with the greatest reluctance. On the other hand, Couton, in his notes to Corneille's *Tite et Bérénice*, presents equally compelling evidence for accepting the Louis-Marie Mancini affair as the actual historicopolitical basis of both tragedies.[13]

That the "true" origin of the plays remains, like all origins, elusive strikes me as of less compelling interest than what the desire for this originary truth reveals. For the desire that propels this search and these arguments for an "origin" of both Racine's and Corneille's dramatic recasting of the (hi)story of Titus and Berenice is not historical but ideological. It seems to me important that we understand the "narrative," the court gossip elevated to the role of (possible) historical truth, as one more "allegorical" twist in the forever-unfolding ideological myth that absolutism recounts to itself. The anecdote about the doomed love of the king and Marie Mancini presents to us just one more example of the impossible contradiction at the heart of all political ideology — the "story" of how the irreconcilable demands of societal law and personal desire are navigated by each individual as she or he becomes a social, that is, political being. Here, of course, the story is focused on the most representative, most highly invested individual in seventeenth-century France, the king, as he exists both in and out of his own body, both (in Kantorowicz's terms) the body royal and the body private.

We have learned from Kantorowicz's classic study as well as from the more recent elaborations of Louis Marin and Jean-Marie Apostolidès, that one of the most prevalent ways of representing both the majesty and mystery of divine-right kingship was in and through the allegory of the "king's two bodies."[14] In simple terms, this representation of the paradox of majesty in which the history, sacred and profane, of the nation is "incorporated" in the physical reality (the body) of the king, constantly had to shuttle between this body as transcendental reality, the body royal representing the transhistorical essence of the monarchy in its mystic dimension, and the actual physical body of the king, the "body private," that like all physical bodies in this sublunary sphere is subject to desire, corruption, and death. The theory of the "king's two bodies" achieved a reasonably sophisticated representation of an impossible contradiction —

an allegory, if we wish — of the "essence" of monarchy that while transcendental was also, like Christ, obliged to take on transient human form and thus be subject to all the pleasures and all the woes of the flesh.

It is in this sense that we must understand the desire for the historical anecdote. For what does the anecdote do but exhibit, under the guise of "doomed love," the internal conflict of majesty, the conflict between the public and the private, between *raison d'Etat* and desire? This anecdote not only teaches us that the king, absolute ruler that he may be, must renounce his pleasure, his chance for happiness, his body, but, on a higher, more political plane, it also teaches us (perversely) that this king is *not* absolute; he is not above the very laws that his body embodies, he is not free to give in to his pleasure. The king too recognizes the law and subjugates himself to it.

At this juncture the myth of Louis XIV and Marie Mancini leaves the realm of the purely romantic and becomes an allegory of an ongoing debate within the confines of French legalo-monarchical discourse. It also extends beyond the limits of France and perversely intertwines with a general hegemonic drive of European culture, which is defining itself to itself over and against a traditional site of cultural difference: the Orient (as we have already seen in *Othello*), most forcibly represented in the European imaginary as the lustful and despotic Ottomans, a haunting specter of power and difference.

Although the European world had lived in fear and jealous envy of the Ottoman East for at least two hundred years, in 1670 (the year in which Racine wrote *Bérénice*) there was, with the visit of the official Turkish embassy to Paris, a paroxysm of interest, a turning point in neoclassical "orientalism":

> It is a well-known fact that a fascination with things Turkish was all the rage. An embassy from the Sublime Porte had paid Louis XIV an official visit in 1670 and these real-life Turks had spawned hundreds of imaginary ones. This innocuous exoticism permitted a dreamlike comeuppance, freed up a taste for fantasy, for folly, that elsewhere in reality had few occasions for satisfying itself.[15]

In Molière's *Le Bourgeois Gentilhomme* and Racine's *Bajazet* (1671) there is obviously a purely picturesque fascination with the East. These exotic fantasies are mise-en-scènes of a cultural appropriation of the more spectacular aspects of foreignness, both an exterior extravagance (the foreign costumes, the bejeweled and turbaned servants) and, on another level, the interior projections of a dark, threatening eroticism (the sexuality of the seraglio, of beautiful, available, passive women and of mute slaves and perverse eunuchs).[16] These picturesque appropriations should not turn us away from the more profoundly ideological sorting out, the tremulous "othering," at work in late-seventeenth-century Europe, of which the theatrical is only the most "spectacular" of the many symptoms.

Although the Ottoman Empire had, at least since the catastrophic fall of Constantinople, been a subject of fear and respect in the West, and although its social, political, and sexual mores had been minutely detailed, especially in the long reports (the *relazioni* that the Venetian ambassadors gave in public audience upon their return from their posting abroad), during the fifteenth and sixteenth centuries the particular form of government of the Turkish state was not described as "despotic" with the overtones that word was to bear in Montesquieu.[17] Neither Machiavelli nor Bodin, those two essential theorists of absolutism, describes the empire of the Turk with Montesquieu's dark tones.[18] During the seventeenth century, through the reports of embassies, missionaries, and savants, the image of the East shifts, going from one of respectful admiration of a powerful but "rightful" monarchical state, to the description of an "unnatural" despotism. The word, in fact, makes its appearance into European vocabulary during the first decades of the seventeenth century:

> From 1634 onward the word [despotic] appears; as an adjective it will be regularly used and associated with "government," "dominion," and "authority."[19]

From the word to the thing: in its most powerful, that is, culturally charged, definition a despotic state is a monarchy that "is ruled by the passions and by (self)-interest."[20] In the Western imaging of the Orient, of the Oriental despot, there is a strong dose of sadomasochistic projection, in which sexuality, a cruel, absolute desire, an unquenchable, unyielding pursuit of pleasure, becomes the image and definition of the Oriental other. In this definition, as Alain Grosrichard has suggested, the chief character of the Oriental, of the despot, would be situated in the involution of the political and the sexual; pleasure, unlimited sexual pleasure, becomes, tautologically, the definition of despotism, as a tyrannical, that is, political, structure. Paradoxically, this supreme right to *jouissance*, Grosrichard tells us, leads to an effective absence of sovereign power at the very center of the political structure. The Oriental despot, condemned to pleasure, condemned to a total unrelenting attention to his body as site of pleasure, to the body's imperious and incessant demands, cannot exercise any real political power in the state:

> Since they are raised in harems with women and eunuchs, Muslim sovereigns are so little able to rule that it is better for the general welfare of the people and for the safety of the state that a subaltern govern in their stead . . . and since these Oriental kings usually only think of satisfying their senses, it is all the more necessary that there be someone who thinks about the preservation and the glory of the empire.[21]

What we have in these images of the Oriental monarchs is essentially a taxonomy of difference, difference between an "eastern" body and a "western" (European/Christian) mind, between body (pleasure) and spirit (reality principle), between, eventually, effeminacy (thus the feminine) and martial vigor (thus masculinity). If we were to contrast the Oriental despot to the "absolute" sovereign as we see the concept developed in the mid to late sixteenth century, we could reduce schematically the opposition the West establishes between itself and its other as one between a body that refuses the law of castration, refuses the Law that would be anything other than the demands of its own pleasure, and the body subjugated to castration, to the "no" of the Law, to the principle of negation and thus sublimation.

For even among those writers in the French tradition who are the theorists of absolutism, and here Bodin will serve as an exemplary figure, although it was admitted that the prince was " 'legibus solutus' in respect to civil law," he was " 'legibus alligatus' in respect to natural law."[22] What this meant, essentially, was that although the sovereignty of the state resided in the prince, who was above civil law, he was not, could not be, above natural law. He could not act contrary to the basic laws of the realm (for France, the "Salic Law," for instance) nor could he infringe upon the property rights of his subjects by expropriating their private domain or levying new taxes upon them. Although sovereign, he was (in/by theory) limited.

> There are three limits: (1) The sovereign is expected to be subservient to the laws of God and nature; (2) he cannot infringe the fundamental laws of the realm ('leges imperii') nor can he change them without the consent of the representatives of the people; (3) finally he must respect the private property of his subjects . . . therefore he cannot impose . . . tributes or taxes without their consent.[23]

The scholarly tradition of the medieval and Renaissance theorists of absolutism, who were, let us remember, jurists and legal scholars, descends, if not in a straight line, at least in a complicated series of transmissions from the legal codes of Ancient Rome, particularly the Justinian Code.[24] Through a series of compilations, transmissions, and textual commentaries of Roman, canon, and medieval law, a "Western" legal subjectivity elaborates itself in and around the concept of "sovereignty," defining the place, figure, and limits of the prince and of those subjected to him. Subjectivity in the West is made to appear the product of an unbroken chain of legal tradition. "Legally" speaking, the Western world, in the person of the greatest avatar of sovereignty, Louis XIV, embodies an entire "corpus" of privilege and duty: the shining body royal that imposes its glory upon the body private. The king, in other words, in the theory of Western tradition, cannot be a slave to his "earthly" body, in which case he would be merely a "tyrant," and thus (although this was hotly debated) removable. He is sovereign precisely because he accepts the castration, the loss of his private body, for the good of the polis. Subjected to the Law of "no," to the law that eliminates the other (body) that inheres in him, he sacrifices this body private in the immolation of his "privates"; (in theory) he becomes sovereign — one, absolute.

Certainly the West's vision of itself, as it will be elaborated in opposition to its projection of the tyranny of the East, is as much a theory of sexuality as of politics. Even after the threat of an Ottoman invasion is successfully parried, the fantasy of Eastern domination continues to haunt Europe in its dreams of Oriental sexuality and violence. It cannot but strike us as uncanny that it is in Vienna — that continually threatened outpost of European/Christian civilization — that Freud elaborates his sexual/political myth of the origins of culture. The "primal" father who possesses all the available females for his own sexual enjoyment and who visits castration and death upon the horde of his randy sons repeats, in more ways than one, the haunting figure of the Oriental satrap.

If the elaboration of a social theory that would distinguish the West from the East is as much sexual as political, if, in other words, the political and the sexual form an inextricable knot in which "difference" is adumbrated in ever-varying shades of distinction, it should not surprise us that when we pass from politicolegal theory to theatrical representation the fantasies of sexuality that were obfuscated in the former should pass to the forefront in those narrations of passionate but doomed love that were written for the stage. To return to Racine's *Bérénice*, what I am suggesting is that we read the literary productions of classicism as continuing in another rhetorical register, a more violently passionate register, the political/sexual theorizing, a refiguring of the myth of Oedipus that is contemporaneously elaborating and solidifying the hegemonic discourse of Western/Christian difference. What I am not suggesting is that a tragedy, especially a highly intricate, multileveled textual construction such as *Bérénice*, be simply read, or read simplistically, as a transcoding of the political. At first glance it would seem incongruous that a tragedy situated in the Roman court of the first century A.D. and that had, at its center, an "elegiac" separation of two lovers, should have anything in common with the struggle for religious/cultural hegemony in seventeenth-century Europe. Even if we accept its "romantic" origins, this love story seems far removed from the truly contemporary and Oriental tragedy, *Bajazet*, that would follow it onto the Parisian stage a year later. But let us not forget our initial desire, our first interpretative strategy of reading *Bérénice* as an allegory — and in allegory, as we know, "that which is apparent is almost never the truth." Racine's first radical move in *Bérénice* was the elimination of the body, of death. When we consider the implications of this gesture, especially in terms of the "passionate" history that the play purports to represent, we cannot but be struck by one further aporia this gesture implies. In a perverse interpretative move on our own part we can take this elimination of "death" from the scene of tragedy as implying, at one and the same time, the impossibility of "sexuality," the desexing of the theatrical scenario, especially when we consider that, according to psychoanalytic theory, it is precisely "castration," one of the metaphoric substitutions of death, that precipitates the individual into language and into desire.

> It has been said that the "invention" of sexuality was one with the discovery of death. In fact, without sexual differentiation — in the absence of "sectioning" — the infinitely repeated scission of the same organism traces a figure of immortality.[25]

This excursion into psychoanalysis is invoked only to underline, theoretically, what Racine himself tells us he is doing, quite consciously, in his tragic rescription of the love affair. Explaining why he felt it unnecessary to end his tragedy with Bérénice's death, Racine symptomatically compares Titus and Bérénice's historical liaison with the mythological passion of Dido and Aeneas:

> In fact, there is nothing more touching in any of the poets than the separation of Dido and Aeneas in Virgil. And who can doubt that what provided matter for a whole canto of a heroic poem, where the action lasts several days, is not sufficient for a tragedy that should not take up more than a few hours? It is true that I have not driven Bérénice to kill herself, like Dido, because Bérénice, not having with Titus the ultimate commitments that Dido had with Aeneas, is not obliged, like Dido, to take her life.[26]

In Racine's dramatization of history, where there is no sex, there is, tautologically, no death. From its inception in Racine's mind, then, there is a deliberate collusion between sexuality and death that is excluded in the composition of this new tragedy. That this is a deliberate choice seems obvious to anyone familiar with the different historical accounts of Titus and Bérénice that Racine possessed. Both of the protagonists of the tragedy had, historically speaking, a reputation for rather rampant sexual activity. Suetonius, for example, had written:

> Perhaps no one ever became emperor with so bad a reputation, or so against the general will of the people . . . Besides his cruelty everyone feared his intemperance because he indulged in orgies with the most jaded of his cronies . . . and not least of all his debauchery was feared because of his groups of favorites and eunuchs and because of

his famous passion for queen Bérénice . . . and finally, everyone feared him to be another Nero.[27]

The stories told about Bérénice by Flavius Josephus paint her as lascivious, incestuous, and sexually insatiable. With his typical gift for understatement, Pierre Bayle writes:

Bérénice left Polemon [her second husband] because of her inordinate need for caresses, which he was incapable of satisfying.[28]

That Racine chose to transform this couple of middle-aged voluptuaries into an ethereal example of noble sublimation and purely platonic passion is not the least of the paradoxes of artistic creation.

Only once we have understood that this precursory elimination of sexuality/death from the universe of the tragedy represents the meanderings of an imperious drive toward an integrity of being that would situate the characters and the tragedy beyond death, in the realm of the unique, can we begin to comprehend the tragedy's involvement in the elaboration of an absolutist aesthetics. If we consider seventeenth-century absolutism as it was perfected in France during the reigns of Louis XIII and Louis XIV as the first form of a modern totalitarian state that Balandier defined as "the submission of all and everything to the state" where "the unifying function of power is carried to its highest degree, and where the myth of unity becomes the strategy controlling political theatrics," then we can begin to understand why the tragedy of *Bérénice*, as an allegorical representation of absolutism, its mise-en-scène, necessarily fixes its characters in those tropes — melancholia and its other, narcissism — most intimately connected to the elaboration of an "image" of lonely but triumphant sublimation.[29]

Of all the psychic phenomena theorized by Freud, surely narcissism remains both the most general, the most elusive, and yet the most seductive for any attempt at analyzing the interrelation between the private and the public valences of political leaders. When we consider that the underlying drive of narcissism is, as André Green says, "the desire for the One," that it represents a "unitary utopia, an ideal totalization," we can establish a rapport between the internal structures of narcissism and the political drives of absolutism.[30] Narcissism, like absolutism, is also a totalizing drive, the desire for a unity of being that necessarily must ignore and repress what precisely would sunder that being, its own desire:

Portrait of Narcissus, all powerful in his body and in his mind, which becomes embodied in his speech, independent and autonomous when he wishes to be so, but upon whom others depend without his feeling in any way needy of them. Residing among his own, the members of his family, his clan, his race, chosen by the obvious indications of a divinity, created in his own likeness. He exists at their head, master of the universe, of time, of death, totally involved in his silent dialogue with the solitary deity who bestows all his blessing upon him — up until the moment of his fall through which he becomes the chosen object of his own sacrifice — an intercessor between God and mortals living in the brilliant isolation of his splendor. This shadow of God traces a figure of the same, of what is unchanging, intangible, immortal, and intemporal.[31]

Green's description of Narcissus, of the narcissistic personality, is eerily consonant with Louis XIV's own self-descriptions in his *Mémoires*, most specifically in the famous passage where he speaks about the choice and imposition of the solar topos as his personal emblem:

It was then that I took this emblem that I have kept ever since and that you see in so many places. I thought that, without stooping to anything baser or commoner, this emblem must represent the duties of a prince and at the same time continually encourage me to fulfill all these obligations. We chose as an emblem the sun, which, according to the rules of this art, is the noblest emblem of them all, and which, by its unique quality, by the brilliance that surrounds it, by the light that it sheds on the other stars that form what we may call its "court," by the equal and equitable sharing of this very light into all the corners of the world, creating life everywhere, spreading joy and action by its eternal movement, but where it nevertheless appears, in its never-swerving path, calm and self-possessed; it is assuredly the most vivid and perfectly beautiful image of a great king.[32]

What I find particularly appealing in the juxtaposition of Louis's self-presentation with Green's description of Narcissus is the way both accentuate "social" positioning. Green's Narcissus is a political leader; he exists in society as its charismatic chief, among the people but above them, radically nondesirous. This "indifference" makes others desire him, attaches them to him. His own lack of contingency is the sign of his divine election. The idol of his people, he is also their victim. Narcissus in his self-sufficient totality is the perfect representation of a desire for closure, for unity, and ultimately for death.[33]

But this unity can be obtained only through the erection and elimination of a difference, an "other." This repression of difference allies narcissism so seductively with political totalitarianism. "Narcissism maintains a profound complicity with power," writes Mikkel Borch-Jacobsen. "Let us be clear about this — tyrannical power, or political madness . . . Narcissistic desire is, by definition, desire for power: the assimilation and thus the subservience of the other to his Majesty the Self."[34] The most highly invested other was the other that inheres in society, the feminine that must be encircled, contained, repressed. Narcissus must remain deaf to Echo, to her, and to his desire.

Both Richelieu and Louis XIV, in very different ways, warn of the troublesome, chaotic consequences of allowing women any influence in the politics of the realm. Louis warns the dauphin not to let sexual passions get in the way of *raison d'Etat*:

> As soon as you give women the liberty of speaking to you about important matters it becomes impossible not to be led astray by them. The tender feelings we have for them makes us appreciate their worst ideas and disposes us, without our even realizing it, to their reasons; their natural weakness makes them often prefer the petty interests of private trifles to more ponderous affairs and almost invariably causes them to choose the wrong side. They are eloquent in their pleas, insistent in their entreaties, and opinionated in their feelings.[35]

This desire for unity, this narcissistic desire for the absolute, must, in order to protect itself from itself and the other that inheres in that self, engage in a dialectic in which a highly charged dose of masochistic self-denial is coupled to an aggressively sadistic desire for subjugation. This dialectic comes to rest on and in the person of the king, his "moi," the image of his own resplendent majesty, which is, as we know, "l'Etat." Although Louis XIV was more often extolled as either a modern-day Apollo or a triumphant Mars, when his publicists descended from the heights of Mount Olympus to the more mundane comparisons with historical heroes, we see that as early as 1660 Louis was already being matched with no less a figure than the Emperor Titus, "délices du genre humain."[36] Nevertheless, I would like to insist that when we look beyond these "images" of martial glory, we see staring back at us the more melancholic figure of Narcissus, who like the king can only gaze on himself as reflected in a spectacular self-enclosure. This desire for closure, for an ego that must constitute itself in as closed a system as possible, is the symptom of narcissism's intimate connection with death.[37] Either as an "individual" personality or as a collective societal impulse, narcissism attempts to effect a closure of the world, a sideration of the body that can best be represented as the body's elimination. The body's radical otherness is cerned, closed, objectified.[38]

In Racine's elimination of the body/death from his tragedy, the absence of this "sectioning," the refusal of difference ("sexuality") will establish a constant pendulum-like oscillation between the two radical poles of narcissism and melancholia that will come to rest on its two protagonists Titus and Bérénice. In an important sense, of course, neither one of the two psychic poles is able to exist independently of the other, in just the same way that Titus and Bérénice's love is portrayed as a mutual interrelation, a relation that both confuses and separates out into gendered sexual and political differences. Nevertheless, we must remember that in our discussion and in the dynamics of the play it is always a question of more or less—that is, it is always a question of how sexuality will be gendered as specifically narcissistic, and thus attached to Titus, or melancholic, and thus the realm of Bérénice. In a further twist to this involution of sexuality and politics we will have to remember that this dyadic declension is further reinforced by still another twist wherein the masculine and feminine of the play are transcoded into that other impossible distinction, the division between the visual and the linguistic, the distinction, if we wish, *grosso modo* between a certain "imaginary" locus and the "symbolic register."

In the textual dynamics of the tragedy this "imaginary" dimension surfaces in the importance of "visioning" for the narcissistic subjectivity of the protagonist. The pole of vision and images works against, or at least is in active opposition to, the symbolic register, which in this most "aphasic" of dramas appears in the difficulty experienced by the characters in breaking out of their silence, in speaking.[39] For by speaking, they are forced out of the realm of a self-enclosed protective view of themselves and the world and into the realm of difference and therefore death. In *Bérénice*, death—that is, loss, exile, abandonment—is introduced not by the glance but by the word.

The characters of Titus and Bérénice function as the most heavily invested "signifiers" in a declensional chain of textual forces that, while striving for "difference," for the liberating, destructive gesture that would separate them and allow them to love and to die, are, nevertheless, incapable of any gesture other than a mutual dance of affirmation and denial, a constant interweaving of polarities that rather than destine them to difference condemn them to act out, as if in a morality play, allegorical roles of an equally impossible complementarity.

Titus and Bérénice appear on stage as mirror reflections in sexual reversal of each other: although they rarely, in the first acts of the drama, share the stage for any length of time, rhetorically the presence of one appeals to and loses itself in the image of the other. Bérénice, we learn in Antiochus's outburst, has eyes only for Titus, sees him even when she gazes on her entourage. She is blind to all else; for her everything "reflects" Titus.

> I flee the name—Titus—that tortures me,
> The name that endlessly your lips repeat.
> What shall I say? I flee your vacant eyes
> Which never saw me, staring into mine.
> (I, iv)[40]

When Bérénice gazes on Titus she is lost in a spectacular staging of his person, of his persona, in which that person becomes an image of the "universe."[41] Titus, filling up the world, masters it, becomes in her imaging of him the masterful image to which, in voluptuous abandon, Bérénice loses herself:

> The splendor of that night did you behold?
> Are not your eyes full of his majesty?
> This pyre, these torches, this inflamed night,
> These eagles, fasces, people, army, and
> This host of kings, consuls, and senators,
> Borrowing their radiance from my beloved;
> This gold, this purple that his glory gilds,
> These laurels, witness of his victory;
> And all these eyes gazing from every side
> Focused on him alone their eager looks;
> This royal carriage and this gentleness.
> Heaven! how gladly, how respectfully,
> All hearts assured him of their loyalty!
> Speak, can one see him and not think like me
> The world would straight acclaim him as their lord
> On seeing him, even were he born obscure?
> (I, v)[42]

This remarkable example of imagistic rhetoric, which Barthes among others has signaled out as a symptomatic moment fixing the Racinian erotic in a confusion of the visual, the martial, the destructive, and the pleasurable, produces a spectacular scenario.[43] The extraordinary density of the scene functions to occasion, simultaneously, an inseparable conjunction, an erotic conjunction between the object of the image — Titus, disseminated across and marked by the entire nighttime scene — and the subject of that image, Bérénice, whose pleasure lies precisely in being in love with/loved by "the world," imaged in its master, Titus.

Although Bérénice protests loudly and at great length to any who will listen to her that she does not love Titus as "emperor," that she loves only the man Titus, the private subject, she is deluding herself. She is in no way able to separate the private from the public as the erotic charge of the just-quoted "imaging" passage demonstrates. Bérénice loves the image of Titus, an image inseparable from his symbolic function of emperor. Her rhetoric, which we must insist is always a re-creation, the past made present, but the past re-created as an image, is lost in Titus's apotheosis. It is his nighttime epiphany, where he is as much the body as the symbol of "Rome" and "empire," that seduces her. That this image is inseparable from the "law" is underlined by Paulin's remark that it was during this same ceremony in which his father Vespasian was "placed among the gods" that Titus was declared "emperor," precisely by the people's giving him his new "name":

> The people stop him, gather round, entranced,
> Applaud the senate's titles [*noms*] to him . . .
> (V, ii)[44]

By and through this "symbolic" process of naming, Titus is confounded with the image he is — emperor. Thus, despite her denial, despite the fact that Bérénice dwells in an image that she would have private, Titus remains not so much hers, but the world's: he is and
represents the desire of the people, the answer of the vox populi to its own
demand for a leader.

Bérénice's visioning of Titus is totalizing. It attempts to exclude the
world, exclude the law of that world, for a capture of Titus in a self-
enclosed embrace. For Bérénice, Titus is the/her world, and that is precisely the problem. When Titus describes Bérénice and his love for her,
she is presented also as an image, but in a strange reversal, an image seen
in isolation, an isolation that becomes for Titus his *tout*, his all, but more
resonantly his "whole," his "integrity," his "absolute":

> In short, all the most powerful bonds of love,
> Gentle reproaches, ever-welling bliss,
> Artless desire to please and constant fear,
> Charm, honor, virtue — I find all [*tout*] in her.
> (II, ii)[45]

Each for the other is the world; and that world is both divided and confused by them and for them along traditional gender lines. Yet, there is
a strange gender reversal that I find significant for the chiasmatic totality
their couple forms. In a further, intriguing twist, the possibility of distin-
guishing either the "subject" or the "object" of their vision is difficult and
tendentious at best. Because each is for the other a *tout*, the world in all
its inclusive appropriations, we can never be sure where to situate the
protagonists in relation either to each other (who is the container, who
the contained?) or to an alterity that is not immediately appropriated in
them. In the inseparable knot they form, in their union, each can occupy
both positions — subject and object — in their desirous network. This in-
nate reversibility of Titus/Bérénice is precisely what destabilizes any inherent gendered sexual division their "love story" would naturalize.

In the Western sexual tradition, active scopophilia appears to be
relegated to the domain of male sexuality. In the West, as much recent
work in art and film history has shown, and as Mary Ann Doane reminds
us, women, when they "look, look good."[46] What this means, of course,
is that in the sexual economy of patriarchy, the active, subjective role of
looking, of seizing and possessing the world, of objectifying it, belongs
to men. Women are, in that economy, only the object of the gaze. In
Bérénice, however, this economy seems to be reversed: Bérénice gazes on

Titus, captures him in her look, and there loses herself. Titus seems to be in the feminine position of offering himself as an image at the same time that image, reflected back to him as "emperor," as "glory," will eventually prove too powerfully seductive to allow him any compromise with an exterior erotic object.

In a certain sense the entire movement of the play will come to appear to us as a chiasmatic reversal: Titus moves from his space as an object of erotic/political imagery to the acceptance of the symbolic dimension of that image as it becomes articulated as the Law, as it is voiced by the Roman people, while Bérénice moves from her position as lost in the erotic contemplation of Titus, to the acceptance of her own removal from that scene and her exile to "l'orient désert," where she will forever be able only to mourn her abandoned vision of an impossible plenitude. How this move is authorized will depend on the particular ideological weight each image bears in the rhetoric of the tragedy.

When Titus describes Bérénice his rhetoric creates an image of an angelic, almost maternal presence. His description strikes us as a bit unusual in the mouth of a lover, for rather than accentuate the passion, that is, the sexual desire she arouses in him, in Titus's speech Bérénice appears singularly "unsexed." In fact, according to Titus, she has been his savior by turning him away from sexuality, from the debauchery at Nero's court. In his depiction of her, she is portrayed not so much as purity incarnate but as an example of efficacious grace. Not only does she save him by leading him out of sexuality, but this "sexless" love has turned him into the generous, humanitarian hero he is today:

> As well you know, fame did not always shine
> With the same lustre on my name as now.
> My youth, Paulin, spent at Nero's court,
> Was by corrupt example led astray,
> Following the primrose path of dalliance.
> Bérénice pleased me. What does one not do
> To please one's love and win one's conqueror?
> I carried all before me on the field.
> In triumph I returned. But blood and tears
> Were not sufficient to deserve her smile.
> I sought a thousand wretches' happiness.
> My charities were lavished far and wide . . .
> (II, ii)[47]

Behind Titus's military prowess and magnanimity stands the image of Bérénice. She leads him away from the easy road of sensual pleasure, away from the monstrous sexuality that reigned at Nero's court and down the thorny path of moral rectitude. In this re-visioning of her, Bérénice stands as (anachronistically speaking) a new Beatrice, leading the errant pilgrim on through the thickets of courtly sexual excess and into the light of (pre)Christian charity; she appears more in a maternal than a passional role.[48] At the same time this "maternal," in the sense of "nonsexual," this wise pedagogue who leads the child-man still captive of his senses out of the prison of his body's pleasure and into the light of mature, that is, sublimated, humanitarianism seems to be the embodiment of a traditional allegory for the Orient: Bérénice is figured here garbed as "Sophia"—the traditional wisdom of the ancient Orient, who has her historic abode in the East (in Egypt).

Thus, the image that each of the lovers has/projects of the other is a narcissistic image of closure. Each for the other presents an image that includes the loved one as container/contained. They present to the world an image of mutually exclusive, self-contained monad, be it "world/emperor" or "mother/child." It is an image impervious to societal desire, impervious to the law. Nevertheless, these positions are precarious because their closure is too fragile to be ensured in a world that with greater and greater insistence is forcing itself upon them. Although Bérénice would like to believe she can live her love as a utopian idyll, the play never lets us forget that idyll is threatened, spied on, commented upon by that invisible presence, the "Roman people," who although unseen are omnipresent. This social impetus, this drive that refuses the pleasure of individual desire, will move the protagonists into the positions that society defines for them. These roles are enigmatically articulated by Paulin in his response to Titus's inquiry, "What is reported of the queen and me?" This "voice," the cutting popular voice of the Law, introduces into this universe of seamless, imaginary indifference, the force and presence of the "symbolic," and will separate Titus and Bérénice forever:

> TITUS: What is reported of the queen and me?
> Speak. What do you hear?
> PAULINUS: I hear on every side
> Your virtues published and, my lord, her charms.
> (II, ii)[49]

The division of the couple Titus/Bérénice by the vox populi into "virtues/charms" ("vertus/beautés") rhetorically reinserts a division of masculinity and femininity that the imaging confounded. This is just the first instance of the imposition of difference, of sexuality, of the Law of renunciation (castration) that will eventually force the final separation of the protagonists.

Paulin's speech is an elaboration on this initial, irreconcilable "othering." Through its obvious echoes, "vertus" establishes an entire chain of sexual/political allusions that are coded as male and Roman. "Beautés," functioning as a metonymy for Bérénice, establishes another chain in hierarchical opposition to the first and which declines an economy of otherness: beauty, female, Oriental. Although articulated by Paulin, the entire speech appears to our ears as oracular: giving voice to what is presented as a timeless truth, it is as if Paulin only served as the receptacle of a sacred affirmation that echoes from some distant, unlocalizable, but ubiquitous and eternal space. Paulin appears here as a political *vates*, inhabited by the god(s), guardians of Roman identity, an identity rendered unique because it refuses contamination, refuses the "other" that by the very gesture of evocation it summons forth:

> No doubt of that. Be it reason or caprice,
> Rome does not see her as its empress. She
> Is known to be enchanting. Such fair hands
> Seem to demand of you the empire's crown;
> She even has, they say, a Roman heart;
> She's every virtue, but she is a queen.
> Rome, by a law that never can be changed
> Admits no foreign blood to blend with it,
> And does not recognize the offspring born
> Of such a marriage which its laws condemn.
> (II, ii)[50]

We may go on to speculate that the place from whence this voice echoes is the same place to which the Roman senate and people have just sent Titus's father, Vespasian.[51]

> You were a witness of this night gone by
> When, in response to his religious wish,
> The senate placed his father midst the gods.
> (II, iv)[52]

Deifying the dead father, placing him in space beyond death, successfully makes Vespasian one with a certain "ideal" that Titus, if he wishes to correspond to the image that Bérénice reflects to him, the universalizing image of "emperor," will have to attain. It is a place that we know Titus desires (because he admits it): "I even coveted my father's place" ("J'ai même souhaité la place de mon père"; II, ii). He wishes to become one with his image, with his father; and the dictates of the voice of this Father, confounded in/as the generalized voice of the people, articulate to Titus the sacrificial gesture by which he may finally arrive there.

In order to make the "sacrifice" palatable, to make it not less painful (after all, suffering is part of the self-congratulatory pleasure that is the premium the ego receives for its loss) but at least communally acceptable, the sacrificial victim must be turned by the speech into a scapegoat. It will only seem that I am stating the obvious to insist that in a highly patriarchal society the relation between sovereignty in both its political forms (monarchy) and its metaphysical imperatives (the relation between God and the world) turns, as Freud suggests, equally on the elevation and sublimation of the figure of the father and his destruction.[53] No divine-right monarchy is possible without the integral backing of a theological view of the universe that unites God, kingship, and paternity along the same metaphoric axis, establishing a universe in which the devolution of power from male to male is mediated through the sacrifice of patriarchy's other, the representation of the other Woman, of the feminine that must be eliminated.

In the case of Bérénice, the conflation of otherness functions sexually, politically, and, we must add, racially. On the first level Paulin announces Bérénice's unacceptability to the Roman populace on the grounds of her royal status: she is a queen. Although the apparent contradiction is obvious to all — Titus is an emperor — it still appears that there is a rhetorical difference between empire as something quintessentially Roman, and furthermore quintessentially Roman precisely because "kings" have been historically eliminated from the Roman political sphere, and thus so have queens. This elimination of king(ship), another primal sacrifice (of the Father), functions as a "historical" memory and reminds Romans of who they are:

> By banishing its kings, as well you know,
> Rome to this title that it once revered
> Forever vowed an unrelenting hate;
> And, though obedient to its Caesars still,
> This hate, my lord, a vestige of its pride,
> Survives in all their hearts since freedom came.
> (II, ii)[54]

From the first enunciation of the historical/mythical *obstat*, the speech passes from the idea of Bérénice as "generic" queen to allusions to a specifically overinvested (for Romans) queen — Cleopatra. Here, to the rather bland political connotations are added the more sulfurously enticing attributes of sexuality, luxury, and Orientalism. *Bérénice* incorporates into its very center the most overdetermined signifier of sexual excess, of the Oriental femme fatale, who, capable of seducing both Julius Caesar and Mark Antony, by her feminine allure almost caused the entire history of the world to swerve from its predestined (Roman) course. Cleopatra's "monstrosity," the foreignness so necessary to authorize her (or her sister's) sacrifice, is introduced rhetorically by a negative comparison with those political monsters Caligula and Nero. Despite Paulin's embarrassment at even mentioning their names ("Monsters whose names I hesitate to cite . . . "), their misdeeds stopped short at the threshold of separating the *heimliche* (Roman law) from the *unheimliche* (marriage to a foreign,

Oriental queen). The *penates* were not contaminated by the intrusion into that most sacred space of racial/political separateness, the marriage bed:

> Since then, my lord, Nero, Caligula,
> Monsters whose names I hesitate to cite,
> With nothing but the figure of a man,
> Trod underfoot all the grave laws of Rome,
> But feared this law alone, and did not light
> The torch of a detested marriage feast.
> (II, ii)[55]

This fear that stopped emperors did not stop the brother of a base free-man, Pallas, from passing, almost miraculously, from the imprisoning chains of Claudius Felix to the marriage bed of not one but two Oriental queens:

> The freedman Pallas' brother, Felix, still
> Bearing the marks, the brand, of Claudius' chains,
> Became the husband of two queens . . .
> (II, ii)[56]

And, as the coup de grâce, the speech ends in a crescendo of rhetorical violence by embracing all the previously mentioned allusions to sexuality, femininity, and Orientalism with the clincher:

> . . . and, if
> I must obey you to the bitter end,
> These two queens were of Bérénice's stock [*sang*].
> (II, ii)[57]

"Blood," that extraordinarily overdetermined signifier for all systems of nobiliary aristocracy, is brought in at the end of the speech to under-line the "contaminating" possibilities of what the words "fruits illégitimes" and "hymen odieux" had already suggested.[58]

The fear of the other that the speech has adumbrated is finally summa-rized in the ultimate rhetorical chiasmus where the theme of the inherent "abjection" of Bérénice, her guilt by association, by association of gender and of race, is expulsed from the realm of Roman possibility:

> And yet you think you might without offense
> Now bring a queen into our Caesar's bed,
> While the East witnesses a slave ascend,
> Fresh from our chains, the couches of their queens.
> (II, ii)[59]

Paulin's speech enunciates the Law of Romanness, which is a law of exclusion and, of course, death. In order to empower this law from the space of enunciation, that place is never relativized. Rather, what is at work is simply the arrogance of power staking out its own limits by defining itself over and against its weaker other. Bérénice is victimized, rendered abject by a sliding series of "naturalized" (for Rome) oppositions that are all implicitly or explicitly validated in and through this exclusion. Ideas of "Fatherland," "History," and racial difference are articulated by stating what they are not: feminine, sexual, Oriental. At the same time, this image of Bérénice as unwitting sacrificial other, her "sacrificeability," is rendered all the more poignant by the love she inspires in Titus. This love, the maternal love as it has been described by Titus, is contrasted to the abject portrait to which the Law/Speech has reduced her.

In Paulin's depiction, therefore, we have the inverted portrait of the picture suggested by Titus. To the passive, demur, and maternal Bérénice of Titus's description is opposed the sultry, aggressive, inherently dangerous Cleopatra. That these two contrasting images of women haunt the dramatic universe of Racine comes as no surprise to modern students reading in the wake of Freud. On a simple level what we have in these antithetical images of Bérénice is the classic dichotomy of the woman as "mother/whore" that Freud discussed in his essay "A Special Type of Object Choice Made by Men." In that essay, Freud opined that "a thing which in consciousness makes its appearance as two contraries is often in the unconscious a united whole."[60] It would seem, however, that what we have here in one protagonist is what is so often presented as separated characters in the bloodier tragedies of Racine—on the one hand, the aggressive threatening phallic woman and, on the other, the submissive, virginal passive female.[61]

In either case, whether we are seduced by one or the other image, or if we allow ourselves to be lost in their complex blurring, Bérénice cannot escape her exile in/as the configuration of the female, Oriental other. It is this other that the text, through an internal dynamic of which it is undoubtedly unaware, must rid itself. Just as unaware as the text, Titus must, if he wishes to attain his father's place, that place beyond contingency, that space of the absolute, rid himself of Bérénice. In order to conform to the narcissistic image Bérénice has projected on him, in order to conform to his ideal image of himself, to his acceptance of his *gloire* and *devoir*, Titus must extirpate the other that is in him, that by its and his desire renders him contingent and desirous, and he must by this sacrifice of a part of himself begin his long, lonely journey into masculine autonomy—into the epitome of Roman *virtù*.

> . . . Ah! cruel recompense.
> All that I owe her will recoil on her.
> (II, ii)[62]

With this extraordinary chiasmus Titus announces his sacrifice of Bérénice. I would suggest that we must turn to the echoing of the one word "all" ("tout"), a word whose pregnant meaning for Titus and for absolutism we have already discussed, if we are to understand the internal dynamics of the tragedy as a drama of sacrifice and loss.

Barthes has opined that the death of Titus's father, Vespasian, and the end of Titus's love for Bérénice are coterminous, but two sides of the same coin:

> The two figures from the past, the father and the woman, . . . are eliminated by a single gesture. It is the same murder that carries away Vespasian and Bérénice. Vespasian dead, Bérénice is condemned.[63]

How are we to understand this enigmatic coupling of the dead father and the erotic object of Titus's desire? As I've already suggested, Vespasian, "placed among the Gods," deified by the Roman people and senate, accedes to the realm of absolute desire, to the realm of the ubiquitous, omniscient "law." From this space "beyond death" Vespasian now exists in and for his son as the most unattainable yet seductive image of masculine desire, sublimated into political imperatives. Vespasian, dead and deified, becomes both an image — of God(s)/emperor — and a voice that from beyond the grave calls to his son, imperiously demanding that he be "emperor." But to be emperor, to be "absolute," means first and foremost that he obey the law, the law of loss, of denial, of death.

Bérénice herself has betrayed this portentous change in her relation to Titus, without, however, being aware of its nefarious and absolute consequences:

> . . . This long
> Mourning imposed by Titus on his court
> Had even frozen his passion at the root.
> No longer had he that assiduous love
> When he would spend days hanging on my eyes.
> Care-laden, silent now, with tearful gaze,
> He only took a sad farewell of me.
> (I, iv)[64]

In her description of Titus's mourning for his dead father, Bérénice describes the loss of his love for her: not only has he ceased burning for her, he has withdrawn into silence. This retreat into mutism marks two important aspects, one dramatic, the other psychoanalytic, for the understanding of Titus and Bérénice's doomed love. On the one hand this retreat into silence describes the present situation of the characters on stage. Each one of the main characters — Antiochus, Bérénice, Titus — is trapped in the same dilemma: to speak or not to speak, to declare one's desire or to continue in an ambiguous silence. This impossibility of speech, the impossibility to define oneself to oneself and thus to the other, the addressee of one's speech, informs the dramatic tension of the play.

Who will say what to whom, and what will be the consequences of this declaration, a declaration that is always a performative in that it immediately forces each character out of self-imposed and delusional relation to the others and into a radically altered intersubjective reality? Paradoxically, when the protagonists do talk about each other it is always to recall a past time, a moment that is, as we have seen, also an "image," a verbal re-creation of an instant of visual shock, of a powerfully erotic encounter. This moment of visual plenitude, when desire and its fulfillment were coterminous, now, in the present, exists only as a fantasy, informed by its impossibility and by the introduction of the Law.

On the other hand, psychoanalytically speaking, this erotic regression that manifests itself as "silence," as a refusal to speak, and therefore as a refusal to situate oneself in a dialectics of erotic desire, betrays a regression of object love into a claustral narcissism.[65] This narcissism refuses to acknowledge the presence and the hold of the other, to acknowledge "desire," and therefore also to admit, if only tangentially, the "lack" and the "split" in the desiring subject, the fact that in and through desire that subject situates itself as a subject of lack, a nonintegral, nonabsolute subject. In a sense, Titus's retreat into silence is the sign of his "mourning" the loss of his father, but also, beyond that loss, a refusal, perhaps an entrapment, in a self-enclosed eroticism, a narcissistic fix on his own image, that refuses an originating loss and thus refuses an origin. This loss, reaching beyond the loss of Vespasian, would perhaps point to the more originary object, that absent object of the tragedy, the "Mother," whose loss can only be repeated in the expulsion from the scene of tragedy, and the expulsion from Rome of her substitute, Bérénice.[66]

Titus, through the mourning for his father, also abandons the "mother." He turns away from the object that relays to him the image of his own contingency, and closes himself off in the contemplation of his own incorruptible, because purely sublimated, image, the new ideal that now presides over his erotic destiny, the image of his *gloire*:

> Though the whole empire spoke to me, the voice
> Of glory had not yet sounded in my heart
> As when it trumpets to an emperor.
> (IV, v)[67]

Once he has seized upon this new image of his own glory, once he has retreated into the realm of the image, the image of his own imperial *corps glorieux*, which is, at one and the same time, a symbolic (that is, political) and an erotic (narcissistic) image, he attempts to expel Bérénice from the realm of speech where act IV has forced them both and to have her retreat from her own indignant outburst, the manifestation of her desire for him,

and into a new visual sphere where she can only contemplate the image
of her desire, which will forever remain beyond her grasp:

> . . . Silence your love for me,
> And, in the light of reason and renown,
> Dwell on my duty at its most austere [*dans toute sa rigueur*]
> (IV, v)[68]

He summons Bérénice to the contemplation/worship of his rigidity, of
his masculine integrity that he brandishes before her eyes. But this vision
of tumescent glory is the last glimpse she will ever have of him. Once she
has been sent back to her "orient désert," he will remain only a memory,
an "absence éternelle" whose evocation can only recall in her ever-
renewed suffering:

> How will we pine a month, a year, from now
> When we're divided by a waste of seas,
> When the day dawns and when the day will end,
> With Titus never seeing Bérénice
> And all day long my never seeing you?
> (IV, v)[69]

Separated forever from her vision, from the image of glory and empire
that inspired her love, Bérénice is bereft of the nurturing, life-sustaining
force of that brandished image. She is betrayed by her own desire,
betrayed by a vision of absolutism that necessarily had to exclude her
from its sphere in order to be absolute.

This sacrifice of "love" condemns all of the protagonists to a death that
is metaphorized as an exile, a banishment, to an absence, an empty space
of loss — "l'orient désert." Titus describes his moral struggle to conform
to Roman dictates as a sacrifice of himself: "far from being my beloved's,
/ I would be forced soon to renounce myself." With the immolation of his
love, the only thing left him is an eternity of internal emptiness at the
heart of the Roman world:

> Swear to her, prince, that always true to her,
> With sorrowing heart, and exiled more than she,
> Bearing even to the grave a lover's name,
> My reign will be one long, long banishment.
> If not content with robbing me of her,
> Heaven still desires to force long life on me.
> (III, i)[70]

It is the same exile that Antiochus had known in Rome and before that
in Caesarea. With Bérénice gone, with the disappearance of the loved object, the world became destitute:

> The East was one vast desert where I pined.
> I wandered long in Caesarea where,

.Drinking enchantment, I had worshiped you.
I asked you back again of your sad realms;
I sought in tears the traces of your steps.
But, in the end, succumbing to my gloom,
Despair guided my steps back to Italy.
(I, iv)[71]

Italy, with Bérénice, becomes the space of love, drawing Antiochus to it/her. Would it be an exaggeration to state that with the image Titus offers us of Bérénice, the wise, maternal Bérénice, we might say that this also infuses a maternal presence into what is essentially the Fatherland of Roman patriotism, into the Law of the Father? With her presence Rome signals itself as the site of love, of life — Roma/Amor. And this is, of course, what Rome, the Rome of masculine sublimation, the Rome of *gloire* and *devoir*, the Rome of empire, cannot accept. By her presence, and this is most probably the secret threat of Bérénice, Rome risks being undermined from the inside by all those heterogeneous forces, the forces of desire, of femininity, of Oriental excess that it must scorn. Now, in the name of the law, Bérénice is to be extirpated from Rome, which turns, as we have seen in Titus's monologue, into an internal desert. At the end, despite his tears and protest, Titus does send his two Orientals back to the outer limits of his/their world. He sends them back to "noth-ingness." Through this sacrifice of his pleasure, of his body's desire, this nothing, this *rien*, is all that is left to him. While the Oriental/femi-nine/other is expelled from Rome, the melancholy that Antiochus fled in-vades the space left absent by love.

In a striking chiasmatic inversion, Bérénice, denied her image, denied the narcissistic image of Titus, turns her being, as she learns and accepts her fate, from the site of loss, the sacrifice of her own image to the Law of the Father, into a perfect example of *la dame méréncolye*, that image of a sad, half-maddened woman that the iconographic tradition of the fifteenth and sixteenth centuries had so studiously elaborated:

But how can you receive him so distraught?
Compose yourself. Come to your senses, and
Let me arrange these veils in disarray
And this disheveled hair that hides your eyes.
Let me repair the ravage of your tears.
(IV, ii)[72]

In order to complete the image of melancholy, in order for the tragedy to incorporate at its center the allegory of melancholia, we only have to see this woman reduced to her traditional seated position. In her last con-frontation with Titus, at that moment when death enters onto the scene of this tragedy only to be rendered forever impossible, only to be internalized as a perpetual, permanent exile of love, is this last avatar, the last iconographic stage detail, put in place to afford us this image of the ultimate transformation of the beautiful queen of Palestine into an eternal vision of Melancholia: "Bérénice sinks into a chair."

Didascalia are rare in classical theater. It is therefore particularly striking that this is the only such example in the play and that it comes at the very end, at the juncture of the penultimate and last scenes of the tragedy. At the moment the characters are closest to death, and yet at that moment when death is forever expelled from the tragic universe, Bérénice is shifted before our eyes into that eternal marker of the presence/absence of death. She is transformed into a monument to Melancholia, the woman who has internalized the death of that object — the vision of her love — that she has lost forever.

Death, which has been stalking the characters from the very beginning, appears in the play as a generalized suicidal impulse. Titus comes looking for his sacrificed love. Instead he finds, as he gazes on his suicidal queen, no longer the object of his love but an image of death:

> I come to you without a fixed design.
> My love swept me along. Perhaps I came
> To find myself and recognize myself.
> What do I find? Death painted in your eyes.
> (V, vi)[73]

In order to turn Bérénice away from death, the only ploy Titus can invent is the threat of his own suicide:

> I'll stop at nothing in my present state
> And in the end it may well be my hand
> Will stain with blood our ill-starred last farewell.
> (V, vi)[74]

Finally, in order to complete the circle, Antiochus arrives, confesses to Titus that he has always been his rival for Bérénice's love, and claims that to repay this treachery he, too, has but one option, suicide:

> More is required to break so many ties;
> Only by dying can I sever them.
> I haste toward death . . .
> (V, vi)[75]

Only by a supreme effort on the part of Bérénice does she rise above death, and accepts her loss and its internalization as her most precious possession. She accepts the loss of Titus, without losing the love that she now has internalized as its impossibility, and that she imposes on both of the men, the compromise of sacrifice and remembrance with which the play ends:

Live. Make a noble effort on yourself.
Model your acts on Titus and on me.
I love but flee him. Titus worships me
But parts . . .
. . . Let us, all three, exemplify
The most devoted, tender, ill-starred love
Whose grievous history time will e'er record.
(V, vii)[76]

And it is as exempla that the three remain in our memory as the tragedy
ends, as the curtain falls on this universe bereft of love, reduced to the
immensity of a desert, to a world of death and disillusion, to the last
word, "Hélas," whose emptiness echoes in our ears, forever.

As we leave the theater we take with us the play's last, most striking
image—the allegorical image, with all that allegory contains of ambivalence. The image engraved in our minds is the almost iconographic
depiction of loss. It is a bivalent image, playing as it does with both the
visual and symbolic codes of the play. We are offered the sight of beauty,
of possible pleasure, Bérénice as the forbidden object of desire, at the
very moment that object is effaced by its inscription/prescription in the
Law. This last image, in its poignant equipoise, captured just when it is
about to disappear, represents simultaneously the absence/ presence of
the body, of pleasure under the rule of the Law—its presence, Bérénice,
but its presence as loss, as that which is forever exiled beyond the limits
of patriarchal monarchy.

To Titus's narcissistic pleasuring in his own image of Roman glory,
the stage leaves us with a melancholic last glimpse of his sacrificed other,
of the abandoned body, which had to be extirpated in order for Rome
to continue to exist, in and as the Law—the Law that said "no" to Titus,
that said "no" to his desire, that said "no" to the excessive, feminine,
Oriental queen ("What! you love me, you protest, and yet I leave"). The
law triumphed over the mightiest man in the universe, the man who although he can make and depose kings cannot dispose of his own
heart/body:

Lord of the world, I guide its destiny.
I can make kings and can unsceptre them,
Yet cannot give my heart to whom I choose.
(III, i)[77]

This would seem to be the pernicious last lesson of this new, "absolute"
tragedy. If we see it in allegorical terms as representing the "tragedy of
divine-right monarchy," then under its melancholic guise it proclaims the
advent of a new era of politically subversive totalitarianism. Upon taking
leave of Marie Mancini, Louis XIV shed tears of loss. "You're crying,

you're the master" were supposedly Marie's parting words to him.[78] Titus also cries as he bids farewell to Bérénice: "Your heart was ravaged, and I saw your tears." Finally, the success of this drama whose "tristesse majestueuse" marks the advent of a new tragic is measured in those plentiful tears shed by the audience:

> But neither can I believe that the public would take it amiss that I have given it a tragedy which has been honored by so many tears and the thirtieth performance of which was as well attended as the first.[79]

We shed our bitter/pleasurable tears for the sad fate of these three exemplary leaders, all of whom have shown us, and have shown the king, the cost of duty, the price we all must pay (but in our different stations) to the Law, to Order, to the desire of the absolute.[80] Might we not suggest that these "tears," the sign of sacrifice and loss, recall Oedipus's teary, bloodied eyes: eyes that have seen the terror and chaos produced by unfettered sexuality. That sight, a vision peering into the abyss, blinds the eyes that have seen what should remain invisible. Their loss signals Oedipus's renouncement of chaotic sexuality, his self-imposed castration and the sublimation of his body's desire. That desire has been sacrificed to the obedience to the Law. It is the law of the Father, the space where Narcissus and Oedipus meet and are confined, the law of no, of renunciation, of difference, and of exclusion that structures the possibilities of social life and that permits its perpetuation within order, within history, within the state.

Bérénice is perhaps Racine's most perverse tragedy because what it summons us to witness and to pleasure in is the melancholy sacrifice of our irreducible otherness, of our bodies and loves, to the love of the Father, which leaves us forever bereft, mourning the most intimate part of our being we have sacrificed for his pleasure and, in a strange twist, for our own as well.

Notes

Preface

1. W. Benjamin, "Theses on the Philosophy of History," in *Illuminations*, trans. H. Zohn, ed. and intro. by H. Arendt (New York: Schocken Books, 1969), 256.

2. See M. Foucault, *Les mots et les choses* (Paris: Gallimard, 1966) and *Histoire de la sexualité* (Paris: Gallimard, 1975); J. Lacan, "L'agressivité en psychanalyse," in *Ecrits* (Paris: Seuil, 1966); and also the article by T. Brennan, "The Age of Paranoia," *Journal of Modern Critical Theory* 14, no. 1 (March 1991). As for the "new historians," mostly working in the English tradition, see S. Greenblatt, *Renaissance Self-Fashioning* (Chicago: The University of Chicago Press, 1980), and *Shakespearean Negotiations* (Berkeley: University of California Press, 1988); J. Goldberg, *James I and the Politics of Literature* (Baltimore: The Johns Hopkins University Press, 1983).

3. S. Greenblatt, *Learning to Curse* (New York: Routledge, 1990), 142.

4. Stephen Heath, in "The Ethics of Sexual Difference," *Discourse* (Spring/Summer 1990): 135–36, delineates the differences in the Foucauldian and Lacanian concepts of the "subject." For Foucault, "the making of the subject as a process of subjectification that can be grasped through an analysis of institutions and the knowledge that supports and enables them"; for Lacan, "the subject as constitutively divided, realized in its in-process-as-subject construction; language, unconscious, sexual all bound up in a history that is the fact of the subject. It is no longer a matter of history, of the sexual for the subject but rather of the

subject in the sexual . . . To say 'subject' is to say 'desire.' " Heath continues: "Where Foucault stresses his displacement of the history of sexuality from any necessary link with the law . . . psychoanalysis makes such a link determining — Lacan's 'Law' is there ab origine: there is no question, therefore, of posing the question of origins — the Law is indeed there from the beginning, ever since, and human sexuality must realize itself by and through it." For a feminist rereading of psychoanalytic positioning of the idea of the "subject," see L. Irigaray, *Sexe et parenté* (Paris: Minuit, 1985), as well as her well-known *Speculum de l'autre femme* (Paris: Minuit, 1976). See also J. Butler's discussion of the theories of the subject in psychoanalytic and philosophical theory, *Gender Trouble: Feminism and the Subversion of Identity* (New York: Routledge, 1990).

Introduction

1. The concept of the general crisis of the seventeenth century was first put forth by a series of articles that appeared in the early 1950s in the British journal *Past and Present*. The majority of these articles, including the controversial "The General Crisis of the Seventeenth Century" by H. R. Trevor-Roper, were collected and republished in *Crisis in Europe, 1560–1660*, ed. T. Aston (London: Routledge and Kegan Paul, 1965). Roland Mousnier in *Les XVIe et XVIIe siècles* (Paris: P.U.F., 1953) had also used the concept of "crise" to define the major intellectual, political, and economic changes of the period. In this study I will be using the term "seventeenth century" in the sense that E. LeRoy Ladurie does in his book *L'Etat royal 1460–1610* (Paris: Hachette, 1987) when he refers to the period 1560–1715 as "le long dix-septième siècle" (61).

2. This sentiment seems so well documented that it barely needs further comment. It suffices to recall the prominent names of Machiavelli, Montaigne, Bacon, and Descartes, all of whom bore literary and political witness to this sense of instability. Donne's "Anatomie of the World," "The First Anniversarie" (1611) will serve as an example from English poetry:

> And new Philosophy calls all in doubt,
> The Element of fire is quite put out . . .
> And freely men confess that this world's spent,
> When in the Planets, and the Firmament
> They seek so many new; then see that this
> Is crumbled out again to his Atomies.
> 'Tis all in pieces, all coherence gone;
> All just supply, and all Relation.

Reading the privileged political actors of the time, Richelieu, Olivares, James I, Louis XIV, we hear the same anxious echoes. This description from Richelieu's *Testament politique* reveals the perceived political chaos: "When your majesty decided both to allow me into his State Councils and to grant me a large measure of his confidence in the direction of his other affairs, I can state unequivocally that the Huguenots shared the State with your majesty, that the grandees of the realm behaved as if they were not subjects, and that the powerful provincial Governors acted as if they were themselves sovereigns in their respective bailiwicks. I can further state that foreign alliances were neglected, that private interests were preferred to public concerns, and that, in a word, the dignity of Royal Majesty was terribly debased and so far from being what it should have been" [*Testament politique*, ed. L. Andreé (Paris: Laffont, 1947), 93–94].

3. See G. Parker, *Europe in Crisis, 1598–1648* (Ithaca: Cornell University Press, 1979). Also, T. Rabb, *The Struggle for Stability in Early Modern Europe* (Oxford: Oxford University Press, 1975); and R. Mandrou, *Sorciers et Magistrats en France au XVII* (Paris: Seuil, 1980).

4. See, for instance, Lieuwe van Aitzema, *Saken van Staet ende Oorlog, III* (Amsterdam, 1669) [quoted in G. Parker and L. Smith, eds., *The General Crisis of the Seventeenth Century* (London: Routledge and Kegan Paul, 1978), 1].

5. Quoted in G. Parker and L. Smith, Introduction, *The General Crisis of the Seventeenth Century*, 3.

6. Louis XIV, *Mémoires*, ed. J. Longnon (Paris: Tallandier, 1978), 33.

7. E. Enriquez, *De la horde à l'Etat: essais de psychanalyse du lien social* (Paris: Gallimard, 1985), 101.

8. See Enriquez, who, elaborating on Freud (particularly on Freud's discussion of the role of the primal father in *Totem and Taboo*), writes: "Freud does not deny that individuals can live alongside each other, he simply believes that they cannot exist as a group, as a 'people' without reference to a 'unique' [subject]; the 'people' is thus formed by individuals who are joined together by libidinal force, and this libido cannot traverse the social sphere unless it emanates from an individual who can conjure it up, or, like the father of the primal horde, reject it" (*De la horde*, 144).

9. See E. Hobsbawm, "The Crisis of the Seventeenth Century," in *Crisis in Europe, 1560–1660*, ed. T. Aston. "Only in one respect did the seventeenth century as a whole overcome rather than experience difficulties . . . Most of Europe found an efficient and stable form of government in absolutism on the French model" (12).

10. See, for example, R. Williams; *The Country and the City* (New York: Oxford University Press, 1973), and *Problems in Materialism and Culture: Selected Essays* (London: N.L.B., 1980).

11. Mousnier, *Les XVIe et XVII siècles*, 249.

12. N. Keohane, *Philosophy and the State in France* (Princeton: Princeton University Press, 1980), 17.

13. G. Balandier, *Pouvoirs sur scène* (Paris: Balland, 1980), 19. I have discussed this problematics in greater detail in my study of French drama of the period, *Subjectivity and Subjugation in Seventeenth-Century Drama and Prose: The Family Romance of French Classicism* (Cambridge: Cambridge University Press, 1992); the following paragraphs are borrowed from the Introduction to that work.

14. M. de Certeau, *La Fable mystique*, vol. 1 (Paris: Gallimard, 1982), 32. See also his *Heterologies: Discourse on the Other* (Minneapolis: University of Minnesota Press, 1985). For a general speculation on the problem, the "other," see François Hartog, *Le Miroir d'Hérodote: Essai sur la représentation de l'Autre* (Paris: Gallimard, 1980).

15. E. Kantorowicz, *The King's Two Bodies: A Study in Medieval Political Theology* (Princeton: Princeton University Press, 1957).

I am using the terms "representation," "deterritorialized," and "boundary-less" as they are employed by G. Deleuze and F. Guattari in *L'Anti-oedipe* (Paris: Minuit, 1972). Enriquez speaks about the symbolic importance of the "leader" in modern-day "party politics" and, it seems to me, nicely summarizes the role the leader/king plays in seventeenth-century Europe: "It is indispensable that this party have at its head a leader who manifests enough charisma and who is at the same time capable of both symbolizing and incarnating the Nation and the State in their permanence so that the majority of the people can have the feeling that the social corpus finds its unity and its identity in a physical body, whose beauty, allure, force, or wealth it can admire" (*De la horde*, 334). Surely this was also the function of all seventeenth-century monarchs.

16. In the Introduction to his edition of R. Filmer's *Patriarcha* (Oxford: Blackwell, 1949), Peter Laslett writes: "the analogy between the family and the state is, of course, so obvious . . . it appears so frequently in the writings of the sixteenth and seventeenth centuries, and it occupies such an important place in so many of them, that it can be justifiably

supposed that its use during this period was one of the reflections of patriarchal institutions"
(27).

17. Ibid., 28: "It is obvious . . . that the use of the family analogy created a presumption in favour of monarchy. It is also to be expected that sooner or later the two societies would be merged into one, and that thinkers would be found who could claim that the King *was* the father and the family *was* the state."

18. Filmer, *Patriarcha*, ed. Laslett, 63.

19. *Mémoires*, 111, 221.

20. J. L. Flandrin, *Le sexe et l'Occident* (Paris: Seuil, 1981), and *Familles, parenté, maison, sexualité dans l'ancienne société* (Paris: 1976); P. Ariès, *L'enfant et la vie familiale sous l'Ancien Régime* (Paris: Seuil, 1973); P. Shorter, *The Making of the Modern Family* (New York: Basic Books, 1975); P. Laslett, *The World We Have Lost* (London: Methuen, 1971).

21. M. Foucault, *The History of Sexuality*, vol. 1, trans. Robert Hurley (New York: Random House, 1978), 108. Cf. also this remark of J. Solé: "The new mercantilist monarchy was as equally concerned with inculcating a moral standard in its subjects as it was about putting them to work. Its struggle against illegitimate sexuality was an integral part of its general policy of close surveillance and control of individuals" [*L'amour en occident à l'époque moderne* (Paris: Albin Michel, 1976), 100].

22. Writing about the intense ambivalences toward the father, the French psychoanalyst Guy Rosolato states: "As for the murder of the father I would offer the hypothesis that in the myths of monotheism it never appears directly. The entire project has, in fact, as its aim to avoid its accomplishment. We must therefore come to the conclusion that this murder remains the hidden kernel, the secret, in relation to which are organized all the sacrificial substitutions through which the alliance comes into being" [*Le sacrifice: repères psychanalytiques* (Paris: P.U.F., 1987), 74].

23. "There was a sense of security when the monarch was personally in charge of things, a trust in the benevolence of his will, which can only be explained by the belief that he apprehended and spoke for the good of the entire society in a way no other human being could approach" (Keohane, *Philosophy and the State in France*, 59).

24. Enriquez, elaborating on Freud's insights, writes: "Both ambivalence of feeling and aggressivity characterize, structurally, the father-son relation. The son is and always remains the person who wants the father's death in order, in his turn, to become a subject and a father" and "the father is always both a censor and an object of identification, the son is always the creator and destroyer of his father" (*De la horde*, 246, 247).

25. I am aware of the long tradition, exacerbated by the religious controversies of the sixteenth century, of antimonarchical writings (*Vindicae contra tyrannos, ou Le Reveille-matin des Gaulois*, or Etienne de la Boétie's *Discours de la Servitude Volontaire*, for instance, in France). Nevertheless, even in these writings the sacred person of the "just monarch" was affirmed at the same time that the evil "king" was effaced under the figure of the "tyrant."

26. Rosolato, in *Le sacrifice*, talks about the ambivalent role of the king/*pharmakos*: "The similarity between the king (we could as well say the monarch or the dictator) and the sacrificial victim has been noticed: his power and ascendancy are effectively exercised precisely in relation to the danger that he attracts, that remains suspended over his head and that he conjures up. His position as an exceptional being binds him to the victim as to an oppositional pole toward which he could easily swing, in a defeat, in an assassination, in a coup d'état" (88). For the particular case of France, see the sociological perspectives of J. M. Apostolidès, *Le Prince Sacrifié: Théâtre et Politique au temps de Louis XIV* (Paris: Minuit, 1985).

27. S. Freud, *Group Psychology and the Analysis of the Ego* (New York: Norton, 1959), 12.

28. Ibid., 13.

29. Enriquez, *De la horde*, 169: "the social contract is a passionate and not a rational bond."

30. See L. Marin, *Portrait of the King*, trans. Martha M. Houle (Minneapolis: University of Minnesota Press, 1988), 237: "Thus the secret of the absolute monarch, the ethical secret, the retreat from the statesman in his portrait, the secret of the all-powerful king, is that he is not so; a hidden thought, never spoken, a thought that is perhaps never thought — and there would be the force of the figure, of the fiction, of the figurative, to think that thought — that of the impossibility of forgetting that he is not what he is." For an analysis of court life, see N. Elias, *The Court Society* (New York: Knopf, 1980).

31. As the most hyperbolic example, consider d'Aubignac's description of Louis XIV: "In conclusion the glory and the grandeur of Spectacles could no better come than from he who himself became the most glorious and the greatest Spectacle in the world" [*La practique du théâtre* (Paris: 1649), 15]. For a modern analysis of representation as power, especially in the English context, see S. Orgel, *The Illusion of Power: Political Theater in the English Renaissance* (Berkeley: University of California Press, 1975); for France (and England), see T. Murray, *Theatrical Legitimation* (New York: Oxford University Press, 1987).

32. For the importance of spectacle in the "construction" of the absolute monarch, see, for England, Orgel, *The Illusion of Power*, and J. Goldberg, *James I and the Politics of Literature* (Baltimore: The Johns Hopkins University Press, 1983); for France, Marin, *Portrait of the King*, and J. M. Apostolidès, *Le roi machine* (Paris: Minuit, 1981), and *Le prince sacrifié* (Paris: Minuit, 1985); for Spain, J. Brown and J. H. Elliott, *A Palace for a King* (New Haven: Yale University Press, 1980), and J. M. Diez-Borque, *Sociedad y teatro en la España de Lope de Vega* (Barcelona: A. Bosch, 1978). The recent book by A.-M. Lecoq, *François I, imaginaire* (Paris: Macula, 1989), is an important new contribution to this discussion.

33. See J. Barish, *The Antitheatrical Prejudice* (Berkeley: University of California Press, 1981), for an overview of the heated debate surrounding the role and social function of theater in the sixteenth and seventeenth centuries.

34. Some of the arguments I developed in the Introduction to *Subjectivity and Subjugation in Seventeenth-Century Theater and Prose: The Family Romance of French Classicism* are reelaborated here. I am readdressing the problems raised in that book and expanding my area of inquiry to the larger European arena.

35. A. Green, *The Tragic Effect*, trans. A. Sheridan (London: Cambridge University Press, 1979), 7–8.

36. Greenberg, Introduction to *Subjectivity and Subjugation*, 9–23.

37. See S. Freud, "Family Romances," *The Standard Edition of the Complete Psychological Works of S. Freud*, trans. J. Strachey (London: Hogarth Press and the Institute for Psychoanalysis, 1981), 9:237–41.

38. S. Mullaney, *The Place of the Stage: License, Play and Power in Renaissance England* (Chicago: The University of Chicago Press, 1988). Here would perhaps be the best place to offer a brief summary of the different approaches taken by contemporary historians to the "general crisis of the seventeenth century." The generalized malaise that distinguishes the seventeenth century has intrigued historical commentators of the period at least since Voltaire. Situated between the world of the Renaissance and the triumph of the Enlightenment, the seventeenth century figures a transitional moment in European history. It is a fraught moment in which competing ideologies, economic systems, religions, and familial structures vie for dominance. Like other great periods of historical transitions it is marked by uncertainty, fear, and trauma, but also, almost perversely, by some of the greatest literary, artistic, and scientific creations in the Western tradition. One has only to think of Shakespeare, Cervantes, Milton, Racine, Velázquez, Rubens, Van Dyck, Descartes, Spinoza, and Newton to realize that this century of trauma was also a period of enormous and breathtaking achievements — in the words of the Spanish social historian J. M. Diez-Borque, a "siglo de oro y de miseria" (*Sociedad y teatro*, 247). The redeployment of human knowledge during the Renaissance marks a high point in Western culture and at the same

time and by the very same token sows the seeds of the turmoil that convulses Europe from the late sixteenth century onward. The great innovations of the fifteenth and early sixteenth centuries resulted in the fracturing of the unity of the Roman church, the discovery of worlds unsuspected by the ancients, and the scientific revolution of the heavens.

European thought was sent reeling as the unity of a millennium was fractured and dispersed. This sense of fragmentation was not limited to metaphysical angst; it was also a horrific and indelible physical trauma. From the last decades of the sixteenth century to Louis XIV's personal reign (1660 — these dates are relative, not absolute) European society was thus brutalized by enormous and conflicting upheavals in the social fabric. (Consider the generalized judgment of H. R. Trevor-Roper in "The General Crisis of the Seventeenth Century," 31: "The middle of the seventeenth century was a period of revolution in Europe . . . To contemporary observers it seemed that society itself was in crisis and that this crisis was general in Europe . . . The various countries of Europe seemed merely the separate theaters upon which the same great tragedy was being simultaneously, though in different languages and with local variations, played out.") Political unrest flares up in isolated but also, at times, national "revolutions." The English Puritan revolution and the French "Frondes" are perhaps the most spectacular but certainly not the only threats to the body politic. In Portugal, Spain, and the "Holy Roman Empire," national revolts only added to the impression that an entire order of things was irrevocably rent. (See Parker, *Europe in Crisis, 1598–1648*; Rabb, *The Struggle for Stability in Early Modern Europe*; and Parker and Smith, eds., *The General Crisis of the Seventeenth Century*.) The sundry reasons underlying this generalized social malaise have been examined in minute detail by historians, without, however, the emergence of any universal consensus. For some, and here E. Hobsbawm, is the most eloquent spokesman, the general crisis of seventeenth-century Europe is essentially an economic one: the period, Hobsbawm argues, marks the transition from the declining economic structures of feudalism to the emerging order of bourgeois capitalism. European economy gradually shifts from an essentially feudal agrarian structure to the (pre)capitalist ventures of the emerging mercantile powers — Holland, England, and, with a bit of a delay, France (see his essay "The Crisis of the Seventeenth Century," in *Crisis in Europe, 1560–1660*, ed. T. Aston, 5–58). For others, the crisis is more directly political: having undergone a period of enormous religious and social upheaval in the sixteenth century, the monarchies of Europe are gradually, under the sway of economic and social forces, moving away from an antiquated, "Aristotelian" concept of shared monarchy — shared between the different feudal orders of the "corporations," the grandees, and the king — to a more modern form of centralized, bureaucratized government. What we see emerging in the England of James I, in the Spain of Olivares and Philip IV, and in the France of Richelieu and Louis XIII, is a new concept of sovereignty. Supported by the writings of sixteenth-century political theorists, of whom Jean Bodin is perhaps the most illustrious example, a new "absolutist" conception of the state and its government emerges and eventually imposes itself on Europe (see in particular Mousnier, "Les nouvelles structures de l'Etat," *Les XVIe et XVIIe siècles*, 110–63). This government, situated in the expanding urban centers of Europe, comes, according to Trevor-Roper, into ever-greater conflict with the more austere ("puritan") strains of the country (see his essay "The General Crisis . . . . " and the responses to it by R. Mousnier, and J. H. Elliott, reprinted in *Crisis in Europe, 1560–1660*, ed. T. Aston). Modern students of this transitional period appear only to echo what was the shocked and anguished sentiment of those seventeenth-century witnesses whose testimonies have come down to us; (see Lieuwe van Aitzema, *Saken van Staet ende Oorlog, III* (Amsterdam, 1669); G. B. Birago Avogadro, *Delle historie memorabili che contiene le sollevationi di stato de nostri tempi* (Venice, 1654); and J. Bisaccioni, *Historia delle Guerre civili di questi ultimi tempi* (Venice, 1653), all quoted in Parker, *Europe in Crisis, 1598–1648*, or Parker and Smith, eds., *The General Crisis of the Seventeenth Century*.

39. For the relation between the theater and institutional (both governmental and ec-clesiastical) authority, see, for England, S. Greenblatt, *Shakespearean Negotiations* (Berkeley: University of California Press, 1988) and Goldberg, *James I and the Politics of Literature*; for Spain, J. A. Maravall, *Teatro y literatura en la sociedad barroca* (Madrid: Seminarios y Edi-ciones, 1972) and Diez-Borque, *Sociedad y teatro en la España de Lope de Vega*; for France, A. Adam, *Histoire de la littérature française au XVII siècle*, 5 vols. (Paris: del Duca, 1962).

40. See A. Ubersfeld, *Lire le théâtre* (Paris: Editions Sociales, 1977), 15: "The theater strikes us as a privileged art form because it shows better than any other form of art how the individual psyche becomes invested in a collective relation. The spectator is never alone, his gaze at the same time that it takes in what is shown to him, takes in all the other specta-tors, who in turn embrace him in their gaze." Also, H. Blau, *Audience* (Baltimore: The Johns Hopkins University Press, 1991), 42: "What is surrendered by the audience in its identifica-tion with (that) character is precisely a personal identity and more unexpectedly, if not scan-dalously, a social identity."

41. Green, *The Tragic Effect*, defines the theatrical situation in the following way: "Be-tween the two, at the meeting-point of the individual and society, between the personal res-onance of the work's content and its social function, art occupies a transitional position, which qualifies the domain of illusion, which permits an inhibited and restrained jouissance obtained by means of objects that both are and are not what they represent" (23).

42. Mullaney, *The Place of the Stage*, 130.

43. F. Moretti, "A Huge Eclipse," *Genre* 15 (1982): 29.

44. L. Althusser, *Positions* (Paris: Editions Sociales, 1970), 103. For an English transla-tion, see L. Althusser, *Lenin and Philosophy and Other Essays*, trans. Ben Brewster (London: MR Press, 1971), 162. Also, "in ideology men represent their real conditions of existence to themselves in an imaginary form" (ibid., 163).

45. F. Jameson, *The Political Unconscious* (Ithaca: Cornell University Press, 1981), 7: "ideology is not something which informs or invests symbolic production, rather the aes-thetic art is itself ideological, and the production of aesthetic or narrative forms is to be seen as an ideological act in its own right, with the function of inventing imaginary or 'formal' solutions to irresolvable social contradictions."

46. See Ubersfeld, *Lire le théâtre*, 15, as quoted in note 40.

47. Green, *The Tragic Effect*, 2.

48. P. Smith, *Discerning the Subject* (Minneapolis: University of Minnesota Press, 1988), 68.

49. In "Function and Field of Speech and Language," in *Ecrits: A Selection*, trans. A. Sheridan (London: Tavistock, 1977), Lacan talks about "rememoration" (that is, the narra-tive by which the analysand re-creates his or her past) and distinguishes between truth (*vérité*) and reality (*réalité*): "in psychoanalytic anamnesis, it is not a question of reality, but of truth, because the effect of full speech is to reorder past contingencies by conferring on them the sense of necessities to come, such as they are constituted by the little freedom through which the subject makes them present" (48). If we consider theater as a collective act, in which and by which a society narrates itself to itself, we can see that although this narration may not be "real" for the purposes of historical accuracy, it will be for the ideology underpinning the narration a "true" (though not necessarily dependable) narration. This is also perhaps the place to indicate my debt to the French theoretician of the theater, Anne Ubersfeld, who in *Lire le théâtre* points out the "a-subjective" role of the theater by underlin-ing its communal nature. But it is precisely in this communal space, the space of the au-dience and the actors, that the theater both avoids individual subjectivity and yet places the individual within a collective "truth": "We can only say [write] what can be heard: positively or negatively [by self-censure] the 'scriptor' responds to the public's demand . . . Every

theatrical text is the response to the public's desire, and it is here that one can most easily articulate the relation of theatrical discourse to history and ideology" (*Lire le théâtre*, 265).

50. This, of course, would be the way Oedipus is defined, as always a "representation" that attempts to harness and circumscribe uncontrollable movements ("flux"), by G. Deleuze and F. Guattari, *Anti-Oedipus*, trans. R. Hurley et al. (Minneapolis: University of Minnesota Press, 1983): "Yes, Oedipus is universal . . . In reality it is universal because it is the displacement of the limit that haunts all societies, the displaced represented (*le représenté déplacé*) that disfigures what all societies dread absolutely as their most profound negative: namely, the decoded flows of desire" (177).

51. I am borrowing the term "lieux de mémoire" from Pierre Nora. See his Introduction to *Les lieux de mémoire, I. La République* (Paris: Gallimard, 1984).

52. See J. J. Goux, *Oedipe philosophe* (Paris: Aubier, 1991), speaks eloquently to my purpose here by talking about the relation uniting Oedipus and "History": "A close tie links Oedipus to History. Ideally in a society without "History" based primarily on the repetitive transmission from generation to generation of an intact tradition, a figure such as Oedipus could not take on an essential meaning. This figure would be but an aberration. Thus, any culture that lives History as a second nature, any society that tears itself away from repetition and experiences something like "progress," "development," permanent "innovation," is oedipal; it is a society torn asunder at its very heart, in its fate and its spirit, by the tragedy of Oedipus" (201).

For a brief history of the Renaissance revival of the Oedipus myth and Sophocles' play, see P. Rudnytsky, *Freud and Oedipus* (New York: Columbia University Press, 1987), 96–97. For more detailed explanations, particularly about the history and influence of Aristotle's *Poetics*, which is in great part responsible for the canonical position of Sophocles' play, see B. Weinberg, *A History of Literary Criticism in the Italian Renaissance* (Chicago: The University of Chicago Press, 1961), 350–52.

53. Rudnytsky, *Freud and Oedipus*, 97. I am indebted to Rudnytsky's work for most of the historical documentation of the play's history and productions. See also N. Lukacher's remark: "I am suggesting that the 'oedipal' is synonymous with the crisis of the subject, and that traces of such a crisis mark all the great texts of the tradition" (238); see his discussion of "Oedipus Politicus" in *Primal Scenes: Literature, Philosophy, Psychoanalysis* (Ithaca: Cornell University Press, 1986), 238–247.

54. The egregious example of Pierre Corneille comes to mind, who in his 1659 version of the play demonstrated that he both knew and refused to know, or rather refused to "see," the full impact of Oedipus. He writes these telling lines in his introduction to explain why he has transformed the story into a drama of love from which the horror of Oedipus's fate, his putting out of his eyes, is excluded: "I understood that what had been considered prodigious in the time of the ancients would seem horrible in our period; that that marvelous and eloquent description that takes up the entire fifth act of how this unhappy prince blinds himself would certainly offend the sensibilities of our ladies, whose discomfit would surely spread to the rest of the audience. It is these reasons that led me to hide so hazardous a sight from the eyes (of my audience)" [Corneille, "Examen" to *Oedipe*, in *Oeuvres complètes*, vol. 3, ed. G. Couton (Paris: Gallimard, 1987), 20].

55. G. Rosolato, "Trois générations d'hommes dans le mythe religieux et la généalogie," in *Essais sur le symbolique* (Paris: Gallimard, 1969), 92. For another reading of the importance of the Oedipus "myth" for (Lacanian) psychoanalysis, see S. Felman, "Beyond Oedipus: The Specimen Story of Psychoanalysis," in *Jacques Lacan and the Adventure of Insight* (Cambridge: Harvard University Press, 1987) 99–159.

56. In this same sense Goux talks about Descartes as an "oedipal" philosopher, marking one more important aspect of the seventeenth century's renaissance of Oedipus. See *Oedipe philosophe*, 165–66: "In no philosopher more than in Descartes can we recognize the oedipal

strategy at work. It is in this sense, and rightly so, that his thought strikes us as the beginnings of a philosophy of modernity. For Descartes the orderly form of the method (of the progression of his thought, its assured forward movement) rigorously imitates the major moments of Oedipus' story. . . . Of course, I am not speaking here of a simple transposition, but of the particular insistence of a configuration of thought, of a decisive deepening of a certain regimen of subjectivity, that was prefigured, in spite of all the differences, by the oedipal stance. 'Murder of the father,' 'response to the Sphinx,' '(sexual) possession of the mother.' Each of these three great moments in the heroic oedipal drama can be recognized in the three major steps in Descartes' progress."

57. J. P. Vernant, "Ambiguïté et renversement. Sur la structure énigmatique d'*Oedipe Roi,*" in J. P. Vernant and P. Vidal-Naquet, *Oedipe et ses mythes* (Brussels: Editions Complexe, 1988), 36: "The God-King, purifier and savior of his people, is confused with the sullied criminal that must be exiled as a 'pharmakos,' a scapegoat so that the newly cleansed city can be saved."

58. Marie Delcourt convincingly demonstrates the inextricable weaving between the Oedipus legend as we know it (that is, she says, already in a late form) with the entire tradition of "habilitation à la royauté," which she shows almost always passes through the winning and espousal of a princess. See *Oedipe ou la légende*, 209: "How can we not remember that the legend of Oedipus, who marries his mother, groups together all the various themes of royal habilitation?" Goux, *Oedipe philosophe*, 30–32, takes up this same point.

59. See Vernant, "Ambiguïté et renversement," 44: "God/King-pharmakos: these are the two faces of Oedipus that give him his enigmatic aspect by joining in him, as in an ambivalent conundrum, two figures, each the opposite of the other."

60. For the role and influence of Oedipus as "philosopher," see Goux, *Oedipe philosophe*, especially chapters 8 and 9, "Philosophie I" and "Philosophie II."

61. Delcourt, *Oedipe ou la légende*, 110: "All these beings (e.g., Sphinx, Erinyes, Keres, Harpies) hunger after food and erotic pleasure."

62. See Goux, *Oedipe philosophe*, 98: "Oedipus could very well have been destined to become the model of the philosopher, the eponymous hero of the complex of the nuclear family and thus the paradigm of the pharmakos, the sacrificial victim." Also: "Oedipus . . . can be seen to represent the bridge to an anthrocentric culture. It is a passage from myth to rationality, the birth of the individual as an autonomous agent and juridical subject, the quest for a compromise of divergent viewpoints, a democratic debate that founds politics . . . " (128).

63. S. Heath, "The Ethics of Sexual Difference," *Discourse* (Spring-Summer 1990): 128.

64. For the role of women and the feminine in ancient Greek society, the recent work of Nicole Loraux is essential; see *Les enfant d'Athéna: Idées athéniennes sur la citoyenneté et la division des sexes* (Paris: Maspero, 1981), *Façons tragiques de tuer une femme* (Paris: Hachette, 1985), and *Les expériences de Tirésias: le féminin et l'homme grec* (Paris: Gallimard, 1989). See also L. Irigaray, " . . . l'éternelle ironie de la communauté," *Speculum, d'autre femme* (Paris: Minuit, 1974), 266–81; and the recent work of P. DuBois, in particular *Sowing the Body: Psychoanalysis and Ancient Representations of Women* (Chicago: The University of Chicago Press, 1988).

65. See Deleuze and Guattari, who, in *Anti-Oedipus*, talk about Oedipus as a form of colonization: "Oedipus is always colonization pursued by other means . . . where we Europeans are concerned, it is our intimate colonial education" (170). Goux, talking about Oedipus at Colonnus, and the political import of this final act of the oedipal myth, writes: "And doesn't Oedipus with this secret to be left to the future kings of Athens who will reign after Theseus, become the founder of a symbolic line, a line that will no longer pass from father to son but from sovereign to sovereign? Isn't Oedipus by this originatory act the inaugurator of the authentic ritual of royal initiation?" (*Oedipe philosophe*, 191–92).

66. Rosolato discusses the political import of this myth in the following way: "By bringing to the light of day the fantasies and the obsessional mechanism centered on the murder of the father, Freud allows us to understand their social purpose, e.g., the covenant or the 'social contract' that is built upon the shared guilt that arises from similar (individual) fantasies" (*Le sacrifice*, 139).

67. See the Introduction to M. Foucault, *Les mots et les choses* (Paris: Gallimard, 1966), passim.

68. Enriquez writes: "The destiny (fate) of the great leader is to be killed. This is the single condition required in order for nations ["peuples"] to exist, thus the following paradox: without a great leader, there can be no nation (people); without the murder of the great leader there can also be no nation" (*De la horde*, 144).

69. Freud, writing in *Totem and Taboo* (*Standard Edition* 13:156), offers an explanation of why tragic heroes are tragic precisely in order to be heroes: "But why did the hero of the tragedy have to suffer? . . . He had to suffer because he was the primal father, the hero of that primordial tragedy the repetition of which here serves a certain tendency, and the tragic guilt is the guilt which he had to take upon himself in order to free the chorus of their own."

70. See Rosolato, *Le sacrifice*: "The sacrificial victim establishes the boundary between the outside and the inside. The sacrifice is effective only within the limits of the tribe" (87) and "each sacrifice must be a point of departure, a new origin" (47).

71. See R. Girard, *La violence et le sacré* (Paris: Grasset, 1972), and *Le bouc émissaire* (Paris: Grasset, 1982), as well as Rosolato, *Le sacrifice*. I am perfectly aware of Girard's attack on the Freudian scenario. It seems, nevertheless, disingenuous on his part to negate a scenario that clearly informs his thinking on the subject. For this reason I insist that his thought is inspired by Freud even if he attempts to reject Freud's notion of the Oedipal myth.

72. Rosolato, *Le sacrifice*, 75: "Let's think about the characteristics of the sacrificial victim: his innocence and humanity, but especially his fragility, are the exact opposites of the all-powerful, savage Ideal Father, collectively hated and guilty for all his arbitrary acts of violence." See also W. Burkert, *Homo Necans* (Berkeley: University of California Press, 1983).

73. R. Girard, *Violence and the Sacred*, trans. P. Gregory (Baltimore: The Johns Hopkins University Press, 1977), 252: "All the episodes of the Oedipus myth are repetitions of one another. Once we recognize this fact it becomes apparent that all the figures in the various episodes are monsters and that their resemblance is far closer than appearance alone might suggest. Oedipus . . . is a monster . . . "

74. Vernant claims that through Sophocles' retelling of the myth Oedipus becomes "the model of the human condition" ("Ambiguïté et renversement," 44).

75. Rosolato, *Le sacrifice*, 83–123.

76. A. Green, *The Tragic Effect*, 210.

77. G. Rosolato, *La relation d'inconnu* (Paris: Gallimard, 1978), 87: "However, psychoanalysts since Freud have revealed in this schema another latent vector, all the more disguised as the patriarchal system is all the more powerful. Beneath the disguise of the slaughter of the son we can insinuate desires for the murder of the father. The sacrificial victim, a substitute, stands in for, represents, the father . . . "

78. As Goux remarks, both sides of this coin exist together in the myth; it is a question of social parameters that privilege one or the other. See *Oedipe philosophe*, 183: "There is no surprise if Freud discovers at the same time both the unconscious and the two oedipal impulses. The self-consciousness (*conscience de soi*) of the modern subject is formed as a 're-sponse to Oedipus,' which leaves, however, in the shadows the two never-extirpated impulses that traverse Oedipus's fate. It is not only this self-consciousness, the self-reflected

egocentricity, that is oedipal, as Hegel so magisterially understood, but it is also the desiring unconscious response that this answer also engenders, as Freud discovered. If consciousness is constituted as 'a response to the Sphinx,' the unconscious is the shadow of instinctual drives that falls across this answer: parricide, incest."

79. Marie Delcourt appears to suggest a similar move in the evolution of the Oedipus myth itself. She sees it evolving from a mainly political myth (Oedipus in his functions as king) to a "sentimental" (i.e., "sexual") component. See *Oedipe ou la légende*, 15: "If all the mythographers have conflated these two dangers (i.e., kill the father, marry the mother) it is because from Aeschylus to them the legend had evolved: political at its origins, it had become more and more 'sentimental,' and the theme of incest had relentlessly become more important."

1. Shakespeare's *Othello* and the "Problem" of Anxiety

All quotations from *Othello* are from *Shakespeare's "Othello,"* ed. D. Bevington (New York: Bantam, 1980).

1. See E. M. Tillyard, *The Elizabethan World Picture* (Hammondsworth: Penguin, 1963).

2. For an overview of the idea of a "crisis" in the seventeenth century, see *Crisis in Europe, 1560-*1660, ed. T. Aston (London: Routledge and Kegan Paul, 1965). M. Foucault's two studies, *Les mots et les choses* (Paris: Gallimard, 1966) and *Histoire de la folie à l'époque classique* (Paris: Gallimard, 1965), provide an essential hypothesis for understanding, philosophically, the changes in the metaphysical apparatus of the period. Interesting histories of sexuality and the family can be found in L. Stone, *The Family, Sex and Marriage in England, 1500-1800* (New York: Harper and Row, 1977); J. L. Flandrin, *Familles, parenté, maison, sexualité dans l'ancienne société* (Paris: Seuil, 1976) and *Le sexe et l'Occident* (Paris: Seuil, 1981); P. Ariès, *L'enfant et la vie familiale sous l'Ancien Régime* (Paris: Seuil, 1973); P. Shorter, *The Making of the Modern Family* (New York: Basic Books, 1975); and P. Laslett, *The World We Have Lost* (London: Methuen, 1971).

3. S. Freud, *The Problem of Anxiety* (New York: Norton, 1963), 65. The proximity of danger is the central point of a Lacanian notion of anxiety, according to S. Zizek, *Looking Awry: An Introduction to J. Lacan through Popular Culture* (Cambridge: M.I.T. Press, 1991), who states: "what provokes anxiety is not the loss of the incestuous object but on the contrary its very proximity" (146). For the particular case of *Othello*, see E. Snow, "Sexual Anxiety and the Male Order of Things in *Othello*," *English Literary Renaissance* 10, no. 3 (Autumn 1980): 384-413; for the idea of the "catharsis" of anxiety, see N. Lukacher, "Anamorphic Stuff: Shakespeare, Catharsis, Lacan," *South Atlantic Quarterly* 88, no. 4 (Fall 1989): 863-98.

4. Examples abound, especially in the writings of religious propagandists such as d'Aubigné, du Bartas, and La Boétie. The now-classical work of E. Kantorowicz, *The King's Two Bodies: A Study in Medieval Political Theology* (Princeton: Princeton University Press, 1957), while concentrating on the medieval aspects of the metaphor in its particular relation to English theological and legal theory, describes in great detail how common the image of the body became in the representation attempts at describing the "commonwealth." For an analysis of the French tradition, see L. Marin, *La parole mangée* (Paris: Klinsckieck, 1986).

5. J. Butler, *Gender Trouble* (New York: Routledge, 1989), goes on to gloss Douglas in the following terms: "All social systems are vulnerable at their margins, and all margins are accordingly considered dangerous. If the body is synecdochical for the social system per se or a site in which open systems converge, then any kind of unregulated permeability constitutes a site of pollution and endangerment" (132).

6. Stone, *Family, Sex and Marriage*, 216-17.

7. S. Greenblatt, *Shakespearean Negotiations* (Berkeley: University of California Press, 1988), 34.

8. Ibid., 137.

9. See, for instance, the several books of René Girard, particularly *La violence et le sacré* (Paris: Grasset, 1972) and *Le bouc émissaire* (Paris: Grasset, 1982). In this chapter I will be influenced, however, by the more directly psychoanalytical approach of G. Rosolato in his *Le sacrifice: repères psychanalytiques* (Paris: P.U.F., 1987) and his essay "Trois générations d'hommes dans la mythologie et la généalogie," *Essais sur le symbolique* (Paris: Gallimard, 1969). Finally, two interesting attempts to interpret the political development of scapegoating in and through psychoanalysis are E. Sagan, *At the Dawn of Tyranny* (New York: Knopf, 1985), and E. Enriquez, *De la horde à l'Etat: essais de psychanalyse du lien social* (Paris: Gallimard, 1983). W. Burkert, *Structure and History in Greek Mythology and Ritual* (Berkeley: University of California Press, 1979) deals with scapegoating as a result of social anxiety in ancient Greek culture.

10. S. Mullaney, *The Place of the Stage: License, Play and Power in Renaissance England* (Chicago: The University of Chicago Press, 1988), 92

11. For the entire complicated question of the shift in world economic and cultural dominance from the sphere of the Mediterranean powers (Venice and Istanbul) to the hegemony of the colonialist countries of the Atlantic (Spain, France, and England), see the essential work by F. Braudel, *La Méditerrané et le Monde Méditerranéen à l'Epoque de Philippe II*, 2 vols. (Paris: A. Colin, 1966) [trans. S. Reynolds, *The Mediterranean and the Mediterranean World in the Age of Philip II* (New York: Harper and Row, 1973)].

12. For the importance of the "myth" of Venice for Elizabethan England, see J. Goldberg, *James I and the Politics of Literature* (Baltimore: The Johns Hopkins University Press, 1983), 74–80; G. K. Hunter, *Dramatic Identities and Cultural Tradition: Studies in Shakespeare and His Contemporaries* (New York: Barnes and Noble, 1978), especially chap. 1, "Elizabethans and Foreigners"; and the essay of A. Rosalind Jones, "Italians and Others," in *Staging the Renaissance: Reinterpretations of Elizabethan and Jacobean Drama*, ed. D. S. Kastan and P. Stallybrass (New York: Routledge, 1991). In her discussion of the "myth" of Italy Jones says: "The Italy of English playwrights from the 1580s on was not a geographic record but a fantasy setting for dramas of passion, Machiavellian politics and revenge — a landscape of the mind. . . . But what Italy mainly signified in Renaissance England was really another country, a country of others, constructed through a lens of voyeuristic curiosity through which writers and their audience explored what was forbidden in their own culture" (251).

13. See, for instance, act II, scene i, which is almost entirely devoted to a rhetoric that both underlines the "sea/land" dichotomy and intermingles them, i.e., "the wind shaked surge, with high and monstrous mane, / Seems to cast water on the burning Bear / And quench the guards of th'ever fixed pole" and "Tempest themselves high seas, and howling winds, / The guttered rocks and congregates sands / Traitors ensteeped to clog the guiltless keel."

14. Anne Ubersfeld remarks on the importance of "scene," that is, the (literal, i.e., represented) "place" of the stage. See her *Lire le théâtre* (Paris: Editions Sociales, 1973), 157: "Thus the stage always symbolizes a sociocultural space. In a certain sense theatrical space is the locus of history."

15. A. C. Bradley, in his influential and much-used *Shakespearean Tragedy* (Cleveland: Meridian Books, 1955), writes: "*Othello* is a drama of modern life: when it first appeared it was a drama almost of contemporary life, for the date of the Turkish attack on Cyprus is 1570" (148). S. Cavell will serve as an example of the second tendency; in *The Claim of Reason: Wittgenstein, Skepticism, Morality and Tragedy* (Oxford: Oxford University Press,

1979), he states: "and there can be no argument with the fact that . . . compared with the cases of Shakespeare's other tragedies, that this one is not political but domestic" (485).

16. See for example, the comments of M. B. Rose, *The Expense of Spirit: Love and Sexuality in English Renaissance Drama* (Ithaca: Cornell University Press, 1988), 115: "Many of the most important Jacobean tragedies focussing on love and sexuality develop a new conception of heroism that depends not on an ideally imagined separation between public and private life, but on the assumption that the two domains should and must be united."

17. Some of the very interesting works by feminist critics of Shakespeare that have informed my discussion of sexuality and marriage include M. B. Rose, *The Expense of Spirit*; C. Kebzm, G. Greene, and C. Neely, eds., *The Women's Part* (Urbana: University of Illinois Press, 1980); C. Kahn, *Man's Estate: Masculine Identity in Shakespeare* (Berkeley: University of California Press, 1981); C. Belsey, *The Subject of Tragedy* (London: Methuen, 1985); A. Loomba, *Gender, Race, Renaissance Drama* (Manchester: Manchester University Press, 1989); C. Neely, *Broken Nuptials* (New Haven: Yale University Press, 1985). To these must be added the pioneering work of French feminists L. Irigaray, *Speculum, de l'autre femme* (Paris: Minuit, 1974) and H. Cixous and C. Clément, *La jeune née* (Paris: 10/18, 1975).

18. For the collusion of femininity and "blackness," race, see the article by K. Newman, " 'And Wash the Ethiop White': Femininity and the Monstrous in *Othello*," in *Shakespeare Reproduced: The Text in History and Ideology*, ed. J. Howard and M. O'Connor (London: Routledge Chapman and Hall, 1988), 143–63. See also the interesting discussion of racism and femininity in Loomba, *Gender, Race, Renaissance Drama*.

19. See Stone, *Family, Sex and Marriage*, and Flandrin, *Le sexe et l'Occident*.

20. Ubersfeld points out in *Lire le théâtre* that the "love-object" in theater is never simply a "personal choice" of the character, but rather is the product of the entire society's ideological intermeshing: "The choice of the 'love-object' is never decided only by the subject's own personal tastes but rather it is chosen by all the sociohistorical determinants in which the subject is inserted" (87). This is just another way of expressing why Desdemona's choice seems so shocking to her father and to her world.

21. Se. Greenblatt, *Renaissance Self-Fashioning: From More to Shakespeare* (Chicago: The University of Chicago Press, 1983), 238.

22. The vexed question of what is and how to interpret a "character" is discussed with persuasive zeal by Ubersfeld, "Le personnage," chap. 3 of *Lire le théâtre*. Particularly important for my discussion are the following remarks: "Beyond any problem of methodology, what is really at stake is the 'Ego' (the 'I') in its autonomous substance, its autonomous 'soul' (being), notions that appear quite ragged after more than eighty years of being worked over by a renewed psychology. Is it possible that what can no longer be said about real human beings caught in the web of their concrete existence, can still be said about literary characters? We will not, therefore, be surprised by the uproarious commonplace that tells us that these characters are 'beings even more alive than certain living beings, more real than the real.' As if one could transpose onto the phantasmatic plane of literary creation the idealist notion of the 'person' when this very notion has been dismantled everywhere else.

"Thus an entire traditional discourse grasps on to the characters in a novel, in the theater—as a substance, as the soul of the transcendental Kantian subject, as universal character, as universal Man, the infinitely renewed hypostasis of the bourgeois conscience, the crowning creation of culture, the most beautiful blossom of dominant ideology" (120–21).

23. See once again Ubersfeld, *Lire le théâtre*, 134: "It is the rhetorical, and even more specifically the metonymical, function of the character that assures the mediation between different historical contexts that are foreign to each other." For a discussion of the psychoanalytical inception of "subjectivity" in the rhetoric of *Othello*, see J. Fineman's brilliantly elliptical "The Sound of O in *Othello*: The Real of the Tragedy of Desire," in his book *The*

Subjectivity Effect in Western Literary Tradition (Cambridge: M.I.T. Press, 1991), 142–64; also, for the relation of Shakespeare and (modern) subjectivity in general, see J. Fineman, *Shakespeare's Perjured Eye: The Invention of Poetic Subjectivity in the Sonnets* (Berkeley: University of California Press, 1986). Patricia Parker discusses the importance of Othello's narrative, the "demand for narrative as the demand to know" in "Shakespeare and Rhetoric: 'Dilation' and 'Delation' in *Othello*," in *Shakespeare and the Question of Theory*, ed. P. Parker and G. Hartmann (New York: Methuen, 1985), 54–74.

24. See R. Girard, *Violence and the Sacred*, trans. P. Gregory (Baltimore: The Johns Hopkins University Press, 1977), 111: "It is the same thing exactly to be a regicide in the political order as it is to be a patricide in the familial order."

25. For the psychoanalytically theoretical aspects of sacrifice, see G. Rosolato, *La relation d'inconnu* (Paris: Gallimard, 1978), where he says: "The sacrificial victim determines the boundary between the outside and the inside. The sacrifice is effective only within the tribe" (87). Also, Girard, *Violence and the Sacred*, 43: "To the violence which has been excluded from the group corresponds the gesture of its outward turn. Since there is no collectivity possible without the establishment of limits, this movement towards the outside tends also to fix these boundaries." As for the question of sacrifice as an originary act, see Rosolato, *La relation*: "There is therefore a symbolic birth or rebirth of the group, which is marked as an origin, either real, historical or mythic, in the sacrifice" (68) and "Any sacrifice must figure as a point of departure, an origin" (46).

26. What I am suggesting here (but only suggesting) is that the tragedy of *Othello*, as a social symptom, is as much a tragedy of a dying world as it is of a new world's birth. F. Moretti has stressed the importance of this way of viewing the tragic situation. See "A Huge Eclipse," *Genre* 15 (1982): "Yet, new ages are not brought into being merely through the development of new ideas; the dissolution or overthrowing of old ideas plays an equal part in their emergence" (7). The same thought appears in a different critical guise in Girard, *Violence and the Sacred*, 43: "We always view the 'tragic flaw' from the perspective of the new, emergent order; never from that of the old order in the final stages of decay." See also the article of T. Murray, "*Othello*: An Index and Obscure Prologue to the History of Foul Generic Thoughts," in *Shakespeare and Deconstruction*, ed. G. D. Atkins and D. Bergson (New York: P. Lang, 1988), 213–42.

27. For recent analyses of Shakespeare and patriarchy, see Kahn, *Man's Estate*; Loomba, *Gender, Race, Renaissance Drama*; and P. Erickson, *Patriarchal Structures in Shakespeare's Drama* (Berkeley: University of California Press, 1985).

28. The standard reference work on the double as death is Freud's essay "The Uncanny" in vol. 17 of *The Standard Edition of the Complete Psychological Works of S. Freud*, trans. J. Strachey (London: Hogarth Press and the Institute for Psychoanalysis, 1981). See also the comment of Rosolato in *Le sacrifice*, 30: "The narcissistic aim is to preserve the unicity and the unity of the Ego. Doubling does away with difference, suppresses the other, and thus loses the foil for unicity."

29. The inextricable interweaving of sexuality and/as death is made by Freud as he elaborates his theory of the death instinct. See in particular *Beyond the Pleasure Principle* (*Standard Edition*, vol. 18); *Civilization and Its Discontents* (*Standard Edition*, vol. 21); and, for the interconnecting of positive and negative sides of the instinct, "Instincts and Their Vicissitudes" (*Standard Edition*, vol. 14). Freud's initial theories have been taken up and expanded by G. Bataille, *L'Erotisme* (Paris: 10/18, 1967). For Lacan, the initial loss (the "division") of the subject, a loss that is coterminous with death, precipitates the subject into both sexuality and language; see "Subversion du sujet et dialectique du désir dans l'inconscient freudien," in *Ecrits* (Paris: Seuil, 1966), 793–828.

30. J. Rose, *Sexuality in the Field of Vision* (London: Verso, 1986), 226.

31. For a rigorous exploration of the "production of" sexual difference, see S. Heath, "Difference," *Screen* 19, no. 3 (1978): 51–113.

32. M. Foucault, *The Order of Things* (New York: Random House, 1970), 43; emphasis in the original.

33. S. Serpieri also argues for a reading of *Othello* based on different epistemic models. See his article "Reading the Signs," in *Alternative Shakespeare*, ed. J. Drakakis (London: Routledge Chapman and Hall, 1985), 119–43. For an extended and acute discussion on the interrelation of power, spectacle, and (nascent) absolutism, see Goldberg, *James I and the Politics of Literature*.

34. Serpieri, "Reading the Signs," refers to Act III as "perhaps the greatest scene of seduction in Shakespeare" (132). I borrow the concept of "acoustic mirror" from K. Silverman, *The Acoustic Mirror: The Female Voice in Psychoanalysis and Cinema* (Bloomington: Indiana University Press, 1988).

35. The classic text on the ear as orifice of seduction is, of course, E. Jones, "The Madonna's Conception through the Ear," in *Essays in Applied Psychoanalysis*, vol. 2 (London: The Hogarth Press, 1951), 266–357.

36. The dialogue between Othello and Iago, an anxious dialogue of sexuality and desire, underlines the point Lacan makes about the production of subjectivity in a dialectic of signification. See "Aggressivité en psychanalyse," *Ecrits*, 102: "Psychoanalytic action is developed in and through verbal communication, that is, in a dialectical grasp of meaning . . . only a subject can understand a meaning; conversely, every phenomenon of meaning implies a subject."

37. André Green's reading of the play is based, in part, on uncovering the repressed "homosexuality" of both Othello and Iago. See *The Tragic Effect*, trans. A. Sheridan (London: Cambridge, 1979), 121: "What basically unites Othello and Iago is their common *méconaissance* of their desire for Cassio." Jonathan Dollimore has discussed the specificity of Iago's supposed homosexual desires in the larger cultural context of the tragedy (in which he also equates Desdemona to the Oriental, Turkish, Other) in "The Cultural Politics of Perversion: Augustine, Shakespeare, Freud, Foucault," *Genders* 8 (Summer 1990): 1–16. See also "*Othello*: Sexual Difference and Internal Deviation," in his *Sexual Dissidence: Augustine to Wilde, Freud to Foucault* (Oxford: Oxford University Press, 1991), 148–69.
My analysis here follows a rather traditional Freudian view that sees repressed homosexual desire as an active component in all paranoia. See Freud, "Psychoanalytic Notes upon an Autobiographical Account of a Case of Paranoia," in *Three Case Histories*, ed. P. Rieff (New York: Macmillan, 1963), 103–87, especially p. 161: "The distinctive character of paranoia (or of dementia paranoides) must be sought for elsewhere, namely, in the particular form assumed by the symptoms; and we shall expect to find that this is determined, not by the nature of the complexes themselves, but by the mechanism by which the symptoms are formed or by which repression is brought about. We should be inclined to say that what was characteristically paranoic about the illness was the fact that the patient, as a means of warding off a homosexual wish-phantasy, reacted precisely with delusions of persecution of this kind." André Green bases his interpretation of the play on Othello's and Iago's suppressed desire for Cassio.

38. That hostility would be a paranoid form of desire is underlined by Freud in his "Psychoanalytic Notes upon an Autobiographical Account of a Case of Paranoia," 165: "Nevertheless, it is a remarkable fact that the familiar principal forms of paranoia can all be represented as contradiction of the single proposition: *I* (a man) *love him* (a man). . . . The mechanism of symptom-formation in paranoia requires that internal perceptions, or feelings, shall be replaced by external perceptions. Consequently the proposition 'I love him' becomes transformed by projection into another one: 'He hates (persecutes) me, which will justify me in hating him.' "

39. Without going into lengthy psychoanalytic excursions we can simply appeal to the social historians who inform us of the profoundly unsettling changes that institutionalized sexuality, i.e., "marriage," was undergoing during this period. See Stone's chapters on sixteenth- and seventeenth-century marriage in *Family, Sex and Marriage*, as well as the comment on Stone's work by Goldberg, *James I and the Politics of Literature*, 86: "Stone's work represents a recent trend, recognizing that a number of family structures exist at any time; discontinuities, disagreements, and multiplicity are the norm."

40. Although Green, *The Tragic Effect*, makes the supposedly repressed homosexuality of Iago and Cassio the crux of his interpretation of the tragedy, other critics, such as L. Fiedler, *The Stranger in Shakespeare* (New York: Stein and Day, 1972), tend to return this theme to the margins of the text and its interpretations. For example, see Fiedler, 153: "Real or fancied . . . such glimmerings of homosexuality belong not to the main plot of *Othello* but to a peripheral action never fully developed."

41. See Freud, "Psycho-analytic Notes on an Autobiographical Account of a Case of Paranoia (dementia paranoides) (Case History of Schreber)," *Standard Edition* 12: "Paranoia is a disorder in which a sexual aetiology is by no means obvious, on the contrary, the striking prominent features in the causation of paranoia, especially among males, are social humiliation and slight" (162). This social slight could be interpreted in Lacanian terms as read by M. Borch-Jacobsen, *Lacan: The Absolute Master*, trans. D. Brick (Stanford: Stanford University Press, 1991), with, it seems, particular relevance to the triad Othello/Iago/Cassio: "And how . . . could it be otherwise, if delirium always pivots on what one could (ideally) like to be and not on what one would like to have (in the name of sexual pleasure)? What I myself am not (namely, a subject; free, autonomous, independent, and so on) is always an other (another subject, rich, famous, admired, recognized) who is taking my place — that place or social position where I would like to be. The problem, of course, is that I will then compete savagely with that other for that 'being,' for that 'place,' because if the other is in my place, it goes without saying that I shall never cease my efforts to dislodge him, in order finally to be myself; what begins in admiration, ends in murder" (24).

42. Rosolato, *Le sacrifice*, 180: "Sacrificial activity takes on an exceptional degree of urgency during periods of crisis when (social) conflicts threaten a particular form of power, . . . when a new ideology begins to develop and belongs only to a minority, which has not as yet the means of successfully accomplishing its goals."

43. Ibid., 75: "Let's think of the characteristics of the sacrificial victim: innocence and humanity, but especially fragility, are the negative opposites of the all-powerful, savage Idealized Father, hated by collective envy and guilty of all his arbitrary acts of barbarity. The victim thus uncovers, through this reversal, the meaning of the substitution and its occluding effects."

44. See the endless discussions on Shakespeare's depiction of women, summarized in the works of feminist critics already cited. In particular, for the sociohistorical analyses of Renaissance misogyny, one could consult M. B. Rose, *The Expense of Spirit*; C. Belsey, *The Subject of Tragedy*, as well as her article "Alice Arden's Crime," in *Staging the Renaissance*, 133–50; K. McLuskie, "The Patriarchal Bard: Feminist Criticism and Shakespeare: *King Lear* and *Measure for Measure*," in *Political Shakespeare: New Essays in Cultural Materialism*, ed. J. Dollimore and A. Sinfield (Ithaca: Cornell University Press, 1985), 88–108.

45. See, for instance, J. Anger, *Her Protection for Women* (1589), as well as those works cited by C. Jordan, *Renaissance Feminism: Literary Texts and Political Models* (Ithaca: Cornell University Press, 1990).

46. Fiedler, *The Stranger in Shakespeare*, points precisely to this aspect of Desdemona's upbringing as ill preparing her for the world of Cyprus: " . . . once she has left her native Venice for the sea-marches of Islam. There neither she nor Cassio will thrive, her courtly witchcraft, like his courtly charms, powerless in a camp of armed men where 'wit' alone can

cope with drunken brawls and casual whores" (142). See too M. Pryse, "Lust for an Audience: An Interpretation of *Othello*," *E.L.H*, 43 (1976): 461–78, where she comments on Desdemona's educated skills: "Desdemona is confident not simply that she can talk to Othello, but that she can outtalk him; she will become his schoolmistress" (467).

47. Feminist critics have all pointed out the "double-bind" of Desdemona's position. Precisely by "choosing" to love Othello she reveals a force of will that will be used in the paranoid accusation of her unfaithfulness. See Neely, *Broken Nuptials*, 111: "The men's profound anxieties and murderous fantasies cannot be restrained by the women's affection, wit, and shrewishness. The play ends as it began, in a world of men — political, loveless, undomesticated." A radically nonfeminist critic such as Fiedler has also written about this paradox; see *The Stranger in Shakespeare*, 145: "For marriage to occur, a girl must abandon her father, and that abandonment necessarily implies revealing capacities for deceiving men which terrify her husband forever, making assurance in marriage impossible."

48. For an elegant analysis of the binary function of the eye in literature, see J. Starobinski, *L'oeil vivant* (Paris: Gallimard, 1961).

49. Freud first describes the importance of the "primal scene" in his analysis of the "Wolf-Man"; see S. Freud, "From the History of an Infantile Neurosis," *Standard Edition*, vol. 17. J. Laplanche and B. Pontalis offer this succinct definition in *The Language of Psychoanalysis*, trans. D. Nicholson-Smith (New York: Norton, 1973), 335: "Scene of sexual intercourse between the parents which the child observes, or infers on the basis of certain indications, and phantasises. It is generally interpreted by the child as an act of violence on the part of the father."

50. See this definition by Rosolato, *Le sacrifice*, 179: "The primal scene remains an inaccessible point because of the impossibility of any return, and of situating oneself at the origin of a sexual act that was the very conception of each human being. The myth covers over this unknown: it narrativizes the origin."

For an elaboration of the "fantasy" of the primal scene, one can consult J. Laplanche and B. Pontalis, *Fantasme originaire, fantasmes des origines, origines du fantasme* (Paris: Hachette, 1985).

S. Cavell, *The Claim of Reason*, 488, and more pointedly J. Kovel, *"Othello," American Imago* (1978): 115, talk about the importance of the primal scene in *Othello*. See also Snow, "Sexual Anxiety."

51. T. Conley, *Film Hieroglyphs: Ruptures in Classical Cinema* (Minneapolis: University of Minnesota Press, 1991), xxii–xxiii. Rosolato first introduced this concept in *Essais de l'interprétation* (Paris: Gallimard, 1985).

52. Burkert, *Structure and History in Greek Mythology and Ritual*, talks about the way sacrifice appeases social anxiety: "The unquestioned effect of the procedure is the salvation of the community from evil and anxiety, which disappears with the doomed victim" (67).

53. I have developed this idea further in the introduction to my *Subjectivity and Subjugation in Seventeenth-Century Theater and Prose: The Family Romance of French Classicism* (Cambridge: Cambridge University Press, 1992).

54. For the symbolism of the male desire to "fix" women, to turn them to stone, see Irigaray, *Speculum, de l'autre femme*, and S. Kofman, *L'énigme de la femme: la femme dans les écrits de Freud* (Paris: Galilée, 1977).

55. For an interesting "neo-Lacanian" reading of the importance of the "gaze" in Shakespearean comedy, see B. Freedman, *Staging the Gaze: Postmodernism, Psychoanalysis, and Shakespearean Comedy* (Ithaca: Cornell University Press, 1991), and Fineman, *Shakespeare's Perjured Eye*.

56. See " 'Oedipe' sans complexe" in J. P. Vernant and P. Vidal-Naquet, *Oedipe et ses mythes* (Brussels: Editions Complexe, 1988), 1–23.

57. The expression is from Girard, *Le bouc émissaire*, 39: "As so many other mythic

figures, Oedipus manages to draw onto himself exterior and interior marginality . . . He is at the same time foreigner, beggar, and all-powerful monarch." Rosolato, in *Le sacrifice*, talks about Oedipus in similar terms: "Oedipus's ignorance is necessary for establishing his being as a sacrificial victim. In fact, he conflates in his being various indications that come together as signs of his appropriateness for sacrifice: he is marked by an infirmity, he limps; he appears to the citizens of Thebes as a stranger, he is a foreigner; he knows that he is the son of a king, even when he is mistaken about his geneology . . . All these diverse traits put him in the category of a "minority" — handicapped, foreigner (without actually being such), at once external and internal to the community, of noble birth, an only son — felicitously necessary for situating him at the focal point of all the violence and rejection that will turn him into a scapegoat" (127).

58. See Rosolato, *Le sacrifice*, 180, as quoted in note 42 of this chapter. Mullaney, *The Place of the Stage*, succinctly defines the role of the theater in times of social crisis: "The Renaissance stage does not merely reflect the larger civilizing process of its times: the destabilizing dialectic between self and other, audience and play, social and psychological constitutions of the subject which defined the complex theatrical transaction we know as Elizabethan and Jacobean drama was in itself an influential forum and laboratory for the production of the modern subject" (103).

59. Ubersfeld, *Lire le théâtre*, 262: "We can only speak (write) in the theater what can be heard: positively or negatively (by self-censure) the scriptor responds to the audience's demand . . . Every theatrical text is the response to the audience's desire, and it is here that the connection joining theatrical discourse to history and ideology can be most easily articulated."

60. In her chapter "Sexuality and Racial Difference" in *Race, Gender, Renaissance Drama*, 38–64, Loomba discusses Elizabethan society's racial attitudes and quotes Queen Elizabeth's expulsion decree: "They are therefore in their Lordship's name required to aide and assist him to take up such blackamoors as he shall find within this realm with the consent of their masters, which we doubt not, considering her Majesty's good pleasure to have those kind of people sent out of her lande and the good deserving of the stranger towardes her Majesty's subjectes, and that they shall doe charitably and like Christians rather to be served by their owne countrymen than with those kind of people, will yielde those in their possession to him" (63, n. 5).

61. For an example of the first, see Fiedler, *The Stranger in Shakespeare*, 185: "Mythologically speaking Othello is really black only before we see him; after his first appearance, he is archetypically white, though a stranger still, as long as he remains in Venice, a white stranger in blackface." For a general criticism of this view of Othello's blackness, see Loomba, *Gender, Race, Renaissance Drama*. For a general overview of the image of blacks in English drama, see E. Jones, *Othello's Countrymen: The African in English Renaissance Drama* (London: Oxford University Press, 1965). For a discussion of Othello as "alien/other," see also K. Burke, "*Othello*: An Essay to Illustrate a Method," in *Perspectives by Incongruity*, ed. S. E. Hymen (Bloomington: Indiana University Press, 1964), 152–95.

62. Mullaney, *The Place of the Stage*, 92.

63. See Stone, *Family, Sex and Marriage*, and Flandrin, *Families* and *Le sexe et l'Occident*, for analyses of the first glimpses of the emergent nuclear family at the end of the seventeenth century.

64. Erickson, *Patriarchal Structures in Shakespeare's Drama*, also points out the importance of the "State" in his interpretation of *Othello*: "The entire action of the play is circumscribed by the presence of the State. It approves Othello's marriage and sends him to Cyprus. . . . As the play's final lines indicate, ultimately the state is the recipient of Othello's story" (81).

65. In a sense, it is "politics" that is the modern state, that assures the same function of the idealized patriarch of primitive societies. See Rosolato, *Le sacrifice*, 189: "In the social

order, the State representing the abstract Father, a dominant ideal, turns each proletarian citizen into a son obligated to perform the most rigorous sacrifices whose first effect is civil submission, the consequence of a 'status quo,' or of a political ideology."

66. Rosolato, both in *Le sacrifice* and in his essay "Trois générations d'hommes," in *Essais sur le symbolique*, underlines the strategic importance for patriarchal societies (with special emphasis on the three great Western monotheisms) of the myth of the sacrifice of the son. He follows Freud in stating that the "murder of the father is at the heart of the sacrificial myth" (*Le sacrifice*, 9), but goes on to show how this murder is disguised and displaced onto the son, so that the (political) power the "father" represents is left intact: "As for the murder of the father uncovered by Freud, I would offer the hypothesis that in the myths of monotheism it never appears directly. The entire project has as its aim to avoid its accomplishment. We must therefore come to the conclusion that this murder constitutes the hidden, fundamental secret in relation to which are organized all the sacrificial substitutions, through which the alliance comes into being" (ibid., 74–75).

67. Goldberg, *James I and the Politics of Literature*, 149–50, talking about Foucault's conception of sovereignty, states: "But this also means — and this is crucial — that whereas the sovereign sees all, since all he sees is, the spectators of the sovereign cannot see the king; they see the mirrors of his power, but in himself the sovereign's visibility is 'scarcely sustainable' because he has another body, the body of his power."

68. These values are, not unequivocally and not unambivalently, shared with the audience, the object "haled" by the sacrificial act. In this sense, Freud seems to have been, as usual, particularly perspicacious when he remarked that "the tragic hero, though still against his will, is made the redeemer of the chorus" (*Totem and Taboo, Standard Edition* 13:157).

2. *Fuenteovejuna*

All Spanish quotations from *Fuenteovejuna* are from *Fuente Ovejuna*, ed. Francisco López Estrada (Madrid: Castalia, 1973). English translations are from *Fuenteovejuna*, trans. A. Flores and M. Kittel, in *Masterpieces of the Spanish Golden Age*, ed. A. Flores (New York: Holt Rinehart Winston, 1968).

1. For a general overview of the history of the period, see J. H. Elliott, *Imperial Spain, 1469–1716* (New York: St. Martin's Press, 1963), *Richelieu and Olivares* (Cambridge: Cambridge University Press, 1984), and *The Count-Duke of Olivares* (New Haven: Yale University Press, 1986); J. Brown and J. H. Elliott, *A Palace for a King* (New Haven: Yale University Press, 1980); A. Castro, *De la edad conflictiva* (Madrid: Taurus, 1963); J. A. Maravall, *Teatro y literatura en la sociedad barroca* (Madrid: Seminarios y Ediciones, 1972), and *Poder, honor y elites en el siglo XVII* (Madrid: Siglo Veintiuno, 1979); J. M. Diez-Borque, *Sociedad y teatro en la España de Lope de Vega* (Barcelona: A. Bosch, 1978).

2. Diez-Borque, *Sociedad y teatro*, 247. For a debate on this "sociological" approach to the literature of the period, see the discussion about W. Cohen's *Drama of a Nation: Public Theater in Renaissance England and Spain* (Ithaca: Cornel University Press, 1985), in "Plays and Playhouses in Imperial Decadence," Special Edition of *Ideology and Literature* 11, no. 1 (Winter/Spring 1986).

3. J. L. Nancy, *La communauté desoeuvrée* (Paris: Galilée, 1986), 122.

4. See M. de Certeau, *The Writing of History*, trans. T. Conley (New York: Columbia University Press, 1988), 21: "History is probably our myth. It combines what can be thought, the 'thinkable,' and the origin, in conformity with the way in which a society can understand its own working."

5. Ibid, 13–19.

6. Elliott, *The Count-Duke of Olivares*, 196–97. Brown and Elliott, *A Palace for a King*,

define why Philip was not "absolute": "In a now famous secret memorandum on the government of Spain which he [Olivares] presented to Philip at the end of 1624, he told him that, although he might be King of Portugal, Aragon, and Valencia and Count of Barcelona, he was not yet King of Spain. The supreme objective of his reign must be to make himself a real King of Spain, the ruler not of disparate kingdoms but of a unified peninsula" (29).

7. de Certeau, *The Writing of History*, 8: "Its discourse will be magisterial without being that of the master . . . they reflect on the power that they lack."

8. Ibid., 7: "power must be legitimized, it must attribute to its grounding force an authority which in turn makes this very power credible."

9. I am borrowing from Althusser's definition of ideological subjugation in "Idéologie et appareils idéologiques d'Etat," in L. Althusser, *Positions* (Paris: Editions Sociales, 1970). I will return to this idea in more detail later in the chapter.

10. See R. Menéndez-Pidal, "Lope de Vega: El arte nuevo y la nueva biografía," in *De Cervantes y Lope de Vega* (Madrid: Espasa Calpe, 1964), 69: "Lope de Vega died cloaked in the greatest glory and respect . . . the great poet of all the glory and ideals of the Spanish empire was dying . . . "

11. This role is pertinently evoked by the French psychoanalyst and critic André Green, who has described the theater as the "meeting-point of the individual and society, between the personal resonance of the work's content and its social function, art occupies a transitional position." See Green, *The Tragic Effect*, trans. A. Sheridan (London: Cambridge University Press, 1979), 23.

12. de Certeau, *The Writing of History*, 60.

13. For a valuable discussion of the ideological, semiotic role of the theater, see A. Ubersfeld, *Lire le théâtre* (Paris: Editions Sociales, 1978), 215: "the theater by its very nature denies the presence of the past or of the future. Theatrical writing is always 'writing in the present' [tense]."

14. Both Elliott, *Imperial Spain*, 76–77, and C. Aubrun, *La Comédie espagnole, 1600–1680* (Paris: P.U.F., 1966), remind us of the similarities that existed between the internecine rivalries of the feudal lords in fifteenth-century Spain and the dramatic situation of the early seventeenth century. See Elliott, 23: "Everything, then, conspired to make the prospects seem gloomy for Castile, and the opening years of the fifteenth century did nothing to dispel the gloom. The Castilian Kings, their title dubious, had become pawns in the hands of the magnates: the Cortes were disunited and ineffectual; government had broken down, public order had collapsed, and the country was in turmoil"; and Aubrun, 32: "There the *comendadores* play the role of the villain — those tyrannical commanders of military order about whose abuses the histories of the fifteenth century speak so eloquently. By this (temporal) detour the playwrights attack other, more contemporary despots."

The "conservatism" of the *comedia* is a leitmotiv in most of the sociologically oriented critics, such as Maravall, *Teatro y literatura*, and Diez-Borque, *Sociedad y teatro*. See also Aubrun, *La Comedie espagnole*, 28: "After having flattered his or her most normative instincts, the *comedia* brings the spectator to applaud extremely conservative solutions to the problems it has formulated on the stage."

15. See Althusser, *Positions*, 101.

16. For this point, I refer the reader to Ubersfeld, *Lire le théâtre*, 266: "How is a new rapport going to be formed between a textual discourse created in relation to a particular audience and an audience that has changed and for whom neither the anxieties, nor the culture, nor the ideology are the same? The simplest tendency is to deny that a problem exists and to maintain that the relation between the discourse of the scriptor and the voice of the spectator can be established on the grounds of some universal human nature, with the same eternal passions. Another trap would be to try to reconstitute the discourse of the author supported by the [elaboration of the] historical conditions of the author's speech,

thus negating, by the very same token, the presence of a contemporary audience with its own specific voice."

17. I am aware of the tendentiousness of these terms: it is precisely, it seems to me, when differences are not clear and visible that all the more energy is exerted into articulating, thus imagining, them as such.

18. See Castro, *De la edad conflictiva*, 34: "In daily life, not in the life portrayed in the *comedias* of Lope de Vega, wrenching drama erupted when a Spaniard realized that he was not considered a *cristiano viejo* [a "true," untainted Christian]." See also A. Sicroff, *Les Controverses des statuts de "pureté de sang" en Espagne du XVe au XVIIe siècle* (Paris: Didier, 1960). For the problelm of othering in Hispanic culture, see P. J. Smith, *Representing the Other: "Race," Text and Gender in Spanish and Spanish American Narratives* (Oxford: Oxford University Press, 1992).

19. L. Spitzer, "Un tema central y su equivalente estructural en *Fuenteovejuna*," in *El teatro de Lope de Vega* (Buenos Aires: Eudeba, 1967), 124.

20. F. López Estrada, ed., *Fuente Ovejuna* (Madrid: Castalia, 1973), 17. See also D. Larson, *The Honor Plays of Lope de Vega* (Cambridge: Harvard University Press, 1977), 85–86.

21. LAURENCIA: ¿A qué efeto fuera bueno
   querer a Fernando yo?
   Casárame con él?
   PASCUALA: No.
   LAURENCIA: Luego la infamia condeno.
   Cuántas mozas en la villa,
   del Comendador fiadas,
   andan ya descalabradas!

For a good analysis of the complex theme of honor, see Larson, *The Honor Plays*; Maravall, *Poder, honor y elites*; and Menéndez-Pidal," Lope de Vega."

22. LAURENCIA: Id con Dios, tras vueso corzo;
   que a no veros con la Cruz,
   os tuviera por demonio,
   pues tanto me perseguís.

23. See Maravall, quoting K. Vossler on Lope, in *Teatro y literatura*, 33: "In his work there are dramatic situations, but there is no intimate drama."

24. R. Girard, *Violence and the Sacred*, trans. P. Gregory (Baltimore: The Johns Hopkins University Press, 1977), 160: "A fundamental principle, often overlooked, is that the double and the monster are one and the same being . . . There is no monster who does not tend to duplicate himself or to 'marry' another monster, no double who does not yield a monstrous aspect upon close scrutiny."

25. See Ubersfeld, *Lire le théâtre*, 265: "Each theatrical text is a response to its audience's desire, and it is there that we can most easily articulate the relation between theatrical discourse and history and ideology."

26. I am thinking of the following works: E. Enriquez, *De la horde à l'Etat* (Paris: Gallimard, 1983); E. Sagan, *At the Dawn of Tyranny* (New York: Knopf, 1985); and S. Moscovici, *L'age des foules* (Paris: Fayard, 1981).

27. de Certeau, "Freudian Writing: What Freud Makes of History," in *The Writing of History*, 293.

28. A su lado, Fernán Gómez,
   vuestro señor, en un fuerte
   melado, de negros cabos,
   puesto que con blanco bebe.
   Sobre turca jacerina,

peto y espaldar luciente,
con naranjada las saca,
que de oro y perlas guarnece. . . .
Ceñida al brazo una liga
roja y blanca, con que mueve
un fresno entero por lanza,
que hasta en Granada le temen.

29. Spitzer also underlines the importance of the repetition of this ritualistic refrain. For the concept of the "king's two bodies," see the classic study of E. Kantorowicz, *The King's Two Bodies* (Princeton: Princeton University Press, 1957).

30. ¡Vivan la bella Isabel,
y Fernando de Aragón
pues que para en uno son,
él con ella, ella con él!

31. La ciudad se puso en arma;
dicen que salir no quieren
de la corona real,
y el patrimonio defienden.
Entróla, bien resistida;
y el Maestre a los rebeldes
y a los que entonces trataron
su honor injuriosamente,
mandó cortar las cabezas;
y a los de la baja plebe,
con mordazas en la boca,
azotar públicamente.

32. In this sense, of course, my analysis corroborates on the level of sexual/political myth Spitzer's argument in "Un tema central" about the essential (platonic) theme of "harmony."

33. . . . . murmura el pueblo todo,
que me miras y te miro,
y todos nos traen sobre ojo.
Y como tú eres zagal
de los que huellan brioso
y, excediendo a los demás,
vistes bizarro y costoso,
en todo el lugar no hay moza
o mozo en el prado o soto,
que no se afirme diciendo
que ya para en uno somos:
y esperan todos el día
que el sacristán Juan Chamorro
nos eche de la tribuna,
en dejando los piporros.

34. This "public" control of adolescent sexuality is quite normal in "premodern" Europe. See the work of J. L. Flandrin, *Familles, parenté, maison, sexualité dans l'ancienne société* (Paris: Seuil, 1976); and P. Shorter, *The Making of the Modern Family* (New York: Basic Books, 1975).

35. Si sabes que es mi intención
el desear ser tu esposo,
mal premio das a mi fe.

Ya te pido yo salud,
y que ambos como palomos
estemos, juntos los picos,
con arrulos sonorosos,
después de darnos la Iglesia . . .

36. . . . Yo me conformo
con mi estado . . .

37. Both Spitzer, "Un tema central," and Larson, *The Honor Plays*, point out the artificiality and the utopian setting of the village.

38. See G. Genette, "Le serpent dans la bergerie," *Figures*, vol. 1 (Paris: Seuil, 1966); M. Greenberg, *Detours of Desire* (Columbus: Ohio State University Press, 1984), especially chapter 4.

39. G. Rosolato, *Le sacrifice: repères psychanalytiques* (Paris: P.U.F., 1987), 78.

40. Ibid., 116.

41. For a good introduction to narcissism and the nefarious effects of the narcissistic personality, see A. Green, *Narcissisme de vie, narcissisme de mort* (Paris: Minuit, 1983).

42. See G. Rosolato, "Le narcissime," *Nouvelle Revue de Psychanalyse, Narcisses* (Spring 1976), 8: "At the very center of its problematics death remains a basic, always present reference point. Even upon the waters of the Styx, Narcissus would search for his own reflection."

43. See Enriquez, *De la horde*, 100–110.

44. No es malo venir siguiendo
un corcillo temeroso,
y topar tan bella gama.

45. COMENDADOR: ¿No se rindió Sebastiana,
mujer de Pedro Redondo,
con ser casadas entrambas,
y la de Martín del Pozo
habiendo apenas pasado
dos días del desposorio?

COMENDADOR: ¿Que hay de Pascuala?
FRONDOSO: Responde
que anda por casarse.

COMENDADOR: ¿Que hay de Inés?
FRONDOSO: ¿Cuál?
COMENDADOR: La de Antón.

46. COMENDADOR: Mujer hay, y principal,
de alguno que está en la plaza,
que dio, a la primera traza,
traza de verme.
ESTEBAN: Hizo mal.
Y vos, señor, no andáis bien
en hablar tan libremente.
COMENDADOR: Oh, ¡qué villano elocuente!

47. The play is, in the words of López Estrada, "the most popular work of the great Spanish writer" (*Fuente Ovejuna*, ed. López Estrada, 10).

48. Estése la boda queda,
y no se alborote nadie.

49. FRONDOSO: Tal me tienen tus desdenes,

bella Laurencia, que tomo,
en el peligro de verte,
la vida.

COMENDADOR: Aquesos desdenes toscos
afrentan, bella Laurencia,
las gracias que el poderoso
cielo te dio.

50. Los hombres aborrecía,
Mengo, mas desde aquel día
los miro con otra cara.
¡Gran valor tuvo Frondoso!
Pienso que le ha de costar
la vida.

51. Vosotros, ¿padres y deudos?
Vosotros, que no se os rompen
las entrañas de dolor
de verme en tantos dolores?
Ovejas sois, bien lo dice
de Fuente Ovejuna el nombre. . . .
Liebres cobardes nacistes;
bárbaros sois, no españoles.
¡Gallinas, vuestras mujeres
sufrís que otros hombres gocen!

52. ¡Y que os han de tirar piedras,
hilanderas, maricones,
amujerados, cobardes!
¡Y que mañana os adornen
nuestras tocas y basquiñas,
solimanes y colores!

53. I find it intriguing that the second most popular spectacle after the theater was bullfights. During these fights the populace would, according to Diez-Borque, often behave in the following way: "Often the spectators would jump into the bullring and stab the bull with daggers and knives. Cruel buffoonery was not lacking, either; the bull would be trussed with spears and lifted into the air . . . There was neither a fixed order nor a particular ceremony in the bullring; the only plan was to come up with ever more bloody tricks to play on the bull/victim in order to satisfy the aficionados from all social ranks who showed themselves to be cruel and bloodthirsty in ways that strike us as (almost) inconceivable" (*Sociedad y teatro*, 249–50). The mob in *Fuenteovejuna* seems to treat the Comendador like the frenzied populace treated the bull, thus establishing a strange chiasmus in which animal sexual imagery and savagery is literally acted out on the body of Fernán Gómez, who is described as a *fiera*.

54. R. Girard, *La violence et le sacré* (Paris: Grasset, 1972; English translation, *Violence and the Sacred*), and *Le bouc émissaire* (Paris: Grasset, 1982).

55. Reyes hay en Castilla,
que nuevas órdenes hacen
con que desórdenes quitan.
Y harán mal, cuando descansen
de las guerras, en sufrir
en sus villas y lugares

a hombres tan poderosos
por traer cruces tan grandes.

56. ¡Vivan la bella Isabel
y Fernando de Aragón
pues que para en uno son,
él con ella, ella con él!
A los cielos San Miguel
lleve a los dos de las manos.
¡Vivan muchos años,
y mueran los tiranos!

57. For the first point, see Rosolato, *Le sacrifice*, 117: "Every sacrifice must serve as a starting point, an origin."

For the second, ibid.: "The role of sacrifice as a therapy for guilt by exploiting it became at the same time a cohesive force thanks to which both the covenant and the community are formed" (77) and "There exists a symbolic birth of the group, or a rebirth whose reference point, as origin — real, historical, or mythic — becomes fixed in/on the sacrifice" (68).

58. See Althusser, *Positions*, 110.

59. For a lengthy discussion of Althusser and interpellation, see P. Smith, *Discerning the Subject* (Minneapolis: University of Minnesota Press, 1987).

60. Althusser, "Ideology and the State," in *Positions*, 180.

61. LAURENCIA: ¿Aquestos los Reyes son? . . .
ISABEL: ¿Los agresores son estos?

62. Señor, tuyos ser queremos.
Rey nuestro eres natural,
y con título de tal
ya tus armas puesto habemos.

63. For discussions of theatrical pleasure as essentially masochistic, see the following works: J. F. Lyotard, "Oedipe Juif," in *Dérive à partir de Freud et Marx* (Paris: 10/18, 1973); P. Lacoue-Labarthe, "Theatrum analyticum," in *Glyph*, vol. 2 (Baltimore: The Johns Hopkins University Press, 1977); S. Freud, "Psychopathic Characters on the Stage," in *The Standard Edition of the Complete Psychological Works of S. Freud*, trans. J. Strachey (London: Hogarth Press and the Institute for Psychoanalysis, 1981), 7:306.

3. *La vida es sueño*

All quotations from *La vida es sueño* are from *Obras completas de D. Pedro Calderón de la Barca*, ed. A. Valbuena Briones (Madrid: Aguilar, 1966). English translations are from *Life's a Dream*, trans. K. Raine and R. M. Nadal (London: H. Hamilton, 1968).

1. A. Valbuena Briones, ed., *Obras completas de D. Pedro Calderón de la Barca* (Madrid: Aguilar, 1966), "Nota Preliminar," 491: "Like . . . *Don Quijote*, Pedro Calderón's *La vida es sueño* is one of the works of Spanish literature of universal appeal."

2. See R. Ter Horst, *Calderón: The Secular Plays* (Lexington: The University Press of Kentucky, 1982), 216–22.

3. See S. Freud, "The Uncanny," in *On Creativity and the Unconscious* (New York: Harper and Row, 1958), 122–61.

4. See G. Parker and L. Smith, eds., *The General Crisis of the Seventeenth Century* (London: Routledge and Kegan Paul, 1978), as well as J. A. Maravall, *Teatro y literatura en la sociedad barroca* (Madrid: Seminarios y Ediciones, 1972) and *Poder, honor y elites en el siglo XVII* (Madrid: Siglo Veintiuno, 1979), and J. M. Diez-Borque, *Sociedad y teatro en la España de Lope de Vega* (Barcelona: A. Bosch, 1978). For a particular slant on Calderón, there is the suggestive book by A. J. Cascardi, *The Limits of Illusion: A Critical Study of Calderón* (Cambridge: Cambridge University Press, 1984), especially pp. 11–23.

5. M. de Certeau, *La fable mystique*, vol. 1 (Paris: Gallimard, 1982), 32: "Such was the situation in the seventeenth century. Divisive conflicts called into question heteronomous social formations. The fatal splitting of what was formerly religious unity gradually shifted onto the State the responsibility of representing for all members of society a reference point of stable unity. A concept of unity gradually emerged based on an inclusionary strategy, subtended by a subtle interplay of hierarchies and mediations."

6. See M. Foucault, *Les mots et les choses* (Paris: Gallimard, 1966), *Histoire de la sexualité: la volonté de savoir* (Paris: Gallimard, 1976), and *Histoire de la folie à l'epoque classique* (Paris: Gallimard, 1972).

7. J. Lynch, *Spain under the Habsburgs*, vol. 1 (New York: Oxford University Press, 1964), 68: " 'a monarch, a kingdom, a sword" ('un monarca, un imperio y una espada'): the ideal expressed in the nobel verses of Hernando de Acuña remained an unfailing attraction to many people in a divided and threatened world."

8. For an elaboration of the connection between the monarchy and the family, see the Introduction to M. Greenberg, *Subjectivity and Subjugation in Seventeenth-Century Drama and Prose: The Family Romance of French Classicism* (Cambridge: Cambridge University Press, 1992).

9. See A. Ubersfeld, *Lire le théâtre* (Paris: Editions Sociales, 1977), 212: "The theater has the same status as the dream: it is an imaginary creation that the spectator knows to be radically separated from the realm of daily life. [The spectator] can watch the laws that control his or her function with the illusion of not being subjected to them because here they are directly attacked in their constricting reality." See also O. Mannoni, *Clefs pour l'imaginaire, ou l'autre scène* (Paris: Seuil, 1969).

10. See S. Freud, *The Interpretation of Dreams*, in vol. 4 of *The Standard Edition of the Complete Psychological Works of S. Freud*, trans. J. Strachey (London: Hogarth Press and the Institute for Psychoanalysis, 1981), and S. Weber, "The Meaning of the Thallus," in *The Legend of Freud* (Minneapolis: University of Minnesota Press, 1982), 65–83.

11. For instance, see A. A. Parker, *The Mind and Art of Calderón* (Cambridge: Cambridge University Press, 1988), 69–85, and W. Cohen, *Drama of a Nation* (Ithaca: Cornell University Press, 1985), 389.

12. Yo, acudiendo a mis estudios,
    en ellos y en todo miro
    que Segismundo sería
    el hombre más atrevido,
    el príncipe más cruel
    y el monarca más impío
    por quien su reino vendría
    a ser parcial y diviso,
    escuela de las traiciones
    y academia de los vicios;
    y él, de su furor llevado,
    entre asombros y delitos,
    había de poner en mí
    las plantas, y yo, rendido
    a sus pies me había de ver
    (¡con qué vergüenza lo digo!)
    siendo alfombra de sus plantas
    las canas del rostro mío.

13. El mayor, el más horrendo
    eclipse que ha padecido
    el sol, despúes que con sangre

lloró la muerte de Cristo . . .
Los cielos se oscurecieron,
temblaron los edificios,
llovieron piedras las nubes,
corrieron sangre los ríos.

14. The work of the French psychoanalyst Guy Rosolato, both in *Essais sur le symbolique* (Paris: Gallimard, 1969) and more recently in *Le sacrifice: repères psychanalytique* (Paris: P.U.F., 1987), has elaborated a theory of paternal sacrifice, particularly as it occurs as a necessary cultural myth in the three dominant Western monotheisms.

15. Rosolato, *Le sacrifice*, 83–123. See another highly suggestive perspective in R. Girard, *La violence et le sacré*, (Paris: Grasset, 1973).

16. See A. Green, *Un oeil en trop, le complexe d'oedipe dans la tragédie* (Paris: Minuit, 1969), 210. [For English translation, see Rosolato, *The Tragic Effect*, trans. A. Sheridan (London: Cambridge, 1979).]

17. Rosolato, *Le sacrifice*, 74: "As for the murder of the father I would offer the hypothesis that in the myths of monotheism it never appears directly. The entire project has, in fact, as its aim to avoid its accomplishment. We must therefore come to the conclusion that this murder constitutes the hidden fundamental secret, in relation to which are organized all the sacrificial substitutions through which the alliance comes into being."

18. . . . si nací, ya entiendo
qué delito he cometido:
bastante causa ha tenido
vuestra justicia y rigor,
pues el delito mayor
del hombre es haber nacido.

19. Pues muerte aquí te daré,
por que no sepas que sé . . .
que sabes flaquezas mías.
Sólo porque me has oído,
entre mis membrudos brazos
te tengo que hacer pedazos.

20. Basilio, que ya, [señora],
se rinde al común desdén
del tiempo, más inclinado
a los estudios que dado
a mujeres enviudó . . .

21. ya sabéis que yo en el mundo
por me ciencia he merecido
el sobrenombre de docto,
pues, contra el tiempo y olvido,
los pinceles de Timantes,
los mármoles de Lisipo
en el ámbito del orbe
me aclaman el gran Basilio.

22. Ya sabéis que son las ciencias
que más curso y más estimo
matemáticas sutiles
por quien al tiempo le quito,
por quien a la fama rompo
la jurisdicción y oficio . . .

23. The concept of the "analogic universe" is developed by Foucault, *Les mots et les choses*.

24. ¿Qüé confuso laberinto
    es éste, donde no puede
    hallar la razón el hilo? . . .
    descubra el cielo el camino;
    aunque no sé si podrá,
    cuando en tan confuso abismo
    es todo el cielo un presagio
    y es todo el mundo un prodigio.

25. Oh vosotros que, ignorantes
    de aqueste vedado sitio
    coto y término pisasteis
    contra el decreto del Rey . . .

26. E. Enriquez, *De la horde à l'Etat* (Paris: Gallimard, 1983), 243: "Without a father there can be no children (in the social meaning of the term); without children, that is, without individuals capable of recognizing the law of the father and of identifying with the ideal that that law conveyed, there can be no such thing as a 'father,' either."

27. Regarding the Spanish *comedia* in general, see C. Aubrun, *La comédie espagnole, 1600*–1680 (Paris: P.U.F., 1966), 103: "No nuns. Many fathers but no mothers (except for some remarkable plays); uncles and cousins, both male and female . . . "

28. Antes que a la luz hermosa
    le diese el sepulcro vivo
    de un vientre (porque el nacer
    y morir son parecidos),
    su madre infinitas veces,
    entre ideas y delirios
    del sueño, vio que rompía
    sus entrañas atrevido
    un monstruo en forma de hombre,
    y, entre su sangre teñido
    le daba muerte, naciendo
    víbora humana del siglo.

29. See especially L. Irigaray, *Ce sexe qui n'en est pas un* (Paris: Minuit, 1977) and *Speculum, de l'autre femme* (Paris: Minuit, 1974); and H. Cixous and C. Clément, *La jeune née* (Paris: 10/18, 1975).

30. Irigaray, *Ce sexe*, 180: "Insofar as 'mother,' woman, remains on the side of reproductive nature, the relation of man to what is termed 'natural' will never be completely overcome."

31. bajé a la cárcel estrecha
    de Segismundo, y con él
    hablé un rato de las letras
    humanas, que le ha enseñado
    la madre naturaleza
    de los montes y los cielos,
    en cuya divina escuela
    la retórica aprendió
    de las aves y las fieras.

32. See J. Derrida, "La double séance," in *Ecriture et Différence* (Paris: Seuil, 1966).

33. See, for example, C. Bravo-Villasante, *La mujer vestida de hombre en el teatro español* (Madrid: Sociedad general española de librería, 1976).

34. . . . yo, sin más camino
    que el que me dan las leyes del destino,

ciega y desesperada
bajaré la aspereza enmarañada
deste monte eminente
que arruga al sol el ceño de su frente.
Mal, Polonia recibes
a un extranjero, pues con sangre escribes
su entrada en tus arenas . . .

35. Tu voz pudo enternecerme,
tu presencia suspenderme
y tu respeto turbarme. . . .
Con cada vez que te veo
nueva admiración me das
y cuando te miro más
aun más mirarte deseo.

36. Hay que mudando
su nombre, y tomando, cuerda,
nombre de sobrina tuya,
hoy tanto honor se acrecienta,
que dama en palacio ya
de la singular Estrella
vive.

37. The importance of difference/indifference informs the entire analysis of C. Bandera, *Mimesis conflictiva: ficción literaria y violencia en Cervantes y Calderón* (Madrid: Gredos, 1975), 175–260, although given his resolutely Girardian perspective, he does not deal with sexual difference.

38. J. Riviere, "Womanliness as Masquerade," reprinted in *Formations of Fantasy*, ed. V. Burgin, J. Donald, and C. Kaplan (London: Methuen, 1979).

39. . . . que siendo
monstruo de una especie y otra
entre galas de mujer
armas de varón me adornan.

40. En un veloz caballo . . .
en quien un mapa se dibuja atento,
pues el cuerpo es la tierra,
el fuego el alma que en el pecho encierra,
la espuma el mar, y el aire es el suspiro,
en cuya confusión un caos admiro.

41. A. Cilveti, *El significado de "La vida es sueño"* (Valencia: Albatros Ediciones, 1971), 168–72.

42. Tres veces son las que ya
me admiras, tres las que ignoras
quien soy, pues las tres me viste
en diverso traje y forma.
La primera me creíste
varón . . .
La segunda me admiraste
mujer . . .
La tercera es hoy, que siendo
monstruo de una especie y otra . . .

43. For the confirmation of this idea of the play representing a hysterical irresolution, see the suggestive reading of E. Honig, *Calderón and the Seizures of Honor* (Cambridge: Har-

vard University Press, 1972), 167: "She is both hunter and hunted—the hysterical state of many a wronged victim of the honor plays."

44. Mujer, vengo a persuadirte
al remedio de mi honra,
y varón, vengo a alentarte
a que cobres tu corona.
Mujer, vengo a enternecerte
cuando a tus plantas me ponga,
y varón, vengo a servirte
con me acero y mi persona.
Y así, piensa que si hoy
como mujer me enamoras,
como varón te daré
la muerte en defensa honrosa
de mi honor, porque he de ser,
en su conquista amorosa,
mujer para darte quejas,
varón para ganar honras.

45. For the importance of mirroring, especially in the creation of the absolutist subject, I refer the reader to Althusser's classic definition of "ideology" found in "Idéologie et appareils idéologiques d'Etat," in *Positions* (Paris: Editions Sociales, 1970). See also my *Subjectivity and Subjugation*, where the implications of Althusser's work for the seventeenth century are elaborated.

46. . . . y el vulgo,
penetrando ya y sabiendo
que tiene rey natural,
no quiere que un extranjero
venga a mandarle.

47. . . . de uno en otro bando se dilata
por las calles y plazas dividido,
(verás) tu reino en ondas de escarlata
nadar, entre la púrpura teñido
de su sangre, que ya con triste modo
todo es desdichas y tragedias todo.
Tanta es la ruina de tu imperio, tanta
la fuerza del rigor duro, sangriento,
que visto admira y escuchado espanta.
El sol se turba y se embaraza el viento;
cada piedra un pirámide levanta
y cada flor construye un monumento;
cada edificio es un sepulcro altivo,
cada soldado un esqueleto vivo.

48. It is interesting that the descriptions of Segismundo and of his tower correspond hauntingly to the ancient Greek descriptions of Tartarus as "a dark abyss . . . surrounded by an iron wall with iron gates set up by Poseidon and by a trebly thick layer of night, and it served as the prison of the dethroned Cronus, and of the conquered Titans" [O. Seyffert, "Tartarus," *Dictionary of Classical Antiquities* (New York: Meridian Books, 1956, 612)].

49. This is perhaps how we are to take R. Ter Horst's comments on Calderón's ambivalent relation to absolutism: "Calderón's adherence to the absolute should not be interpreted as a taste for totalitarianism. The attachment is complex, involving repulsion as

much as attraction" ["A New Literary History of D. Pedro Calderón," in *Approaches to the Theater of Calderón*, ed. M. McGaha (Washington: University Press of America, 1982), 39].

50. See S. Freud, "A Neurosis of Demoniacal Possession in the Seventeenth Century," in *On Creativity and the Unconscious*, 277–78.

51. Cf. Rosolato, *Le sacrifice*, 87: "Psychoanalysts since Freud have, however, uncovered another vector within this schema, all the more disguised as patriarchy becomes all the more powerful. Under the guise of the slaughter of the son we detect the desire for the death of the father. The sacrificial victim, a substitute, stands in for, symbolizes, the father."

52. Si a mí buscando vas,

[*A Segismundo, arrodillándose.*]

ya estoy, príncipe, a tus plantas,
sea dellas blanca alfombra
esta nieve de mis canas;
pisa la cerviz y huella
mi corona; postra, arrastra
mi decoro y mi respeto;
toma de mi honor venganza;
sírvete de mí cautivo;
y tras prevenciones tantas,
cumpla el hado su homenaje,
cumpla el cielo su palabra.

53. . . . Señor, levanta, [*Al Rey.*]

dame tu mano, que ya
que el cielo te desengaña
de que has errado en el modo
de vencerla, humilde aguarda
mi cuello a que tú te vengues:
rendido estoy a tus plantas.

54. Rosaura está en mi poder,

su hermosura el alma adora;
gocemos, pues, la ocasión;
el amor las leyes rompa . . .
Esto es sueño . . .
Acudamos a lo eterno, . . .
Rosaura está sin honor;
más a un príncipe le toca
el dar honor que quitarle.

55. The "exchange" of women among men has of course been the center of much critical debate. Perhaps the most important texts that launched this debate are M. Mauss, "Essai sur le don," in *Sociologie et Anthropologie* (Paris: P.U.F., 1950), and C. Lévi-Strauss, *Les structures élémentaires de la parenté*. See also J. Mitchell's comments on Lévi-Strauss in *Psychoanalysis and Feminism* (New York: Random House, 1975).

4. Playing Dead

All quotations from works by Corneille are from *Théâtre choisi de Corneille*, ed. M. Rat (Paris: Garnier frères, 1961). English translations are from *The Chief Plays of Corneille*, trans. L. Lockert (Princeton: Princeton University Press, 1952).

1. For an overview of the history of French dramaturgy in the seventeenth century and for Corneille's innovative theater, see A. Adam, *Histoire de la littérature française au XVIIe siècle*, vol. 1 (Paris: del Duca, 1949).

2. For a recent contribution to this aspect of the problem, see W. Beik, *Absolutism and Society in Seventeenth-Century France* (Cambridge: Cambridge University Press, 1989).

3. For the choice of the "four great plays," see the remarks of O. Nadal, *Le Sentiment de l'Amour dans l'oeuvre de Corneille* (Paris: Gallimard, 1948), 21: "Finally, they did nothing more than to corroborate the judgment of the 'Grand Siècle,' which, quite early on, and with but a few exceptions, had chosen the rarest treasures from the enormous mine of contemporary productions. Voltaire's comments merely reduced a bit further an already slim selection."

4. See R. Mousnier, *Les institutions de la France sous la monarchie absolue, 1598–1789*, 2 vols. (Paris: P.U.F., 1974).

5. See, for example, Cardinal de Richelieu, *Testament Politique*, ed. L. André (Paris: Laffont, 1947), 93–94: "When your majesty decided both to allow me into his state councils and to grant me a large measure of his confidence in the direction of his other affairs, I can state unequivocally that the Huguenots shared the state with your majesty, that the grandees of the realm behaved as if they were not subjects, and that the powerful provincial governors acted as if they were themselves sovereigns in their respective bailiwicks. I can further state that foreign alliances were neglected, that private interests were preferred to public concerns and that, in a word, the dignity of Royal Majesty was terribly debased and so far from being what it should have been."

6. L. Marin, *La parole mangée* (Paris: Klincksieck, 1986), 215: "And we should never lose sight of the fact that the desire for absolute power is one of the manifestations of the death drive."

7. The best examples of this historical criticism are, to my mind, G. Bénichou, *Morales du Grand Siècle* (Paris: Gallimard, 1948); and G. Couton, *Corneille et la Fronde* (Paris: Belles Lettres, 1955) and *La Vieillesse de Corneille* (Paris: Maloine, 1949). See also the recent work by D. Clarke, *Pierre Corneille: Poetics and Political Drama under Louis XIII* (Cambridge: Cambridge University Press, 1992).

8. See J. P. Vernant's discussion in "Death in the Eyes: Gorgo, Figure of the Other," in his *Mortals and Immortals*, ed. F. Zeitlin (Princeton: Princeton University Press, 1991), 111.

9. In a Hegelian perspective, S. Doubrovsky has written suggestively on the creation of the Cornelian hero as a confrontation with death in *Corneille ou la dialectique du héros* (Paris: Gallimard, 1963).

10. T. Laqueur, *Making Sex: Body and Gender from the Greeks to Freud* (Cambridge: Harvard University Press, 1990).

11. See Laqueur, *Making Sex*, 25–114 (chaps. 2 and 3).

12. Ibid., 62: "In a public world that was overwhelmingly male, the one-sex model displayed what was already massively evident in culture more generally: man is the measure of all things, and woman does not exist as an ontologically distinct category. Not all males are masculine, potent, honorable, or hold power, and some women exceed some men in each of these categories. But the standard of the human and its representations is the male body."

13. See G. Rosolato, "Perspective de la mort dans la tragédie," in *Essais sur le symbolique* (Paris: Gallimard, 1969), 185: "That death can be considered the perspectival vanishing point implies that it controls tragedy not only as a theme but as the organizing principle of the entire tragic system."

14. S. Freud, *Beyond the Pleasure Principle*, in vol. 18 of *The Standard Edition of the Complete Psychological Works of S. Freud*, trans. J. Strachey (London: Hogarth Press and the Institute for Psychoanalysis, 1981): "Our views have from the very first been dualistic, and today they are even more definitely dualistic than before — now that we describe the opposition

as being not between ego instincts and sexual instincts but between life instincts and death instincts" (53).

15. Freud, *Beyond the Pleasure Principle*, 63.

16. See J. Lacan, *Les quatre concepts fondamentaux de la psychanalyse* (Paris: Seuil, 1973) and "Fonction et champ de la parole et du langage en psychanalyse," in *Ecrits* (Paris: Seuil, 1966).

17. G. Bataille, *L'Erotisme* (Paris: Minuit, 1957).

18. See V. Jankélévitch, *La Mort* (Paris: Flammarion, 1977), 7-8: "Death is the extraordinary order par excellence. . . . But, as opposed to immortality (and God), death is a provable fact, a natural and familiar evidence . . . it has never happened that a 'mortal' has not died, has escaped the common destiny, or has accomplished the miracle of living forever, or never disappearing, or that longevity passing all limits, or heading toward infinity, becomes eternity: for the absolute is of an entirely different order than life." See also M. de Certeau's discussion of death as a locus in seventeenth-century mystic discourse in *La Fable mystique* (Paris: Gallimard, 1982); and J. Laplanche, *Life and Death in Psychoanalysis*, trans. J. Mehlman (Baltimore: The Johns Hopkins University Press, 1976).

19. See S. Weber, *The Legend of Freud* (Minneapolis: University of Minnesota Press, 1982), 32-33: "And yet, Freud's entire theoretical effort to articulate the importance of the unconscious belies the clear-cut distinction between 'inner impulse' or gratification, and 'other people.' If the unconscious means anything whatsoever, it is that the relation of self and others, inner and outer, cannot be grasped as an interval between polar opposites but rather as an irreducible dislocation of the subject in which the other inhabits the self as its condition of possibility."

20. See Vernant, *Mortals and Immortals*, 98: "When women did not yet exist—before Pandora was created—death did not exist for men either. Mingling with the gods, living like them in the Golden Age, men ever remained young like the gods throughout their existence, and a kind of gentle sleep took the place of death for them."

21. S. Freud, "The Unconscious," *Standard Edition* 14:177.

22. S. Freud, "Instincts and Their Vicissitudes," *Standard Edition* 14:127: "The reversal affects only the aims of the instincts. The active aim (to torture, to look at) is replaced by the passive aim (to be tortured, to be looked at). Reversal of content is found in the single instance of the transformation of love into hate."

23. S. Freud, "Repression," *Standard Edition* 14:150: "In this connection we can understand how it is that the objects to which men give most preference, their ideals, proceed from the same perception and experiences as the objects which they most abhor and that they were originally only distinguished from one another through slight modifications . . . Indeed . . . it is possible for the original instinctual representative to be split in two, one part undergoing repression, while the remainder, precisely on account of this intimate connection, undergoes idealization."

24. I am indebted to Vernant, *Mortals and Immortals*, for the following discussion of Greek concepts of death.

25. Ibid., 95.

26. Ibid., 96.

27. Ibid., 95-96.

28. P. Ariès, *L'homme devant la mort*, 2 vols. (Paris: Seuil, 1977), 2, 42: "One can therefore understand the enormous difference that separates the feeling of life and death of the sixteenth and seventeenth centuries from that feeling in the latter Middle Ages."

29. Ibid., 2, 129: "What macabre art reveals to sight was precisely what was not seen, what happened underground, the hidden work of decomposition, not the result of a direct observation, but the product of a particular imagination"; and ibid., 1, 115: "the half-

decomposed cadaver will become the most frequently used representation of death: the sculpted figure of a body eaten away by worms."

30. This is evident in Descartes, as brought out by F. Barker, *The Tremulous Private Body* (London: Methuen, 1984). One could also use Bakhtinian terminology to underline the shift from a "grotesque carnivalesque body" to the individuated body of the bourgeois subject; see M. Bakhtin, *Rabelais and His World*, trans. H. Iswolsky (Cambridge: M.I.T. Press, 1965).

31. For a history of the imposition of the neoclassical imperative in French literature, see R. Bray, *La formation de la doctrine classique en France* (Paris: Nizet, 1957), and A. Adam, *Histoire de la littérature française au XVIIe siècle*, 5 vols. (Paris: del Duca, 1949–56).

32. See T. Eagleton, *Criticism and Ideology* (London: Verso, 1976), 101: "Literature, one might argue, is the most revealing mode of experiential access to ideology that we possess. It is in literature, above all, that we observe in a peculiarly complex, coherent, intensive and immediate fashion the workings of ideology in the textures of lived experience of class-societies."

33. We should not forget that Corneille began his tragic career with *Médée* in 1635 but quickly moved away from "myth" to history. See M. Greenberg, *Corneille, Classicism and the Ruses of Symmetry* (Cambridge: Cambridge University Press, 1986) and "The Grateful Dead: Corneille's Tragedy and the Illusion of History," in *Subjectivity and Subjugation in Seventeenth-Century Drama and Prose: The Family Romance of French Classicism* (Cambridge: Cambridge University Press, 1992), 48–64.

34. Là, par un long récit de toutes les misères
    Que durant notre enfance ont enduré nos pères,
    Renouvelant leur haine avec leur souvenir,
    Je redouble en leurs coeurs l'ardeur de le punir.
    Je leur fais des tableaux de ces tristes batailles
    Où Rome par ses mains déchirait ses entrailles, . . .
    Je les peins dans le meurtre à l'envi triomphants,
    Rome entière noyée au sang de ses enfants:
    Les uns assassinés dans les places publiques,
    Les autres dans le sein de leurs dieux domestiques:
    Le méchant par le prix au crime encouragé,
    Le mari par sa femme en son lit égorgé;
    Le fils tout dégoutant du meurtre de son père,
    Et sa tête à la main demandant son salaire.

35. Ils n'aspirent enfin qu'à des biens passagers,
    Que troublent les soucis, que suivent les dangers;
    La mort nous les ravit, la fortune s'en joue;
    Aujourd'hui dans le trône, et demain dans la boue;
    Et leur plus haut éclat fait tant de mécontents,
    Que peu de vos Césars en ont joui longtemps.
    J'ai de l'ambition, mais plus noble et plus belle:
    Cette grandeur périt, j'en veux une immortelle,
    Un bonheur assuré, sans mesure et sans fin,
    Au-dessus de l'envie, au-dessus du destin.

36. Saintes douceurs du ciel . . .
    Vos biens ne sont point inconstants;
    Et l'heureux trépas que j'attends
    Ne vous sert que d'un doux passage
    Pour nous introduire au partage
    Qui nous rend à jamais contents.

37. Elvire, m'as-tu fait un rapport bien sincère?
Ne déguises-tu rien de ce qu'a dit mon père?
Tous mes sens à moi-même en sont encor charmés:
Il estime Rodrigue autant que vous l'aimez;
Et si je ne m'abuse à lire dans son âme
Il vous commandera de répondre à sa flamme.

38. Ma valeur n'a point lieu de te désavouer;
Tu l'as bien imitée, et ton illustre audace
Fait bien revivre en toi les héros de ma race:
C'est d'eux que tu descends, c'est de moi que tu viens;
Ton premier coup d'épée égale tous les miens . . .

39. See G. Rosolato, "La difference des sexes," in *Essais sur le symbolique*, 19: "The law is not only corporal, anatomical, but also, in its very principle, a pact, a gesture toward the future, a symbolic agreement." See my discussion of the creation of a masculine "essentiality" in *"Le Cid* Father/Time," in *Corneille, Classicism and the Ruses of Symmetry*.

40. O rage! ô désespoir! ô vieillesse ennemie!
N'ai-je tant vécu que pour cette infamie?
Et ne suis-je blanchi dans les travaux guerriers
Que pour voir en un jour flétrir tant de lauriers?

41. Mon bras, qu'avec respect toute l'Espagne admire,
Mon bras, qui tant de fois a sauvé cet empire,
Tant de fois affermi le trône de son roi,
Trahit donc ma querelle, et ne fait rien pour moi?
O cruel souvenir de ma gloire passée!
Oeuvre de tant de jours en un jour effacée!

42. I would suggest, following the French psychoanalyst Guy Rosolato, that this multiplicity of mythic echoes accounts in large measure for the play's hold over its initial audience and over us. The recourse to myth, Rosolato says, "fundamentally concerns the relation that unites within the subject himself both his unconscious fantasies and the conscious myths that preside over his existence" (*Essais* 60).

43. Ce grand coeur qui paraît aux discours que tu tiens
Par tes yeux, chaque jour, se découvrait aux miens;
Et croyant voir en toi l'honneur de la Castille,
Mon âme avec plaisir te destinait ma fille.

44. "don Fernand étant le premier roi de Castille, et ceux qui en avaient été maîtres auparavant lui n'ayant eu titre que de comtes, il n'était peut-être pas assez absolu sur les grands seigneurs de son royaume . . . " (*Examen* 14).

45. LE COMTE: Monsieur, pour conserver tout ce que j'ai d'estime,
Désobéir un peu n'est pas un si grand crime;
Et quelque grand qu'il soit, mes services présents
Pour le faire abolir sont plus que suffisants.
D. ARIAS: Quoi qu'on fasse d'illustre et de considérable,
Jamais à son sujet un roi n'est redevable. . . .
LE COMTE: Un jour seul ne perd pas un homme tel que moi.
Que toute sa grandeur s'arme pour mon supplice.
Tout l'Etat périra, s'il faut que je périsse.

46. In this regard, see G. Rosolato, *Le sacrifice: repères psychanalytiques* (Paris: P.U.F., 1987), 74: "As for the murder of the father I would offer the hypothesis that in the myths of monotheism it never appears directly. The entire project has, in fact, as its aim to avoid its accomplishment. We must therefore come to the conclusion that this murder remains

the hidden kernel, the secret, in relation to which are organized all the sacrificial substitutions through which the alliance comes into being."

47. Quoi! sire, pour lui seul vous renversez des lois
Qu'à vu toute la cour observer tant de fois!
Que croira votre peuple, et que dira l'envie,
Si sous votre défense il ménage sa vie,
Et s'en fait un prétexte à ne paraître pas
Où tous les gens d'honneur cherchent un beau trépas?

48. Rodrigue maintenant est notre unique appui,
L'espérance et l'amour d'un peuple qui l'adore,
Le soutien de Castille, et la terreur du More. . . .
Tu poursuis en sa mort la ruine publique.

49. CHIMÈNE: Rodrigue, qui l'eût cru? . . .
RODRIGUE: Chimène, qui l'eût dit? . . .

50. Rosolato, *Essais*, 189: "La mort reste liée aux effets de Double" ("Death remains attached to the effects of the Double"). See S. Freud, *On Creativity and the Unconscious* (New York: Harper and Row, 1958).

51. See Doubrovsky's analysis in *Corneille* of the stances as the most overdetermined imperative in Cornelian theater.

52. For a more detailed analysis, see my *Corneille, Classicism and the Ruses of Symmetry.*

53. Je dois tout à mon père avant qu'à ma maîtresse;
Que je meure au combat, ou meure de tristesse,
Je rendrai mon sang pur comme je l'ai reçu.
Je m'accuse déjà de trop de négligence;
Courons à la vengeance.

54. Sire, mon père est mort; mes yeux ont vu son sang
Couler à gros bouillons de son généreux flanc;
Ce sang qui tant de fois garantit vos murailles, . . .
Son flanc était ouverte, pour mieux m'émouvoir,
Son sang sur la poussière écrivait mon devoir.

55. CHIMÈNE: Mais n'est-il point blessé?
ELVIRE: Je n'en ai rien appris.
Vous changez de couleur! reprenez vos esprits.

56. D. FERNAND: Si de nos ennemis Rodrigue a le dessus,
Il est mort à nos yeux des coups qu'il a reçus:
Rendez grâces au ciel qui vous en a vengée.
(A D. Diègue)
Voyez comme déjà sa couleur est changée.
D. DIÈGUE: Mais voyez qu'elle pâme, et d'un amour parfait,
Dans cette pâmoison, sire, admirez l'effet.

57. See H. Cixous and C. Clément, *La jeune née* (Paris: 10/18, 1975), and L. Irigaray, *Speculum de l'autre femme* (Paris: Minuit, 1974).

58. Dedans mon ennemi je trouve mon amant;
Et je sens qu'en dépit de toute ma colère
Rodrigue dans mon coeur combat encor mon père.

59. For the "querelle du *Cid*," see Adam, *Histoire de la littérature*. What appeared most to upset the *doctes*, was Chimène's scandalous, that is, nontraditional behavior: "Too sensitive a beloved, and too unnatural a daughter. For however violently her passion might shake her, it is certain that she would never have slackened her quest to revenge her father, and even more certain that she should never have resolved to marry the man who killed her father. It is at this point that we must admit that her morals are quite scandalous, if

indeed they are not entirely perverse" [quoted from Chapelain, *Les Sentiments de l'Académie française sur la tragicomédie du Cid*, in Pellison, *Histoire de l'Académie française* (Paris, 1700)].

60. See R. Girard, *La violence et le sacré* (Paris: Grasset, 1972); M. Serres, *Rome ou le livre des fondations* (Paris: Grasset, 1983).

61. Nous sommes vos voisins, nos filles sont vos femmes,
    Et l'hymen nous a joints par tant et tant de noeuds,
    Qu'il est peu de nos fils qui ne soient vos neveux;
    Nous ne sommes qu'un sang et qu'un peuple en deux villes.

62. Ingrate, souviens-toi que du sang de ses rois
    Tu tiens ton nom, tes murs, et tes premières lois.
    Albe est ton origine; arrête, et considère
    Que tu portes le fer dans le sein de ta mère.

63. Combattre un ennemi pour le salut de tous,
    Et contre un inconnu s'exposer seul aux coups,
    D'une simple vertu c'est l'effet ordinaire,
    Mille déjà l'ont fait, mille pourraient le faire;
    Mais vouloir au public immoler ce qu'on aime,
    S'attacher au combat contre un autre soi-même,
    Attaquer un parti qui prend pour défenseur
    Le frère d'une femme et l'amant d'une soeur,
    Et, rompant tous ces noeuds, s'armer pour la patrie
    Contre un sang qu'on voudrait racheter de sa vie
    Une telle vertu n'appartenait qu'à nous.

64. Mais quoique ce combat me promette un cercueil.
    La gloire de ce choix m'enfle d'un juste orgueil.

65. S. Freud, "Thoughts on War and Death," *Standard Edition* 14:293.

66. Rome a choisi mon bras, je n'examine rien.
    Avec une allégresse aussi pleine et sincère
    Que j'épousai la soeur, je combattrai le frère.

67. Qu'est-ce ceci, mes enfants? écoutez-vous vos flammes?
    Et perdez-vous encor le temps avec des femmes?
    Prêts à verser du sang, regardez-vous des pleurs?
    Fuyez, et laissez-les déplorer leurs malheurs. . . .
    Et ce n'est qu'en fuyant qu'on pare de tels coups.

68. Je suis Romaine, hélas! puisque Horace est Romain;
    J'en ai reçu le titre en recevant sa main;
    Mais ce noeud me tiendrait en esclave enchaînée,
    S'ils m'empêchait de voir en quels lieux je suis née.
    Albe, où j'ai commencé de respirer le jour,
    Albe, mon cher pays, et mon premier amour, . . .
    Rome, si tu te plains que c'est là te trahir,
    Fais-toi des ennemis que je puisse haïr.
    Quand je vois de tes murs leur armée et la nôtre,
    Mes trois frères dans l'une, et mon mari dans l'autre,
    Puis-je former des voeux, et sans impiété
    Importuner le ciel pour ta féliciter?

69. Je sens mon triste coeur percé de tous les coups
    Qui m'ôtent maintenant un frère ou mon époux.
    Quand je songe à leur mort, quoi que je me propose,
    Je songe par quels bras, et non pour quelle cause,

Et ne vois les vainqueurs en leur illustre rang
Que pour considérer aux dépens de quelle sang.

70. For an analysis of the symbolic role of the *pontif*, see P. Legendre, *L'amour du censeur* (Paris: Seuil, 1979), 70: "He represents simultaneously both an all-powerful being and a being of radical sexual privation. He is the father, but castrated. Thus pontifical representation is the sign of an order of absolute ambivalence because the pope is at once put forth as the bearer of the phallus and as deprived of all sexual capacity."

71. Faites-vous voir sa soeur, et qu'un même flanc
Le ciel vous a tous deux formés d'un même sang.

72. Ma soeur, voici le bras qui venge nos deux frères
Le bras qui rompt le cours de nos destins contraires,
Qui nous rend maîtres d'Albe; enfin voici le bras
Qui seul fait aujourd'hui le sort de deux Etats.

73. Rome, l'unique objet de mon ressentiment!
Rome, à qui vient ton bras d'immoler mon amant!
Rome, qui t'a vu naître, et que ton coeur adore!
Rome enfin, que je hais parce qu'elle t'honore!
Puissent tous ses voisins ensemble conjurés
Saper ses fondements encor mal assurés!
Et si ce n'est assez de toute l'Italie,
Que l'Orient contre elle à l'Occident s'allie;
Que cent peuples unis des bouts de l'univers
Passent pour la détruire et les monts et les mers!
Qu'elle-même sur soi renverse ses murailles,
Et de ses propres mains déchirer ses entrailles;
Que le courroux du ciel allumé par mes voeux
Fasse pleuvoir sur elle un déluge de feux!
Puissé-je de mes yeux y voir tomber ce foudre,
Voir ses maisons en cendre, et tes lauriers en poudre,
Voir le dernier Romain à son dernier soupir,
Moi seule en être cause, et mourir de plaisir!

74. La mort seule aujourd'hui peut conserver ma gloire:
Encor la fallait-il sitôt que j'eus vaincu,
Puisque pour mon honneur j'ai déjà trop vécu
Un homme tel que moi voit sa gloire ternie,
Quand il tombe en péril de quelque ignominie; . . .
Permettez, ô grand roi, que de ce bras vainqueur
Je m'immole à ma gloire, et non pas à ma soeur.

75. Corneille, *Examen*, 91–92.

76. Assez de bons sujets dans toutes les provinces
Par des voeux impuissants s'acquittent vers leurs princes;
Tous les peuvent aimer, mais tous ne peuvent pas
Par d'illustres effets assurer leurs Etats;
Et l'art et le pouvoir d'affermir des couronnes
Sont des dons que le ciel fait à peu de personnes.
De pareils aussi sont au-dessus des lois.
Qu'elles se taisent donc; que Rome dissimule
Ce que dès sa naissance elle vit en Romule.

77. Puisqu'en un même jour l'ardeur d'un même zèle
Achève le destin de son amant et d'elle,

Je veux qu'un même jour, témoin de leurs deux morts,
En un même tombeau voie enfermer leurs corps.

78. See, for example, the most recent scholar to repeat this appreciation, M. Prigent, *Le héros et l'état dans la tragédie de Pierre Corneille* (Paris: P.U.F., 1986), where *Cinna* is defined as "the political tragedy par excellence, the tragedy of the State" (57). Also, Doubrovsky, *Corneille*, who calls *Cinna* "the very tragedy of politics" (221).

79. Doubrovsky, *Corneille*, 203.

80. Quand je regarde Auguste au milieu de sa gloire,
Et que vous reprochez à ma triste mémoire
Que par sa propre main mon père massacré
Du trône où je le vois fait le premier degré;
Quand vous me présentez cette sanglante image
La cause de ma haine, et l'effet de sa rage,
Je m'abandonne toute à vos ardents transports,
Et crois, pour une mort, lui devoir mille morts.

81. Editor's note to *Cinna*, in *Corneille, Théâtre choisi*, 148.

82. See O. Seyffert, *Dictionary of Classical Antiquities* (New York: Meridian Library, 1956), 224; P. Grimal, *Dictionnaire de la mythologie Grecque et Romaine* (Paris: P.U.F., 1958).

83. Quoique j'aime Cinna, quoique mon coeur l'adore,
S'il me veut posséder, Auguste doit périr;
Sa tête est le seul prix dont il peut m'acquérir.

84. . . . Qu'il achève et dégage sa foi
Et qu'il choisisse après de la mort ou de moi.

85. Joignons à la douceur de venger nos parents
La gloire qu'on remporte à punir les tyrans,
Et faisons publier par toute l'Italie:
'La liberté de Rome est l'oeuvre d'Aemilie'.

86. Souviens-toi du beau feu dont nos sommes épris,
Qu'aussi bien que la gloire Aemilie est ton prix;
Que tu me dois ton coeur, que mes faveurs t'attendent . . .

87. Eh bien! vous le voulez, il faut vous satisfaire,
Il faut affranchir Rome, il faut venger un père,
Il faut sur un tyran porter de justes coups;
Mais apprenez qu'Auguste est moins tyran que vous.
S'il nous ôte à son gré nos biens, nos jours, nos femmes,
Il n'a point jusqu'ici tyrannisé nos âmes;
Mais l'empire inhumain qu'exercent vos beautés
Force jusqu'aux esprits et jusqu'aux volontés.

88. Seigneur, pour sauver Rome, il faut qu'elle s'unisse
En la main d'un bon chef à qui tout obéisse.
Si vous aimez encore à la favoriser
Otez-lui les moyens de se plus diviser. . . .
Vous la replongerez, en quittant cet empire,
Dans les maux dont à peine encore elle respire,
Et de ce peu, seigneur, qui lui reste de sang,
Une guerre nouvelle épuisera son flanc.

89. Par les peines d'un autre aucun ne s'intimide:
Salvidien à bas a soulevé Lépide;
Murène a succédé, Cépion l'a suivi:
Le jour à tous deux dans les tourments ravi

N'a point mêlé de crainte à la fureur d'Egnace,
Dont Cinna maintenant ose prendre la place.

90. J'ai souhaité l'empire, et j'y suis parvenu;
Mais, en le souhaitant, je ne l'ai pas connu:
Dans sa possession j'ai trouvé pour tous charmes
D'effroyables soucis, d'éternelles alarmes,
Mille ennemis secrets, la mort à tous propos
Point de plaisir sans trouble, et jamais de repos.

91. Octave, n'attends plus le coup d'un nouveau Brute;
Meurs, et dérobe-lui la gloire de ta chute;
Meurs; tu ferais pour vivre un lâche et vain effort,
Si tant de gens de coeur font des voeux pour ta mort. . . .
Meurs, puisque c'est un mal que tu ne peux guérir;
Meurs enfin, puisqu'il faut tout perdre, ou mourir.

92. O Romains! ô vengeance! ô pouvoir absolu!
O rigoureux combat d'un coeur irrésolu
Qui fuit en même temps tout ce qu'il se propose!
D'un prince malheureux ordonnez quelque chose.
Qui des deux dois-je suivre, et duquel m'éloigner?
Ou laissez-moi périr, ou laissez-moi régner.

93. CINNA: Le sort vous est propice autant qu'il m'est contraire;
Je sais ce que j'ai fait, et ce qu'il vous faut faire.
Vous devez un exemple à la postérité,
Et mon trépas importe à votre sûreté.

EMILIE: Et je vous viens, seigneur, offrir une victime,
Non pour sauver sa vie en me chargeant du crime:
Son trépas est trop juste après son attentat,
Et toute excuse est vaine en un crime d'Etat:
Mourir en sa présence, et rejoindre mon père,
C'est tout ce qui m'amène, et tout ce que j'espère.

MAXIME: Vous voyez le succès de mon lâche artifice;
Faites périr Euphorbe au milieu des tourments,
Et souffrez que je meure aux yeux de ces amants.

94. Souffrez que ma vertu dans mon coeur rappelée
Vous consacre une foi lâchement violée,
Mais si ferme à présent, si loin de chanceler,
Que la chute du ciel ne pourrait ébranler.

95. Vous avez trouvé l'art d'être maître des coeurs.
Rome, avec une joie et sensible et profonde,
Se démet en vos mains de l'empire du monde;
Vos royales vertus lui vont trop enseigner
Que son bonheur consiste à vous faire régner:
D'une si longue erreur pleinement affranchie,
Elle n'a plus de voeux que pour la monarchie,
Vous prépare déjà des temples, des autels,
Et le ciel une place entre les immortels . . .

96. Le ciel a résolu votre grandeur suprême;
Et pour preuve, seigneur, je n'en veux que moi-même:

J'ose avec vanité me donner cet éclat,
Puisqu'il change mon coeur, qu'il veut changer l'Etat.

97. Mais vous ne savez pas ce que c'est qu'une femme;
Vous ignorez quels droits elle a sur toute l'âme
Quand, après un long temps qu'elle a su nous charmer,
Les flambeaux de l'hymen viennent de s'allumer.

98. Pauline, sans raison dans la douleur plongée,
Craint et croit déjà voir ma mort qu'elle a songée;
Elle oppose ses pleurs au dessein que je fais,
Et tâche à m'empêcher de sortir du palais.

99. Ainsi du genre humain l'ennemi vous abuse:
Ce qu'il ne peut de force, il l'entreprend de ruse.
Jaloux des bons desseins qu'il tâche d'ébranler,
Quand il ne les peut rompre, il pousse à reculer;
D'obstacle sur obstacle il va troubler le vôtre,
Aujourd'hui par des pleurs, chaque jour par quelque autre;
Et ce songe rempli de noires visions
N'est que le coup d'essai de ses illusions:
Il met tout en usage, et prière et menace;
Il attaque toujours, et jamais ne se lasse;
Il croit pouvoir enfin ce qu'encore il n'a pu,
Et que ce qu'on diffère est à demi rompu.
Rompez ses premiers coups; laissez pleurer Pauline.
Dieu ne veut point d'un coeur où le monde domine.

100. Mon abord en ces lieux
Me fit voir Polyeucte, et je plus à ses yeux;
Et comme il est ici le chef de la noblesse,
Mon père fut ravi qu'il me prît pour maîtresse . . .
Il approuva sa flamme, et conclut l'hyménée:
Et moi, comme à son lit je me vis destinée:
Je donnai par devoir à son affection
Tout ce que l'autre avait par inclination.

101. Quelque reste d'amour s'y fait-il encor voir?
Quel trouble, quel transport lui cause ma venue?
Puis-je tout espérer de cette heureuse vue?
Car je voudrais mourir plutôt que d'abuser
Des lettres de faveur que j'ai pour l'épouser.

102. See C. Lévi-Strauss, *Structures élémentaires de la parenté* (Paris: Plon, 1967), and J. Mitchell's commentary on the importance of Lévi-Strauss for psychoanalysis in *Psychoanalysis and Feminism* (New York: Random House, 1975), especially 370–77.

103. Mais puisque mon devoir m'imposait d'autres lois,
De quelque amant pour moi que mon père eût fait choix,
Quand à ce grand pouvoir que la valeur vous donne
Vous auriez ajouté l'éclat d'une couronne,
Quand je vous aurais vu, quand je l'aurais haï,
J'en aurais soupiré, mais j'aurais obéi.

104. Ah! mon père, son crime à peine est pardonnable;
Mais s'il est insensé, vous êtes raisonnable; . . .
Un père est toujours père, et sur cette assurance
J'ose appuyer encore un reste d'espérance.

105. Ils n'aspirent enfin qu'à des biens passagers,

Que troublent les soucis, que suivent les dangers;
La mort nous les ravit, la fortune s'en joue;
Aujourd'hui dans le trône, et demain dans la boue . . .

106. J'ai de l'ambition, mais plus noble et plus belle:
Cette grandeur périt, j'en veux une immortelle,
Un bonheur assuré, sans mesure et sans fin,
Au-dessus de l'envie, au-dessus du destin.

107. Le Dieu de Polyeucte et celui de Néarque
De la terre et du ciel est l'absolu monarque,
Seul être indépendant, seul mâitre du destin,
Seul principe éternel, et souveraine fin.

108. Mon époux en mourant m'a laissé ses lumières;
Son sang, dont tes bourreaux viennent de me couvrir,
M'a dessillé les yeux, et me les vient d'ouvrir.

Je vois, je sais, je crois, je suis désabusée. . . .
Mène, mène-moi voir tes dieux que je déteste;
Ils n'on ont brisé qu'un, je briseral le reste.

On m'y verra braver tout ce que vous craignez,
Ces foudres impuissants qu'en leurs mains vous peignez,
Et, saintement rebelle aux lois de la naissacne,
Une fois envers toi manquer d'obéissance.

109. Nous autres, bénissons notre heureuse aventure:
Allons à nos martyrs donner la sépulture,
Baiser leurs corps sacrés, les mettre en digne lieu,
Et faire retentir partout le nom de Dieu.

5. Racine's *Bérénice* and the Allegory of Absolutism

French quotations from Racine's work are taken from Racine, *Théâtre complet*, ed. M. Rat (Paris: Garnier, 1960). All English translations are from *Jean Racine: Andromache, Britannicus, Berenice*, trans. J. Cairncross (Baltimore: Penguin, 1967).

1. I am referring to the many diverse, mythological, semiotic, structural analyses (Barthes, Mauron, Goldmann) that attempt a general, overarching synthesis of the Racinian corpus.

2. See Aristotle, *The Poetics*, ed. S. H. Butcher (New York: Dover, 1951). In chap. 6, the famous chapter defining the essence of a tragedy, Aristotle specifies that "tragedy, then, is an imitation of an action that is serious, complete, and of a certain magnitude; in language embellished with each kind of artistic ornament, the several kinds being found in separate parts of the play; in the form of action, not of narrative; through pity and fear effecting the purgation of these emotions" (23). Nowhere does he specify that death must be an integral part of this representation.

3. Racine, "Préface," *Jean Racine*, trans. J. Cairncross, 299.

4. See M. Foucault, *Surveiller et Punir, naissance de la prison* (Paris: Gallimard, 1975).

5. Racine, "Préface," 300: "There are people who think that this simplicity is a sign of poor inventive capacity. It does not occur to them that, on the contrary, the essence of inventive capacity consists in making something out of nothing."

6. Ibid., 300: "Neither can I believe that the public would take it amiss that I have given it a tragedy which has been honored by so many tears . . . "

7. "an elegy rather than a tragedy"; from preface to *Oedipe*, quoted in Racine, *Théâtre complet*, ed. M. Rat, 298.

8. R. Barthes, *Sur Racine* (Paris: Seuil, 1963), 99.

9. "Funeste" appears and reappears throughout the tragedy: "cet hymen si funeste?" (I, iii); "Depuis cette journée/Dois-je dire funeste" (II, ii); "quel funeste entretien!" (II, v); "fuyons un spectacle funeste" (III, ii); " A ma funeste vie aviez-vous destiné?" (V, iv), and so on.

10. S. Freud, *Mourning and Melancholia*, in *General Psychological Theory* (New York: Macmillan, 1963), 166: "This, indeed, might be so even when the patient was aware of the loss giving rise to the melancholia, that is, when he knows whom he has lost but not *what* it is he has lost in them."

11. See W. Benjamin, *The Origin of German Tragic Drama*, trans. J. Osborne (London: New Left Books, 1977).

12. G. Couton, ed., *Corneille, oeuvres complètes*, 3 vols. (Paris: Gallimard, 1987), 3:1604.

13. See R. Picard, *La Carrière de J. Racine* (Paris: Gallimard, 1961), 158: "I will limit my remarks to stating that for my part this is rather a debatable hypothesis that is not provably false but which meets with many serious objections"; and also Couton, *Corneille* 3:1608–9.

14. E. Kantorowicz, *The King's Two Bodies: A Study in Medieval Political Theology* (Princeton: Princeton University Press, 1957); L. Marin, *Le Portrait du Roi* (Paris: Minuit, 1981); J-M. Apostolidès, *Le Roi machine* (Paris: Minuit, 1981).

15. Picard, *La Carrière de J. Racine*, 168.

16. See A. Grosrichard, *Structure du sérail* (Paris: Seuil, 1979).

17. For a detailed study of these accounts, and of elaborations of the term despotic and the image of the despotic Oriental, see L. Valensi, *Venise et la Sublime Porte, La naissance du despote* (Paris: Hachette, 1987). I am indebted to Valensi for much of the information that makes up these paragraphs.

18. Ibid., 80–81. See also P. Anderson, *Lineages of the Absolute State* (London: New Left Books, 1975).

19. Valensi, *Venise*, 99.

20. Ibid., 81 (quoting Bodin).

21. J. Chardin, *Voyage en Perse* (Amsterdam, 1711) (réédition du *Journal de voyage du chevalier Chardin en Perse et aux Indes orientales*, London, 1686), 235; quoted in Grosrichard, *Structure du sérail*, 96.

22. See R. E. Giesey, "Medieval Jurisprudence in Bodin's Concept of Sovereignty," in *Jean Bodin*, Verhandlungen der internationalen Bodin Tagung in München (Munich: Verlag C. H. Beck, 1973), 181.

23. R. Dérathé, "La place de J. Bodin dans l'histoire des théories de la souveraineté," in *Jean Bodin*, 249.

24. Giesey, "Medieval Jurisprudence," 172–74.

25. A. Green, *Narcissisme de vie, Narcissisme de Mort* (Paris: Minuit, 1983), 259.

26. Racine, "Préface," 299.

27. Quoted by Couton in *Corneille*, 3:1598.

28. Ibid., 3:1599.

29. G. Balandier, *Pouvoirs sur scène* (Paris: Balland, 1980), 19.

All the theorists of narcissism beginning with Freud have shown the dyadic coupling of narcissism and melancholia. In *Mourning and Melancholia* Freud writes: "The disposition to succumb to melancholia . . . lies in the narcissistic type of object choice" (171). See also J. Kristeva, *Soleil noir, dépression et mélancolie* (Paris: Gallimard, 1987); Grunberger, *Le Narcissisme, Essais de psychanalyse* (Paris: Payot, 1975) and Green, *Narcissisme de vie*.

30. Green, *Narcissisme de vie*, 55.

31. Ibid., 51.

32. Louis XIV, *Mémoires*, ed. J. Longnon (Paris: Tallandier, 1978), 135–36.

33. M. de Certeau, *La Fable mystique*, vol. 1 (Paris: Gallimard, 1982), 32: "Such was

the situation in the seventeenth century. Divisive conflicts called into question heteronomous social formations. The fatal splitting of what was formerly religious unity gradually
shifted onto the state the responsibility of representing for all members of society a reference
point of stable unity. A concept of unity gradually emerged based on an inclusionary
strategy, subtended by a subtle interplay of hierarchies and mediations."

34. M. Borch-Jacobsen, *Le Sujet Freudien* (Paris: Aubier Flammarion, 1982), 120.

35. Louis XIV, *Mémoires*, 259.

36. Couton, *Corneille*, 1608: "His contemporaries saw in the image of Titus Louis XIV,
as military conqueror . . . his contemporaries also saw in Titus Louis XIV as lover."

37. See Green, *Narcissisme de vie*, 164. Also, L. Marin, *La parole mangée* (Paris: Klincksieck, 1986), 215: "And we should never lose sight of the fact that the desire for absolute
power is one of the manifestations of the death drive."

38. For a general discussion of the subjugation of the body in the seventeenth century,
see F. Barker, *The Tremulous Private Body* (London: Methuen, 1984).

39. Barthes, *Sur Racine*, 98: "The voice is sexualized in Racinian theater, and especially
in *Bérénice*, the tragedy of aphasia."

40. Je fuis Titus: je fuis ce nom qui m'inquiète,
   Ce nom qu'à tous moments votre bouche répète.
   Que vous dirai-je enfin? Je fuis des yeux distraits,
   Qui me voyant toujours, ne me voyaient jamais.

41. See Barthes's comment of Bérénice's being seduced by the image of Titus, in *Sur
Racine*, 94.

42. De cette nuit, Phénice, as-tu vu la splendeur
   Tes yeux ne sont-ils pas tout pleins de sa grandeur?
   Ces flambeaux, ce bûcher, cette nuit enflammée,
   Ces aigles, ces faisceaux, ce peuple, cette armée,
   Cette foule de rois, ces consuls, ce sénat,
   Qui tous de mon amant empruntaient leur éclat;
   Et ces lauriers encor témoins de sa victoire;
   Tous ces yeux qu'on voyait venir de toutes parts
   Confondre sur lui seul leux avides regards;
   Ce port majesuteux, cette douce présence . . .
   Ciel! avec quel respect et quelle complaisance
   Tous les coeurs en secret l'assuraient de leur foi!
   Parle: peut-on le voir sans penser, comme moi,
   Qu'en quelque obscurité que le sort l'eût fait naître,
   Le monde en le voyant eût reconnu son maître?

43. Barthes, *Sur Racine*, 28–32.

44. Le peuple avec transport l'arrête et l'environne,
   Applaudissant aux noms que le sénat lui donne . . .

45. Enfin tout ce qu'amour a de noeuds plus puissants,
   Doux reproches, transports sans cesse renaissants,
   Soin de plaire sans art, crainte toujours nouvelle,
   Beauté, gloire, vertu, je trouve tout en elle.

46. M. A. Doane, *The Desire to Desire* (Bloomington: Indiana University Press, 1987),
168. See also J. Rose, *Sexuality in the Field of Vision* (London: Verso, 1987); and L. Irigaray,
Ce sexe qui n'en est pas un (Paris: Minuit, 1977), 25: "la prévalence du regard et de la discrimi-
nation de la forme, de l'individualisation de la forme, est particulièrement étrangère à
l'érotisme féminin."

47. Tu ne l'ignores pas: toujours la renommée
   Avec le même éclat n'a pas semé mon nom;

Ma jeunesse, nourrie à la cour de Néron,
S'égarait, cher Paulin, par l'exemple abusée,
Et suivait du plaisir la pente trop aisée.
Bérénice me plut. Que ne fait point un coeur
Pour plaire à ce qu'il aime, et gagner son vainqueur!
Je prodiguai mon sang: tout fit place à mes armes:
Je revins triomphant. Mais le sang et les larmes
Ne me suffisaient pas pour mériter ses voeux:
J'entrepris le bonheur de mille malheureux:
On vit de toutes parts mes bontés se répandre . . .

48. C. Mauron talks about the maternal role of Bérénice, as well as about the feminine ambivalence she embodies for the Racinian corpus, in his *L'inconscient dans l'oeuvre et la vie de Racine* (Paris: Corti, 1969), 82–94.

49. TITUS: De la reine ou de moi que dit la voix publique?
        Parlez: qu'attendez-vous?
     PAULIN: J'entends de tous côtés
        Publier vos vertus, seigneur, et ses beautés.

50. N'en doutez point, seigneur: soit raison, soit caprice,
    Rome ne l'attend point pour son impératrice.
    On sait qu'elle est charmante, et de si belles mains
    Semblent vous demander l'empire des humains;
    Elle a mille vertus, mais, seigneur, elle est reine:
    Rome, par une loi qui ne se peut changer,
    N'admet avec son sang aucun sang étranger,
    Et ne reconnaît point les fruits illégitimes
    Qui naissent d'un hymen contraire à ses maximes.

51. This locus of the voice—this voice become one with the dead father—can be compared to that "atopical voice" that Derrida attributes to Socrates as the founding moment in the Western tradition of metaphysics as a metaphysics of presence. In this way, Racine's gesture of inscribing Titus's image of himself—his masculine self-image—repeats the founding gesture that situates its origin (the origin of his "I") in the space of the dead (oedipal) father. As N. Lukacher writes in *Primal Scenes: Literature, Philosophy, Psychoanalysis* (Ithaca: Cornell University Press, 1986), 46: "The voice of the Logos is the echo within the self of an earlier incarnation. Through the Logos, the origin of the self, the absolute earliest incarnation of the self, remains present to the self." This "incarnation" of Vespasian/Father/Emperor calls to Titus, with a seduction more powerful than Bérénice's.

52. Vous fûtes spectateur de cette nuit dernière,
        Lorsque, pour seconder ses soins religieux,
        Le sénat a placé son père entre les dieux.

53. S. Freud, "A Neurosis of Demoniacal Possession in the Seventeenth Century," in *On Creativity and the Unconscious* (New York: Harper and Row, 1958), 277–78.

54. . . . vous le savez, en bannissant ses rois,
    Rome à ce nom, si noble et si saint autrefois,
    Attache pour jamais une haine puissante;
    Et quoiqu'à ses Césars fidèle, obéissante, . . .
    Cette haine, seigneur, reste de sa fierté,
    Survit dans tous les coeurs après la liberté.

55. Depuis ce temps, seigneur, Caligula, Néron,
    Monstres dont à regret je cite ici le nom,
    Et qui, ne conservant que la figure d'homme,
    Foulèrent à leurs pieds toutes les lois de Rome,

Ont craint cette loi seule, et n'ont point à nous yeux
Allumé le flambeau d'un hymen odieux.

56. De l'affranchi Pallas nous avons vu le frère,
Des fers de Claudius Félix encor flétri,
De deux reines, seigneur, devenir le mari . . .

57. Et, s'il faut jusqu'au bout que je vous obéisse,
Ces deux reines étaient du sang de Bérénice.

58. See the discussion of blood in M. Foucault, "Le dispositif de sexualité," *La Volonté de Savoir* (Paris: Gallimard, 1976), 99–175.

59. Et vous croiriez pouvoir, sans blesser nos regards,
Faire entrer une reine au lit de nos Césars,
Tandis que l'Orient dans le lit de ses reines
Voit passer un esclave au sortir de nos chaînes!

60. S. Freud, "A Special Type of Object Choice Made by Men," in "Contributions to the Psychology of Love," reprinted in *Sexuality and the Psychology of Love* (New York: Macmillan, 1963), 54.

61. For an elaboration on this concept, see Mauron's analysis in *L'inconscient dans l'oeuvre*, 82–94.

62. Je lui dois tout, Paulin. Récompense cruelle!
Tout ce que je lui dois va retomber sur elle.

63. Barthes, *Sur Racine*, 97.

64. Ce long deuil que Titus imposait à sa cour
Avait, même en secret, suspendu son amour;
Il n'avait plus pour moi cette ardeur assidue
Lorsqu'il passait les jours attachés sur ma vue;
Muet, chargé de soins, et les larmes aux yeux,
Il ne me laissait plus que de tristes adieux.

65. See Kristeva, *Soleil Noir,* 157: "To speak, to situate and establish oneself within the legal fiction of symbolic acivity is, in reality, to lose the thing itself." Also Green, *Narcissisme de vie,* 68: "If speech is a mediation between body and language, a psychic 'corps à corps,' speech is, therefore, a mirror (psyche). A mirror, or rather a play of deforming prismatic mirrors, undoing the light of the body or recomposing the spectrum of illuminating rays. But speech is also the relation between one body and another, one language and another, between One and Another."

66. See G. Rosolato, "L'axe narcissique des dépressions," in *La relation d'inconnu* (Paris: Gallimard, 1978): "the mother, the central object of depressions" (95); and "The image of the father, of his substitutes, only serves to disguise an unchanging relation with the mother. A phallic, all-powerful Mother, archaic destroyer; the ideal father, all the while giving the illusion of having detached himself from her, is intimately imbricated in this image" (9). For Kristeva as well it is the lost "mother," the figure behind narcissistic melancholia; see *Soleil Noir*, 19. See also Green, *Narcissisme de vie*, 40: "Freud allows us to suggest that narcissism is itself but an appearance, and that behind this image is hidden the shadow of the invisible object."

67. Tout l'empire parlait: mais la gloire, madame,
Ne s'était point encor fait entendre à mon coeur
Du ton dont elle parle au coeur d'un empereur.

68. Forcez votre amour à se taire;
Et d'un oeil que la gloire et la raison éclaire
Contemplez mon devoir dans toute sa rigueur.

69. Dans un mois, dans un an, comment souffrirons-nous,
Seigneur, que tant de mers me séparent de vous;

Que le jour recommence, et que le jour finissse,
Sans que jamais Titus puisse voir Bérénice,
Sans que, de tout le jour, je puisse voir Titus . . .

70. Ah! prince! jurez-lui que, toujours trop fidèle,
Gémissant dans ma cour, et plus exilé qu'elle,
Portant jusqu'au tombeau le nom de son amant,
Mon règne ne sera qu'un long bannissement,
Si le ciel, non content de me l'avoir ravie,
Veut encor m'affliger par une longue vie.

71. Dans l'orient désert que devint mon ennui!
Je demeurai longtemps errant dans Césarée,
Lieux charmants où mon coeur vous avait adorée.
Je vous redemandais à vos tristes Etats;
Je cherchais en pleurant les traces de vos pas.
Mais enfin, succombant à ma mélancolie
Mon désespoir tourna mes pas vers l'Italie.

72. Mais voulez-vous paraître en ce désordre extrême?
Remettez-vous, madame, et rentrez en vous-même.
Laissez-moi relever ces voiles détachés,
Et ces cheveux épars dont vos yeux sont cachés.
Souffrez que de vos pleurs je répare l'outrage.

For more on the tradition of *la dame méréncolye*, see the classic work of R. Klibansky, E. Panofsky and F. Saxl, *Saturn and Melancholy* (New York: Basic Books, 1964), especially 217–74.

73. Je suis venu vers vous sans savoir mon dessein:
Mon amour m'entraînait; et je venais peut-être
Pour me chercher moi-même, et pour me reconnaîrre
Qu'ai-je trouvé? Je vois la mort peinte en vos yeux.

74. En l'état où je suis je puis tout entreprendre:
Et je ne réponds pas que ma main à vos yeux
N'ensanglante à la fin nos funestes adieux.

75. Il faut d'autres efforts pour rompre tant de noeuds;
Ce n'est qu'en expirant que je puis les détruire;
J'y cours . . .

76. Vivez, et faites-vous un effort généreux.
Sur Titus et sur moi réglez votre conduite:
Je l'aime, je le fuis; Titus m'aime, il me quitte; . . .
. . . Servons tous trois d'exemple à l'univers . . .

77. Maître de l'univers, je règle sa fortune;
Je puis faire les rois, je puis les déposer;
Cependant de mon coeur je ne puis disposer.

78. Couton, *Corneille* 3:1609.

79. Racine, "Préface," 300.

80. Our tears, the body's mourning for a loss and its sublimation to conscience, repeat, as Lukacher reminds us, the primal scene of oedipal renunciation: "Our aesthetic and intellectual response to the tragedy of Oedipus is, in effect, our unconscious repetition of the primal scene of the call of conscience" (*Primal Scenes*, 81).

Index

Mitchell Greenberg is chair of the Department of French and Italian at Miami University in Ohio. He is the author of *Subjectivity and Subjugation in Seventeenth-Century Drama and Prose: The Family Romance of French Classicism* (1992); *Corneille, Classicism, and the Ruses of Symmetry* (1986); and *Detours of Desire: Readings in the French Baroque* (1984). He has written numerous articles on history, propaganda, desire, androgyny, and textual conundrums in sixteenth- and seventeenth-century literature.